Silencing The Past

The Arab Spring, Israel and the Jews of Tunisia

Ron Boublil

ISBN-13: 978-1492191421

ISBN-10: 1492191426

TPI Publishers
cybertpi@gmail.com, Montreal, Quebec, Canada
Printed in the U.S.A

In memory of my parents

Printed in the U.S.A
Éditions TPI
Amazon.com

CONTENTS

Preface

In 2011, I moved into a house whose previous owner, a senior university history professor, left me with over a thousand books neatly arranged and completely filling the garage. Most of the books were about colonialism, the history of American First Nations, Europe and the new world. Many of the books were rare and others never opened, written in either English or French. So I started reading, refreshing my memory and knowledge gained from my years of studying history and political science. This new textual treasure expanded my existing personal collection of books. I probably had the largest home library in the world dealing with the history of colonialism. I was also equipped with the power of internet searches, referencing and cross-referencing, archival searches, as well as access to online university libraries around the globe. I knew how to exploit this technology because for many years I have worked in this industry, and developed the first public online information retrieval system in Israel. I had no excuse in delaying the writing of this book, which quickly became a personal journey. Within a few weeks I found myself devoting all my time to researching and writing.

The Internet played a major role in the Arab Spring (Jasmine) Revolution in Tunisia, and it has also helped the Jews in Arab lands present their story to the world, because frankly, local media and media organizations everywhere were not interested or blatantly ignored it. Web sites were set up to inform the world of the new generation of Jewish civilizations that existed in almost every country of the Arab Muslim world. One of these sites is called JIMENA, "Jews Indigenous to the Middle East and North Africa"; another is Amit, a Tunisian Israeli site where its aging members meet regularly. There are others in French, such as Harrisa and Dafina, in Hebrew, such as Moreshet Morocco, and others in Arabic and English. When the Internet first started, people began connecting with families and friends who were scattered all over the world. Tunisian forums for Jewish and non-Jewish people in both French and Hebrew were flooded with requests for lost relatives and friends, and I read them all. I have seen the many pictures posted of their schoolmates, their families and of their cities. Like orphans, they were searching for meaning for what had happened. Every individual had a story to tell, and a few researchers have recently become interested and started to listen. Still, the newer generations born in Israel and elsewhere find it difficult to relate to what happened. It all seems like it took place centuries ago and totally irrelevant to present life and politics. Yet, I argue throughout this book that the history of Jewish people of the Middle East and North Africa has a crucial role to play not just in defining Israel's future character but also in resolving the Israeli-Palestinian conflict and Israel's relations with the rest of the Arab and Muslim world. It is also evident that the future of the Jasmine Revolution in Tunisia is also dependent on how Tunisians come to view their history, including the history of its indigenous Jewish population.

Most, if not all, of the existing literature deals with personal stories and the ethnic aspect of the mass exile of Jews from Lands Conquered by Arabs (LCA). This book is an attempt to further examine the political implications of the stories and the history of North African Jews, with a special focus on the Tunisian experience. It is this dimension of the story which for decades had been often ignored—and at times silenced.

The following work is a result of personal analysis, reflections and sometimes eyewitness accounts of the political history of Tunisia and Israel, and how this history has affected current events in the Middle East and North Africa.

On Silence and Silencing

"Effective silencing does not require a conspiracy, not even a political consensus. Its roots are structural."

Michel-Rolph Trouillot

The Jasmine Revolution in Tunisia, which sparked the Spring Revolutions across the Arab world, practically forced us to revisit the history of Tunisia and reanalyze the treatment of its minorities, especially its indigenous Tunisian Jewish population. This book unravels how Tunisian Jews were pushed out of their homeland by Islamist nationalist forces determined to build a homogenous, all-Muslim Tunisian society. I will attempt to reveal the reasons behind the current struggle for democracy in Tunisia and why it is failing miserably. This book is about the indigenous people of Tunisia who no longer live in the country that was their home and where they lived for thousands of years. This is the story of a people who are about to disappear completely, leaving behind little trace of their history and no friends anywhere, only decades of silence in Tunisia, Israel and elsewhere. The silencing of the past has happened elsewhere as well, in other LCA (Lands Conquered by Arabs) countries and in identical forms of silence. We will follow the evolution of this Tunisian community over the centuries, breaking myths and giving voice to silences along the way. After all, Tunisian Jews were not a small minority in Tunisia. *They were Tunisia.*

In order for our story to be complete, we have to follow Tunisian Jews and their lives in Israel since 1948, revealing how waves of Jews pushed from Tunisia were directly linked to Israeli-Arab wars. We must also examine how Tunisian leaders have led a suicidal political path by letting the country be hijacked by Palestinians and the Palestinian cause, and of course by radical political Islam. Once in Israel, Tunisians and other North African Jews simply retreated into a 65 years of deafening silence and silencing. The book is about the reasons behind this long silence and why it has to be broken. It is the story of a prosperous people reduced to an ethnic group in need of emancipation, a process which has led to their complete disappearance. The Tunisian Jewish story is not unique in this sense. Jews of Yemen, Iraq, Iran, Egypt, Libya, Algeria, Morocco, Syria and other countries all share fundamentally similar experiences and history, both in their country of origins and in Israel.

Discussing Tunisian Jewish history was for decades limited to the examination of cultural heritage: religion, food, music and other cultural and ethnic aspects. But, this is all politically inflected and inherently mixed with the political and historical situation in the Middle East, Europe and Africa. It is therefore impossible to understand our story without embarking on a long journey beyond Zionism and colonialism, beyond the Palestinian question, and even beyond Islam, Christianity and even ancient Israel. As we will see, the history of Tunisia, and hence Tunisian Jews, is inseparable from the history of Europe and its links to Africa; it is inextricably linked to the history of the heart of the world, ancient and modern.

The rise of Islam as a religion and as a political religious movement is obvious, as Islam's world population has surpassed 1.5 billion people and counting. What also appears obvious is that Islam as a state actor and state-empire religion in the post-colonial era has been resistant to appreciating and accepting others with different religions. Millions of Christians have fled North African and Middle Eastern countries. Syrian and Lebanese Christians, once at the forefront of these territories, now reside in North and South America and are preoccupied with building new communities. Egyptian Coptic Christians today are doing all they can to escape the present situation of war, poverty and persecution in their country. In South America alone, there are tens of millions of people from the Middle East, 99 per cent of them Christian. Jews from the same region were also migrating, but suffering even greater persecution, under fear from both the Christians and the Islamists.

This book will demonstrate how this persecution process was done in Tunisia to Tunisian Jews, shattering some of the myths of both Israeli and Tunisian historians and politicians that Tunisian Jews just immigrated to Israel of their own free will or as part of a messianic prophecy, a belief which presumably was held by members of that community. Jews of Tunisia were instead largely pushed out by Islam and Islamic nationalism and have completed an exiling process with the aid of Zionist and Jewish organizations, as well by French colonial interests. I will demonstrate that Tunisian Jews, like their counterparts across North Africa, were mostly an urban population who held free professions and had a unique history that was completely misunderstood by Israel's political and cultural apparatus, which was pushing (as in Tunisia) for a homogenous society. This book will show how fragile the Jewish community in Tunisia became after WWII, emerging from a long and brutal Nazi and Fascist occupation, as well as a racist French Vichy colonial government, which incidently was no less destructive. We will also embark on a political journey claiming boldly that the history of Jews of LCA has a political significance which directly affects current peace processes between Israel and its neighbors, including the negotiations for peace with the Palestinians. Acknowledging this history in itself could play a decisive role in Israel's future as a viable society in the heart of the Middle East. So far, more than half of Israel's population has found no political platform to deal with the injustices, myths and prejudices in their new home. Indeed, the absence of a political voice has forced them into pre-designated ethnic roles. Politically they were part of the silent people of the world, just like the Berbers of North Africa and the North American Indians (First Nations). Still, the history of Jews from LCA is important for Israel's moral and physical survival and for the transformation of energies from war to peace, peacefully. This was important in 1948, but even more so today.

A meaningful change in the region cannot happen without the acknowledgement of this unique history of over half of Israel's population. In fact, I argue that continuing to ignore their history had been disastrous for Israel and for the region, leading to 65 years of continuous violence. After all, the Jews of North Africa were more influenced by Berber heritage than by Arab and Muslim colonialism, and their perennial oppression. Their tradition and languages, their music and customs were all feeding off thousands of years of coexistence with the other indigenous tribes and peoples who stood strong to counter foreign Arab, Muslim and Christian invasions. Taking into account their story will necessarily lead to the unraveling and deeper appreciation of the Palestinian story as well.

The ethnicity of Tunisian Jews is the dominant narrative in Israel. All discussions of North African Jews have been centered on the folkloric side of these ethnic groups, as is the case with indigenous populations everywhere in the world. Social scientists and anthropologists have often described the ethnic character of these communities, avoiding at all cost the big historical picture of the region and the political implications inherent in their story. In many books, articles and studies published in Israel, ethnic diversity, the melting pot and other exotic terms have been used to describe the integration of LCA Jews into Eastern-European Israel. It did not matter that an ancient, non-European Jewish community was always had a presence in Israel, a community that had nothing to do with Zionism as a political philosophy, or with nationalism of any kind. A philosophical discussion of early Zionism is not my objective here, but it is evident from the history books, literature and popular culture that the Zionist ideology lacked the ability to comprehend the complexities and richness of the world outside of its Eastern-European framework in politics, culture and mentality. The nationalist and socialist fervor in the early days of Israel, combined with the new economic and military realities, proved to be disastrous to the ideals inherent in the original Zionist dream.

Venturing beyond the European heritage of Israel into the history of Israelis from LCA makes the current political situation even more complex. Dealing with external Arab threats was easy compared with issues dealing with the internal influences of Jews from LCA who carried with them the languages and customs from their countries of origins and who looked and behaved quite similar to the enemy across the border or across the street. Thus, race, color, religion, tribalism and ethnic composition played, and continue to play, a central role in Israel's political life. Since the 1950s everything in Israel has been based on ethnicity. All of Israel's political leadership including its ideology—Left, Right, religious or non-religious—was and still is ethnically driven, including the teachings of Professor Leibovitz.

The racial conflict was (and is) real, as Jews of Muslim lands with thousands of years of history in the "heart of the world" were now politically governed by new political and ethnic elites from Eastern Europe. Iraqis, Tunisians, Moroccans and others from other Middle Eastern and North African countries confronted a wall of unjust and unacceptable social and political order. Eastern Europeans in the early days of Israel's existence controlled the politics and economic life of the country, leaving little room for anyone to change anything. Above all they controlled the country's ideology. Social injustices and discrimination left Jews of LCA to wonder quietly about as to their future in the Holy Land, and a sizable number of them simply left for new places elsewhere. They silently kept to themselves, unable to compete with the horrors of the Holocaust as to "who suffered more" in Jewish history and who as a consequence had more political and economic rights. Jewish people of LCA identified with the suffering of Israelis of European background; but none of them had gone through the same horrific experiences—except the Jews of Tunisia. Yet, although these ethnic groups were torn by a sense of compassion, they still needed some sort of acknowledgment that they as a community did not suffer comparable catastrophes and that their history was different. The quest for recognition and acknowledgment was sometimes viewed, rightly or wrongly, as proof that they came from different kind of world. This view of their life in LCA was part of their defense mechanism: nostalgia, survival and urgency under fast eroding memory (individual and collective). They somehow knew that their unique non-European experience meant something in Israel, but what? Obviously, this was just wishful thinking in the early days of Zionism, as no one had any intention of attaching significant meaning to any of it; they were the poor immigrants, at times refugees, uneducated folk who should be thankful for this East European emancipation, they were viewed as people without history. After all, Pogroms, tribal wars and other violent clashes in LCA by Muslims and Christians cannot be equaled or even come close to what had happened in European concentration camps during the Second World War. It did not matter that what happened to Tunisian Jews during the war was no different than what happened to most Jews on the European continent. In Israel's political life the history of Jews of the Middle East and Africa meant nothing. It had no moral, political or historical significance. No value was attached to it anywhere in Israel's political life and especially in Israel's relationship with the Palestinians and the rest of the Arab world. Their story had no place in the education system, and it had no place in the Jewish psychic life. In fact, it was completely ignored. And if anyone dared mention it, it was paramount to treason and subjected to a "silencing treatment." After all, North Africans Israelis in Israel had no license to practice any form of independent political expression. The exception to this rule was the religious messianic cover story to their existence in Israel. We should remember here that over 50 per cent of the Israeli Jewish population comes from the Middle East and North Africa.

According to Israel's mainstream ideology, it was a merely a coincidence in history that Jews were not slaughtered in Tunisia, Morocco, Iran, Iraq, Lebanon, Egypt, Turkey, Algeria, and Libya. According to this logic, the Islamists, Arabs and

Palestinians would not hesitate to exterminate the Jews in Israel if given a chance, "never again". This basically sums up Israel's political philosophy of paranoia in the Middle East. This limited political thinking environment has led to the development of all kinds of strange political, social and religious movements, as well as to an overblown ghetto mentality and a physical ghetto reality of being a country encircled by fences. Even the political Left is in disarray, demanding higher fences to separate them from the Palestinians, their idea of two-state solution in miniature. Here is a recent example of this type of thinking. When Shamir, the former Prime Minister of Israel passed away on July 1, 2012, Benjamin Netanyahu, the current PM of Israel, in a government opening session, related to his famous statement uttered in 1991 before the Madrid Conference ("the Arabs are the same Arabs and the sea is the same sea"). Netanyahu pointed out that Shamir stuck to the fundamentals of Israeli politics and today many more appreciated the way he (Shamir) saw the political situation in the region. From our perspective, the above statement shows an unwillingness to understand the past and an inability to take control of the future. Anyone who sailed the Mediterranean Sea could also tell us how the Mediterranean Sea is constantly changing and affecting lives of the people living on its shores.

Everyone in Tunisia—Muslim, Jews and Christians—lived in submission to the Arab Aristocratic classes, the Sultans and the religious ruling class within the Ottoman Empire, the longest surviving empire in history. Those who refused to convert to Islam lived in a situation of submission. It is this part of Islam which concerns us in this book. Even the small island of the Maldives, now greatly threatened as a result of global warming, had recently entered the world of radical Islam in force: "No Law Contrary to Islam Can Be Enacted in the Maldives; Only

Muslims Can Be Citizens of the Maldives; Article 67(g) of the Constitution Obliges All Citizens to Preserve and Protect Islam." The same people who in the very near future will be pleading the world to be accepted as citizens elsewhere see no contradictions in drafting this pure and radical Islamic clause.

A day after the Muslim Brotherhood took power in Egypt during the 2012 presidential election, the White House published a written statement congratulating the winner, Mohammed Morsi. Interestingly, they also wrote: "We believe in the importance of the new Egyptian government upholding universal values, and respecting the rights of all Egyptian citizens—including women and religious minorities such as Coptic Christians. Millions of Egyptians voted in the election, and President-elect Morsi and the new Egyptian government have both the legitimacy and responsibility of representing a diverse and courageous citizenry." This statement has to be acknowledged as a remarkable improvement over how the "Spring Revolutions" were handled and viewed by the US administration and the media to that point. Alan West (a Republican Congressman), however, went a step further, not buying "all this nonsense," stating that, "Clearly, the Arab Spring is nothing more than a radical Islamic nightmare, now we need to unequivocally reiterate our support to the Coptic Christians and Israel." West could not have said the same about Tunisia because there, the job had been 100 percent complete, as no minorities were left to be counted.

Thinking about the issues we will be tackling could make one's head spin in despair and confusion: The Second World War, the Holocaust, the creation of Israel in 1948, the Palestinian refugees, wars, cold and hot (many of them: 1948, 1956, 1967, 1970, 1972, 1973, 1982, 1992, 1996, 2006, not to mention the various intifadas and Gaza wars of attritions), and the disappearance of ancient indigenous communities of Jews from Muslim countries, all in fewer than 65 years. How do we make sense of it all? Which political theory can even begin to put things in order? How do we interpret the history of the Jews of the Muslim world? What can we learn? How do we prevent further escalation of an extremely fragile situation in Israel and in the region as a whole? Our sons and daughters, Muslims, Jews and Christians, are tired of this inherent inability to live in peace.

The Jasmine Revolution in Tunisia was a turning point which helped demonstrate the real motives behind the expulsion of the Jews of Tunisia. The distorted and very confused narrative which was painted for decades by Israelis and Tunisians was no longer a sufficient cover for what had happened to the Jews there. The Tunisia revolution reminded us of the forces at work in the Arab world, not just in that country. The same forces were operating when the Jewish population fled during the 1950s. Egypt is undergoing almost identical problems, with identical results, now that the President of Egypt, as in Tunisia, is also from the Muslim Brotherhood. Nothing in our theory will change if he is removed and replaced by an Islamic military rule. Our perspective here, although a bit different from critics of the Islamic world, will help shed some light on the present on-going events in North Africa.

The history of the Jews of North Africa, the history of Zionism and the Israeli Palestinian problem are all interconnected. A North African-Israeli perspective on history and events in the region may be unique and may even lead to further confusion. But what other choice do we have? We cannot continue studying only Jewish history in Poland and Hungary and hope that this will somehow lead to better understanding and relations with

Arab states. North African countries were under occupation over the years not just by the French, English, Turks, Spaniards, Romans and Phoenicians and many others, but also by Arabs and Islam who invaded the area in the seventh century and have been the principal conqueror to this day. This is why we call the whole of North Africa and most of the Middle East LCA, Lands Conquered by Arabs.

Religious rulers, conquerors and nationalists throughout history have eliminated traces of unacceptable history; it is the first thing conquerors do, whether Christian, Jewish or Muslim. The Arab Spring in Egypt is undergoing similar tendencies, as religious interest groups have targeted historical documents housed in museums and basements everywhere making sure they disappear. Muslim nationalists and radical Islam have a problem with the large Islamic country of Egypt because of the rich pre-Islamic history which exists everywhere, under every stone and sand dune, in every landscape, artwork and cultural artifact. Islamists would make the pyramids disappear if only they could. And they would do this just to make sure that nothing existed before Islam, as nothing is meaningful outside of Islam. One Imam in Egypt was even contemplating covering the pyramids with wax, out of sight of the ordinary people of Egypt in order to avoid corrupting their minds with non-Islamic historical evidence and issues. In Syria, Abraham's Safe, the historic mausoleum of the Prophet Abraham, was recently (in June 2013) bulldozed, eliminating thousands of years of history, some of which are shared by Muslims as well. Similarly, Omar Ja'ara, a lecturer at Al-Najah University in Nablus, offered a skewed interpretation of the Bible on Palestinian TV, stating a few days before the Jewish Passover in 2012 that "Moses led the Muslims out of Egypt" and that "the conquest of Israel consequently was the first Palestinian Liberation of Palestine." But he has not lost his mind; he simply reminds us how easy it is to bend history.

Destroying historical evidence and traces of unwanted history has long roots in the Islamic tradition from Iran to North Africa. The actions of radical Islamist disrespect are manifest in the breaking up of monuments (e.g. cemeteries and synagogues in Libya and Tunisia this year) and various sites in Afghanistan for the past 100 years. "Based on the verdict of the clergymen and the decision of the supreme court of the Islamic Emirate (Taliban), all the statues (Buddhist) around Afghanistan must be destroyed," said a recent decree.[1] "All we are breaking are stones," the Afghan militia leader claimed. "Only Allah, the Almighty, deserves to be worshipped, not anyone or anything else," Mulla Omar's decree said. And in 2011, "Egypt lost an important part of its cultural heritage after important manuscripts and up to 200,000 books were destroyed by fire in the building of the Egyptian Scientific Institute in Cairo."[2] Similarly, ancient documents in Mali were purposefully destroyed in recent attacks by Islamists (2013). In Tunisia, very little is left of the documents and monuments of native Tunisian Jews. What was not looted by the Germans in 1943 was burnt by radical Islamists, such as the Synagogues burned in 2001, Gebes 2002, Djerba in 1985, 1958, 2012 and so on. Jews had been living in Djerba for more than 3,000 years before being looted by the Nazis in 1943, and well before the calls for their extermination again by the Salafists in 2012. In Sfax, as well, two synagogues were completely destroyed and looted, a reaction to the recent (2012) confrontation between Israel and Hamas in Gaza.

In 1958, only two years after Tunisia's independence, new measures were taken and a new series of anti-Jewish government decrees were promulgated. In 1958, Tunisia's Jewish Community Council was abolished by the government, and ancient synagogues, cemeteries and Jewish quarters were destroyed for "urban renewal," they said. The destruction of Jewish monuments, artifacts documents and synagogues in the whole of the Arab world is not very well documented because only recently has anyone taken notice. The destruction has replicated itself in identical forms in all Islamic countries—only the degree of destruction varied. Simply put, there is no one left to document or contest the destruction, and no one was there to contest either.

The Arab Spring has resulted in the Muslim Brotherhood becoming the dominant political group in the area. They took control of the state in both Tunisia and Egypt in presumably fair and democratic elections. Their objective as a religious group is to institute Sharia law. Yet, in the West it was called a revolution. How can we call an Islamic takeover of the state and the implementation of Sharia law a revolution? From our perspective, it is simply a continuation of the long historical trend of cleansing all minorities and expanding a Bey-like (Turkish Sultan) power base. Apparently, there is no place for minorities and other religions in the newly created nationalist Islamic states in Africa and the Middle East. The more powerful radical Islam had become, the less minorities were able to survive. In Egypt and Tunisia, the banners of new demonstrations of the very few now read: "No to the hijacking of the revolution! No to a new dictatorship!" These very few are trying to hold to some form of sanity in the sea of distortions.

For the first time, an 'amazingly' "fair election" was held in Tunisia in 2011, and El Ennahda, a "moderate" Islamic Party won a majority. This was also an actual headline in most newspapers in Tunisia and in the West. It was exactly the same in Egypt. The terms "fair elections," "moderate Islam" and "Arab Spring Revolutions" infiltrated our political jargon. The number of unemployed in Tunisia has exceeded 800,000 out of a work force of 3.8 million, an alarming figure in a country of about 10 million. The unemployment rate has reached 18 percent, compared to 14 percent in 2010, and in the South the unemployment rate has reached 30 percent. This additional unemployment has further worsened the economic situation and deepened the social crisis as well. All this in a country that has never gone to war and basically has no heavy military expenditures.

Despite the obvious reasons for optimism, Tunisians after the revolution have not yet noticed significant change. The same problems remain. State institutions are still weak amidst the sensation of freedom felt by many: "Security forces and other control services have failed to ensure stability and public order. Even civil servants have sometimes felt insecure in their offices due to the use of violence at protests, as the government is still not controlling the country properly."[3] Who can expect social and economic reforms under such a fanatical religious regime? Tunisians are torn between this revolution going forward towards modernization, and adhering to radical political Islam with its restrictive and depressive nature. They cannot have both at the same time. But the tendencies of religious fanatics trying to run the state are not unique to Islam. Israel is suffering from a similar reality with its own nationalist religious Jewish groups, who are becoming stronger every day. It somehow seems as though extremists, both Muslim and Jewish, are competing with one another throughout the region.

In the not so distant past, the burka and the veil generally worn in some parts of the Arab world were limited in Tunisia to a few from the older generations and were rarely seen in the city of Tunis. Tunisia was the European face of Africa and the Middle East, more so than Cairo or Alexandria.[4] Yet, the current Islamist agenda in 2012 has transformed the country into something Tunisia had never known before. In reference to Sharia law, Omar Bakri gives us a glimpse of this: "I invite them, and if they accept the command of Allah, then they may do so. If they don't accept, and kick me out of the country, then we will fight against them. The relationship between us is either a pact of belief in Allah, or a peace treaty, or war."[5] This belief was a constant but unimplemented theme in Islamic history throughout North Africa, but it had been reinforced under the current Islamic nationalism.

Breaking the Silence

Fighting extremism and violence in the long run can only be achieved through education. Universities will have a decisive role to play in the new Tunisia. Academics are now called upon to fight their laziness.

Dr. Hammouda Salhi, University of Tunis

The story of Tunisian and North African Jews matters because over one million of them were forced to leave their homelands and country of origins. They all left behind their homes and belongings, their lands, their culture, languages, history and their territorial identity. The traces they left behind have been eliminated over the years. These same communities have been betrayed by the intellectual classes everywhere, including Israel, who for decades refused to acknowledge this event and place it in its proper historical perspective. This is the part of Jewish history which has been silenced for decades. How is it possible that more than 1.2 million people indigenous to the regions of North Africa and the Middle East disappeared and no one in the international community took notice?

What happened to Jews of LCA is clearly no less tragic than what had happened to the Palestinians in Israel. Yet, they are looked upon as marginal and unimportant events. But what happened to the Jews in each of the Muslim countries was not altogether different from what happened to the Palestinians in both intensity and in numbers. The Jews of North Africa and the Middle East were part of the population of these countries for centuries, only to be forced out completely within a span of 30 years and disappear into thin air within 65 years. It is a big issue, ignored for decades by Israelis and by Western countries, as well by as every international organization from human rights groups to the United Nations. Jews of North Africa and the Middle Ease have been ignored and silenced for as long as they can remember.

However, placing the history of Jews of North Africa and the Middle East in its historical perspective has important implications on how we view everything in the contemporary political and social situation of the nations in these regions, including Israel. It can positively affect peace talks between the Palestinians and Israelis, and it can help unmask the false support given to shady organizations and regimes in Tunisia, Israel and elsewhere. It can affect how we view Islam and how Islam views itself. It will necessarily affect how Israelis view Zionism, as well. This issue is probably the single most important factor in curtailing Jewish and Muslim radicalism in the quest for peace in the Middle East. So far, the whole issue was completely silenced. What were the reasons behind the silence and silencing?

Of all the Muslim countries, only Tunisia was occupied by the Nazis during the Second World War. During this time hundreds of thousands of German and Italian soldiers occupied the country, which was already under French Vichy control. The occupation lasted a little over six months, and the Allied Forces captured a staggering 275,000 German and Italian prisoners of war. This was a period of complete turmoil for Tunisian Jews. If not for the Allied victory they would have ended up in European and African concentration camps—victory was not self-evident. Throughout its history, Tunisia has been strategically important, and attempts to capture it were a reoccurring event, from the Phoenicians, Romans, Arabs, and Turks, to the Germans and Italians. And now radical Islamic forces all over again. It is situated only a few hours by boat from Malta and not much farther from Sicily. The Germans calculated the advantages in controlling Tunisia, not just in circling Europe around the Mediterranean but also as part of their future expansion plans into Africa and the Middle East in the quest for a global colonial empire. Conquering and colonizing Africa, most of which was under European colonial rule, was tempting for both the Germans and the Italians, each for its own historic and political reasons. Having colonies and building empires was always a dream for the Germans, and even more so for the Italians, who had already tried and failed twice in colonizing Ethiopia; they wanted to make up for their inability to exert colonial control.

Once in Tunisia, the Germans wasted no time in executing their final solution for the local Jewish population. The Jewish community as a result was totally devastated, as they lost the French protectorate that helped stabilize their situation in the face of Muslim uprising. There was also a large Italian Tunisian population, who found themselves in a tragic collaboration with Nazis and Italian Fascists. Thousands of Jews were rounded up; some were sent to work camps within Tunis, while others were sent to camps in Europe to never return. By 1943, Jews had lost faith in their future in the area. Tunisia, like many other colonies, was now entering an era of struggle for independence whereby Jews were almost totally excluded from the new social and political design. By the end of the 1940s, and with the creation of the state of Israel, Jews began their exile. There was no place for them in the struggle for Islamic Tunisian nationalism. Independence meant the return of Muslim religious rule and no Tunisian Jew was longing for this again. Three thousand years of Jewish history in Tunisia came to an end. In addition, the Israeli-Arab wars of 1956 and 1967 led to a greater hardening of the Islamic base, making it perfectly clear that Jews were not wanted and were increasingly unwelcome. Within a span of 35 years all Jews were pushed to leave for Israel, France and America.

Still, Tunisia was seen for many years as a moderate force in the Arab-Islamic political culture. Bourguiba, the first President after independence, did his utmost to convince other Arab countries to recognize Israel's right to exist and was ousted from the Arab League because of that. Bourguiba's position on Israel and on Jews in Tunisia was a curious one. His position of not going along with Pan-Arabism and the Arab League boycott of Israel was a result not of "practical policies,"[6] as some have suggested, but rather a result of his understanding of Tunisia's moderate role and the inseparable historical link Tunisia had with the Jewish people as well as their Berber origins. Bourguiba's stance on Israel lasted until the end of the 1960s. In 1963, he called the Arab states to recognize Israel in return for a solution to the Palestinian problem in a speech given in Jordan. By virtue of the existence of a still considerable large Jewish population, Bourguiba tried to secure economic relations and aid from the West, especially the US, as part of his politics of non-alignment during the Cold War. However, by 1967, when no Jews were left in Tunisia, he had no basis and no need for this ideology and began to toe the line with other Islamic countries. Neverthless, for a brief moment there was even talk of listing him as candidate for the Noble Peace Prize. Obviously, "it was clear from the outset that Bourguiba would not receive the Nobel Prize, which was offered to individuals who actually resolved conflicts."[7]

His position and contribution to resolving the Israeli-Palestinian problem was noticed but not given credit nor encouragement. But his real motives were completely unclear. His administration's secret negotiations with Israelis and Jewish economic organizations were interesting. Israelis, including Golda Meir, actually thought in 1965 that Israel was in a position to help Tunisia with the development of Jewish tourism from the US. But Golda Meir was wrong on many levels, and her ideology was based on a fundamental absurdity: you first help take the Jews who lived in Tunisia for more than 3,000 years out for the slums of Israel and then arrange for rich American Jews to help Tunisia through tourism. But then, Golda Meir's prophecy-like approach eventually became a reality. Thousands of Tunisian Jews, including Israelis, started travelling to Tunisia every year for the Lag Baomer celebration, or out of curiosity and nostalgia. (Tunisia also became a favorite tourist place for Germans visiting the Mareth Museum, built along the defensive lines where many German soldiers died during WWII.) For Golda Meir, like her predecessors, there was no such a thing as a "Palestinian problem," nor was there an Israeli Black Panther movement. For her, there were only ungrateful North African Jews living in Israel and not appreciating what was being done for them. There was no Yom Kippur war developing as she stalled the emergency call for army deployment until it was too late resulting in tens of thousands of casualties in the only real war Israel fought in its short history. In her capacity as Foreign Minister, she felt she was in a position to help Tunisia through the tourist industry. Unfortunately, Israel in 1965 was in no position to help anybody, especially not Tunisia. Even still, Bourguiba saw an opportunity not to be missed in all this: Tunisia without Jews but with Jewish American tourism. He could not believe how easy the whole thing was. Not only that no one noticed how he was Islamizing Tunisia by ridding it of its Jewish population but also being rewarded by Meir's blessings and the promise of tourist money. Even the few remaining Tunisian Jews believed he was protecting them against Islamic extremists.

While analysing the recorded conversations Bourguiba had with Jewish leaders such as WJC, Eastman, the foreign ministry and others, it became clear that the question of Tunisian Jews was not discussed nor was it mentioned. It was non-existent. The only concern Jewish organizations and the Israeli State had was to get as many Jews out of Tunisia to Israel, and this was discussed on numerous occasions. This policy is one of the foundations of Zionism and it continues to this day. The Israeli government, along with various Jewish Agencies, will push for Jewish immigration wherever Jews exist and wherever and whenever possible. In the early years of the state of Israel, the interests of Islamic nationalism and Israeli nationalism met in a truly unholy alliance that has carried on until today.

Bourguiba could not develop an open relationship with Israel, and Israel was in no position to understand how to develop such a relationship with Tunisia or with any of the North African and Middle Eastern countries. For Israeli elites Tunisia was Arab and so was its Jewish population, who were in desperate need of emancipation and incapable of contributing to any dialogue with their countries of origin. There were some 140,000 Tunisian Jews living in Tunisia by late 1940s. By the late 1960s, all had been pushed out by three powerful forces: Colonialism, Islamic nationalism and Jewish nationalism (Zionism). No Israeli of Tunisian origin was involved or had any say in any of the negotiations taking place between Bourguiba and Israel over many number of years. By 1982, Tunisia was committed to helping the Palestinian Liberation Organization (PLO) set up base in Tunis, and this was followed by two Israeli raids inside the country. Bourguiba was afraid of the Islamists and radical Islamists in his country, but he did not realize that the Palestinian movement was heavily if not completely manipulated by radical Islamic interests. The Palestinian cause was a heavy ideological burden and was instrumental in making people forget about important local issues, such as poverty and corruption. Support for the Palestinian cause was also a way of easing the deep-rooted guilt brought on by the disappearance of Jewish Tunisia. Bourguiba subsequently misinterpreted the degree of these influences, and the thousands of Palestinians that were welcomed into the country proved to be disastrous for Tunisia, Tunisian politics and his own legacy.

There is no doubt that Zionist activities in Tunisia influenced the Jewish community and affected the fragile equilibrium of its long-standing existence as the ancient people of Tunisia. Every segment of the Zionist movement had its representation in Tunisia in the form of youth organizations. Zionist political leaders were particularly after the young Jewish population of Tunisia, many of whom participated but had not made the ultimate move to settle in Israel. In 1956, Tunisian authorities started to question the logic of these exiling processes to Israel, which they had gladly created. For a brief moment, a sense of guilt was surfacing as hundreds of Tunisians were coming back from the Holy Land with terrible stories of racism and discrimination, extreme poverty and hardship and other strange reasons. One Tunisian official was worried because Tunisian Jews in Israel were treated as second-class citizens and decided to slow down emigration. Egypt forced their Jews to leave despite harsh criticism by Bourguiba, who in turn opened the doors to *Aliyah* (Jewish absorption) agents to operate freely in Tunisia and to do exactly the same thing. The results of both policies were the same: the elimination of local and ancient Jewish communities.

Bourguiba, in fact was the only leader of the Arab world who was clear, writing in his journal that the "Jews are our brothers," and outlining the exceptional relations Jews and Muslim had in Tunisia.[8] Through his new Destour party he acknowledged that Zionism was a political movement that "did not contribute positively to Arab Jewish relations anywhere." However, his opponents knew very well how to capitalize on the Palestinian question to advance a radical Islamic agenda. In 1938 he understood the difference between the two national movements taking place in the land of Palestine. He was open about the conflict, and in a 1965 speech in Jericho he claimed that everyone should understand that there is no such a thing as an "all or nothing" approach in politics. He encouraged moderation and the acceptance of a peace treaty with Israel, even if it meant major concessions by the Palestinians, so things would not get worse. If the goal was the creation of a Palestinian homeland then concessions had to be made to attain this. There was no other way. This practical approach was adopted many years later by Abu Mazan, the Palestinian leader who claimed just before Passover in 2012 that he and his administration were committed to peace since "there is no other way." Israel's reaction to Bourguiba's peace initiative was best described by Aba Eban in 1965 stating on Israel's state radio that: "Israel's reaction must be prudent and measured,"[9] indeed a typically shortsighted, diplomatic and highly limited and unintelligent response.

North African countries, preoccupied with anti-colonial movements, were free to push out the undesirable minorities in favor of Islamic homogenous societies. They rejected colonialism "en bloc" (Albert Memmi), so the Italians, French, the Jews and the Maltese all had to be pushed out. Thus post-colonialism in North African Islam provided the framework for the total elimination of the Jewish populations, and there was no outcry and no questioning by anyone inside or outside of the country. The international community did not view this as an issue. From Egypt to Morocco, indigenous Jewish populations were pushed out, each under similar circumstances and under various degrees of violence. This had a tremendously negative impact on the political and economic development of the whole of North Africa, and even throughout the entire African continent and the Middle East. This was not so much because this segment of the population would have been beneficial economically (an argument which can easily be supported historically), but because the green light to rid themselves of the Jews was also a green light for the development of radical Islam and the further ousting of other minorities, leading to turmoil in North and sub-Saharan Africa. As mentioned above, North African Jews were not strangers to the region, nor were they refugees or temporary residents, yet in this context it was easy to push out close to a million people of indigenous local population. And, if we include Jews of the Middle East as well, we reach the staggering number of over one million people. No one contested or cried foul, and no one questioned the long-term ramifications of such actions.

As Tunisia ousted all its minorities, to become a truly homogenous Islamic country, it was engaging in a total reversal of its character, which it had held for the past 30 centuries. Bourguiba, the first President, thought he was in his position for life, like many leaders across Africa, North and South. The Jews also tended to believe, at least in the first years of independence, that he would guard their interests and their rights against the Islamists. By the end of the 1950s, they were increasingly becoming afraid of what would become of them after Bourguiba's rule, as pressure from radical Islamic groups was mounting. It was also obvious that their faith was directly linked to what was happening in the Middle East, between the Jewish state and their Arab Muslim neighbors. Bourguiba under-estimated the powers of radical Islam and under-emphasized the social and legal measures, which should have been taken after independence. He spent his energy convincing the Jewish population that they were equal citizens under a new Islamic institution, forgetting that this large minority was tired of Islam, Islamic laws, Sharia law and its view of human relationships. For Tunisian Jews, anti-colonialist struggles were the beginning of the end of their existence as people and as an identifiable group.

Only international interference by colonial powers could have ensured and enforced governments in North Africa to accept their minorities. In the case of Tunisia, nothing short of the government declaring that Tunisia is not a religious state—that it would accept its Jews as part of what Tunisia is and was—would have calmed the minorities in the country. Obviously, this could not have happened considering the rapid expansion of radical Islam in the whole of the North African continent, and considering that the Palestinians were able to link all Jews in the world with their conflict with Israel. In addition, the Cold War was of no help in this respect. Dictators, both religious and non-religious, were more than happy to comply with this theme as it became central for their attempts to exercise absolute authority. It also permitted these governments to continue doing nothing about poverty and underdevelopment. Just recently, during the 2012 Egyptian presidential election, the Muslim Brotherhood candidate was using the same methods trying to energize the base and the masses, hoping that the anti-Israel rhetorical magic would work again, and thus diverting the calls for real change.

The new Muslim states of North Africa linked the faith of their Jewish indigenous population to the Palestinian conflict with Israel. They did not see the contradiction and irony of pushing Jews out of their homes and at the same time calling for Palestinian rights. Tunisia was uniquely situated to become a center for technological advancement, as well as the study of Islam, Judaism and of Christianity all at the same time. It was an opportunity that even Bourguiba knew existed, but he could not implement it. Instead it had become a tourist attraction for the French, Germans and others, including a handful of nostalgic Tunisian Jews. Today it has become a hotbed for radical Islamists from the rest of the Arab world. In a way it is stuck with this trend, the outcome of an ethnic cleansing policy, which deprived Tunisia of one of its most vibrant population; it could have led to a totally different country, because Tunisia without its Jews and its Berber is simply not Tunisia.

Was it primarily Islam that pushed Jews out of Tunisia? Or was it the incompetent dictatorial post-colonial leaderships? Ultimately, it was the result of multiple factors, including Islam, post-colonial thinking, the Israeli-Palestinian conflict and Pan-Arabism. Still, Tunisia was uniquely positioned to handle these questions and interests, and become a model for tolerance and cultural and religious pluralism. It is difficult to think of another majority Muslim country that could have permitted their Jews the freedom it needed to thrive. In 1948, radical Islam was only emerging and was not a factor in preventing a different Tunisia.

Tunisia today includes the Jews in their tourist guides, which remind the world that the country *once* had a Jewish population, nothing more. Travelers can see synagogues (most of which were looted or burned) and Jewish cemeteries (the few remaining ones) as evidence—but that is all they can do. They will not find anyone teaching Jewish Tunisian history in school, neither in Tunisia nor in Israel. Tunisians cannot even turn to Israel for morale support for their politics of ethnic cleansing, because 20 percent of Israel's population is Palestinian, mostly Muslims, but also Christians and others. Can you imagine Tunisia having 20 percent of its population Jewish? From archives and speeches, it is more than obvious that Bourguiba struggled with these issues. But he was only one of a few who did. Even the communist party of Tunisia had no interest in this 'Jewish Quetion'. In fact, Bourguiba was afraid of them too, jailing many of their members and outlawing their activities.

Unfortunately, Bourguiba and his government are credited with ensuring that no Tunisian Jews remained in the country. All were accepted as equal citizens in Israel, France, Canada, the US and other countries, and in the process they slowly vanished from world maps as a community and as a people.

Silence and the Jasmine Revolution

Revolutions are taking place in North African countries and in countries of the Middle East, and Islamists have taken over— "moderate Islamists," the headlines screamed. No one seems to notice the incredible contradiction of Islamists producing revolutions in modern times. No one is concerned with the fact that radical Islam was never really out of power for the last 1,300 years, at least not in Tunisia. These so called religious-political powers had simply consolidated their holds and now have full and total control over the lives of Tunisians who, after the ethnic cleansing described in the above sections, are for all intents and purposes 100 per cent Muslim. Islamists taking complete control of the state means one thing and one thing only: "Spring Revolution" or "Jasmine Revolution" means nothing but an Islamic rule under the guise of a "revolution" in the Western sense of the word, with the support of Western media and other geopolitical forces. The fantastic part is the Islamic ability to combine the word revolution with radical Islam almost perfectly. The people got their revolution, and with it they got what they deserve. The young and liberal forces who worked for these "revolutionary" changes throughout area are now speechless, frustrated and writing in blogs that no one reads. Others just gave up and left for the other side of the Mediterranean in worn-out fishing boats. These young liberal forces that held strong for change at the outset no longer have the language and ideals to fight this failed revolution, no history to rely on.

Similar phenomena occurred in Iran years ago and in Egypt recent failed revolution. The young people who "googled," "tweeted" and "facebooked" during the overthrow of their beloved leaders have basically disappeared from the net. They still have their keyboards but lack the words to express their anger and frustration. Western media and intellectuals everywhere agreed that a revolution had taken place and that the people have voted in totally "free elections." Now what? The disappointment was crushing; the young aged physically and mentally all in a matter of weeks. The intelligentsia in their academic institutions was also not helping. A young Tunisian, Ghazi Beji, wrote a book in secret titled *The Illusion of Islam*, and soon after the so-called revolution he decided to publish it, believing that freedom of speech in the new Tunisia was a reality. This landed him in court for insulting Islam, and he received a seven-year prison sentence. Totally confused, he fled Tunisia and is now in Greece without money, passport or a job (there are no jobs at all in Greece), seeking asylum. His father was no less confused, and he stated in an interview: "My son is an unemployed graduate who hurt no one. Is he more dangerous than those who killed during the revolution? Is he more dangerous than the Trabelsis, the Ben Ali's, and the snipers? If they had work they would have never been involved in such a story. But they have the right to speak their mind. What's the problem if they are non-believers?" According to State persecutor Foued Cjeikh Al Zouali, the crime committed is worse than committing murder and he hopes that the new constitution will severely punish these types of crimes in order to protect Muslim Tunisian sentiments.[10] This lawyer sees no contradiction between what freedom of expression is and the need to guard against blasphemy. Everyone is free as long as they are "respectful." Their examination of the published document stated his crime: Beji doubts the existence of God; doubts the existence of a religion called Islam; doubts the existence of the Prophet Muhammad.

There was another case of a teacher, Mejri, who wrote a book called *Dark Land* and was sentenced to prison for transgressing morality, defamation and disrupting public order and morality. This is not new in Tunisia; history is full of punishments for insulting Islam. Every Tunisian Jew knew the limits of expression. They never enjoyed the concept of free expression throughout their history. In 1857, we have a recorded incident about Samuel Sfez, a Tunisian Jew, who was accused of insulting Muslims (not Islam) and was sentenced to an exceptionally cruel and bizarre death: molten lead was poured down his throat and "his head was severed from his body, and kicked through the city by Muslim boys, and then smashed by the men with stones."[11]

What was amazing in these court cases is that the language was exactly the same during the Bey and Ben Ali eras, but in reverse; the persecuted are now the persecutors almost overnight. And, as argued through these pages, little has changed in this respect since the Arab invasion in the seventh century, except the level or degree of oppression and the peaceful transfer of powers from the Bey to the Islamists.

Tunisian Jews could have told these young men the outcome before the so-called revolution started. We all knew the outcome in Tunisia, Egypt, Libya, Syria—and soon Algeria and Jordan and Lebanon. We could have told them that under no conditions should Imams be allowed to preach politics. The ordinary Jews never let their Rabbis speak politics in synagogues. We could have taught them how to distinguish between the language of revolutionary aspirations and the language of religious deceit. But Israel is also very close to being overtaken by ultra-nationalistic religious elements. They, thankfully have not found too much success, but they are hard at work waiting for the Messiah, waiting for the heavens, waiting to own everyone's soul and waiting to take full control of the State and its resources.

In 2011, I met a dear friend, a hard-core Leftist professor of political science, on a freezing morning in Montreal and he asked me, "What do you think about these amazing revolutions taking place in Egypt and Tunisia?" "What revolutions? I see no revolutions there." I answered. He left soon after to walk his dog, confused by my total disagreement with him. He really believed that progressive Leftist revolutions were developing in Arab countries. But, the Left trembles at the mention of revolution anywhere. We heard the same news and read the same newspapers, but understood the events in completely different ways. A few weeks later I met him again at a time when Christians were being attacked in Egypt, and Islamists had taken control of the State in "free and democratic" elections. He did not dare speak about the subject again.

Yusra Ghannushi, a journalist and daughter of Rashid Ghannushi, leader of the Tunisian Renaissance Islamic party, was speaking on CBC radio in 2012, trying to convince Westerners that Islamic values would not be "forced upon the people of Tunisia." She has repeated again and again that democracy and Islam can coexist, stating, "I know my father and he is not like that!" She was well-educated in English universities and knew how to do things with words to suit liberal Western audiences. The *New York Times*, in an article dated April 9, 2012, was also searching for something to hang on to in analyzing events in Tunisia: "But of all the Arab states, it may have been the best positioned for a successful transition to a liberal democracy, with its relatively small and homogenous population of about 12 million, comparatively high levels of education, an apolitical military, a moderate Islamist movement and a long history of a unified national identity."[12] Why is it not happening? They cannot figure it out. However, Tunisia has a liberal tradition because of its Jewish and Berber heritage, not because of Islam. The *Times* had to turn to a of bit history, not in Tunisia, but the 1912 Fez Pogrom in Morocco, when Muslim Moroccans blamed the Jews for the "agreement between the French authorities and Sultan Malai Hafiz making Morocco a French protectorate."[13] The whole of North Africa and the Middle East knew about this pogrom from national newspapers at the time. According to Paul Fenton, a researcher at the Sorbonne, this traumatic experience contributed much to a general uneasiness among Jews in the whole of North Africa. But he falls short from proclaiming that ethnic cleansing happened there too. By the 1940s there were more than 400,000 Jews living in Morocco and today, as in Tunisia, only a handful (2,500) of them remained. Morocco, like Tunisia, is also for all intents and purposes 100 percent Muslim. The *Times* just had to look at the massive anti-Israel and anti-Jewish demonstration in March 2012 in celebration of

Palestinian "Land Day." Muslims were looking for scapegoats; the Jews fit the occasion, even when there were none around.

No one bothered to speak up when Jews were pushed out of the whole of North Africa and the Middle East. No one asked why, and under what right? Little did they know that this would come back to haunt them later, with demands for Sharia law. Islamic expansionism went unchecked when minorities were thrown out of the so-called Arab countries with the help of third-world political theorists and others who called themselves revolutionaries. Tunisian Jews were a target in well-thought-out ethnic cleansing movement. This same movement is now no longer bound by national borders as the same demands and the same outdated political Islam is now inside Europe. It is a numbers game for the radical Islamists, who no longer bother to count their members. Silencing the history of Jews of North Africa came with a heavy price tag.

Asked at a 2010 White House event if she had any comments about Israelis, Helene Thomas, a famous pro-Palestinian journalist said: "Tell them to get the hell out of Palestine. . . Go home, to Poland, Germany, America and everywhere else." It is impossible to be more ignorant when speaking of the Middle Eastern conflict. Palestinians know the story of the Jewish people in WWII, the Holocaust and European anti-Semitism. Most also know a little about the other Jews, from the Middle East and North Africa. But, this part of the Jewish story is too confusing because it is also a part of the history of Islam. Unfortunately, the history of these Jews fits neither the Islamist nor the Jewish narrative.

During the Second World War, the Jews of Tunisia were looted, tortured, raped, killed, deported and bullied during the Nazi occupation. They were singled out, as elsewhere in Europe, for slave work and were taxed to death. The Muslims, for fear of reprisals and uprisings, were left alone. The Bey, the French and the Italians in Tunisia, as well as the Muslims (both nationalist and religious), took part in this system without much enthusiasm. Some helped the Germans and others just stalled the various decrees. Yet, singling out the Jews of Tunisia worked in favor of the various nationalist movements, which could not wait to have a Tunisia "free of Jews" and completely Muslim. The Jews of Tunisia understood what was required of them facing the new beasts of outright colonialism, Nazism and Islamic nationalism. The French were unreliable; the Muslim nationalists could not be counted on for anything; the religious elements of Islam were waiting for the Jews to leave; and the Berbers were too poor to raise their voices, and many converted to Islam for social benefits and greater opportunity. This was Tunisia in the aftermath of the Second World War.

The African Theater of War in WWII

I was born in Tunis to a family with deep roots in Tunisia and grew up in Israel, first in a tent, later in tin barracks, and then in a modest Palestinian house in Acre and Vadi Salib. I knew these were Palestinian houses at a very early age. We all knew this, adults and children in my family and in other families up and down the street. Every North African kid in the neighborhood knew whose houses these used to belong to. The houses there are still occupied by poor Jewish families; there are many poor people in Israel, like everywhere else, maybe even more—the imported, "ready-made" poor. One did not have to listen to Moshe Dayan's speeches to know that "Jewish villages were built in the place of Arab villages. You do not even know the names of these Arab villages, and I do not blame you because geography books no longer exist. Not only do the books not exist, but the Arab villages are no longer there either. Nahlal arose in the place of Mahlul; Kibbutz Gvat in the place of Jibta; Kibbutz Sarid in the place of Huneifis; and Kefar Yehushua in the place of Tal al-Shuman. There is not a single place built in this country that did not have a former Arab population."[14] I presumed that in Tunis some of the houses where we used to live are still standing, occupied by Tunisians who hopefully knew whose houses they once belonged to. The older generation knew, and some were even afraid, that Jews *would come back one day to reclaim their houses and streets, at least those that were not destroyed during the quest for "urban planning." This is mainly the reason why Tunisian Muslims are afraid of Jewish Israeli tourism. Many Jews lived in terrible conditions in the Tunis neighborhood of El Hara, a daily historical reminder for Muslims on who had to live in total submission. This did not prevent those Jews from embracing the Allied Forces in World War II. At the end of the Tunisian Campaign, it was the Jewish women of Tunisia who received the English army entering the city of Tunis in 1943 with smiles and Jasmine flowers, lots of them. The Americans also received their quotas of Jasmine flowers from Tunisian Jews when entering the city of Kairouan. The Jasmine symbolism was a Jewish Tunisian tradition exercised every Friday by rich and poor alike in Israel and in Tunisia, celebrating centuries of Berber culture.*

The history of the Holocaust has little to say about Tunisia and Tunisian Jews. Only a few hundreds of Tunisian Jews were taken to gas chambers by the Nazis, and only a few thousand died in the various work (slave) camps, the official count; *no one has real numbers in this story*. The Germans did not keep records on the numbers of deaths or on the level of destruction in this African country. In the greater tragedy of WWII, where tens of millions of people were killed and exterminated, Tunisia and Tunisian Jews did not matter. The magnitude of the Jewish tragedy in the Holocaust in Europe had overshadowed all other tragedies in the history of humanity. The Tunisian war was viewed as happening far away, somewhere in Africa in a place that had no effect on the big picture of world events. For decades this was the narrative accepted by historians and political scientists everywhere. Yet the big event that marked the outcome of WWII happened in Tunisia, once home to one of the most ancient

Jewish populations in the world. Like everything about Tunisian Jews, their story under the Nazis has also, to a large extent, been silenced in both Israel and Tunisia. But before we examine the story of Tunisian Jews under Nazism, it is important to further set the stage of the Tunisian Campaign. This will allow us to better understand what happened to Tunisia and to the Jewish community there during this destructive war. Indeed, Tunisia's delicate social fabric was destroyed completely during that time, and the country as a whole had not really recovered to this day.

The Second World War was largely about the colonial world order. At the turn of the twentieth century, an empire was measured and valued by its ability to acquire and conquer colonies in Africa, Asia and the Americas. In 1935, the leader of Ethiopia, the only African country never to be colonized by European powers (and which also had a large Jewish population), came to Geneva to plead with the League of Nations, as a member state, for actions against Italy's brutal invasion and attempts at colonization. Emperor Haile Selassie of the ancient and proud country of Ethiopia stood in front of the 54 member nations of the League of Nations and gave a dramatic and emotional speech, deploring the inaction of its members, crying for help to save his people from extermination and destruction. Italy's Mussolini had not forgotten the humiliation the Italian army suffered when it tried to attack and colonize Ethiopia in 1896, when Ethiopia defeated Italy and humiliated its army in a brilliant military campaign. Italy had not recovered from this defeat by a black African nation. The Italian General responsible for this fiasco was court-martialed and never commanded an army again. This time, however, Italy wanted to regain its international standing as a colonial power and aspiring empire by resuming its attempts at colonization, and Ethiopia again became the target.

Selassie's main argument during this famous speech was that the role and future of the League of Nations was at stake if no action was taken to stop Italy's aggression. Leaders of the League nodded in agreement while listening to this African Emperor but did nothing to prevent Italy's brutal attack. The inaction of the League of Nations basically ended its international role as peacekeeper and upholder of some form of international justice, post-WWI. Italy's aggression went unchallenged, signaling the deep-rooted weaknesses of its member States, and especially its colonial members, eventually leading to the Second World War. In essence, Europe gave Italy the green light, in "celebration" of colonialism, to invade this ancient civilization in East Africa. The main colonial powers were dividing Africa and the world among themselves, and Italy, like England and France, felt it was also entitled to colonial glory.

Germany also exercised her "God-given right" to Africa by claiming Namibia as their colony, called South West Africa, beginning in 1890s. This German colonial experience led to the almost total and complete genocide of the Herero indigenous people in 1904, the first genocide of the twentieth century. The Germans later accepted responsibility for the atrocities committed during that time, but never agreed to reparations, claiming that Germany provides enough aid to African countries through the various international organizations. When France decided to take Tunisia, it too received the blessing of other European nations. Tunisia was then under Turkish colonial Islamic control of the Ottoman Empire, the declining and longest-lasting Empire in history.

Another of Italy's failed colonial dreams was Libya, which Italy invaded in 1910 following fierce battles against Turkish and Arab forces, as well as local Berber tribes. They later integrated

Muslims into their military. Two divisions comprising of some 30,000 native Muslims were fighting alongside Italians against the British army in the Egyptian offensive. In 1937, Mussolini visited Libya and declared himself the "protector of Islam," expanding the military and native participation to 100,000 soldiers. All dictators in the region since then have claimed they were the "protector of Islam" and later the protector of Palestinian rights, which has greatly marked the political situation of the region.

By far the biggest player in this era of colonialism was France, with colonial interests spanning east to west across the African continent. Economic interests and historical economic ties continue to dominate France's relations with the colonies, even after the countries' various struggles for independence. France's unique form of colonialism meant the establishment of long-lasting economic and cultural ties with their colonies, irrespective of past, current and future local politics.

On November 8, 1942, the Allies landed in North Africa, 1,000 miles away from their Tunisian target, in Morocco. A naval task force consisting of five aircraft carriers, three battleships, seven cruisers, 38 destroyers, and various support vessels were dispatched there to lead the attack against Axis Forces. Three additional attack groups, totaling some 50,000 soldiers, landed at Safi, Fedala, Mehedia-Port and Lyautey. Other landings occurred at Oran and Algiers. They met sporadic but determined French Vichy resistance, which claimed 556 American lives, as well as the lives of about 300 British and 700 Free French soldiers. This part of the invasion was largely a success, despite the difficult logistical and military terrain conditions. Within months, the total Allied Forces rose to over 400 warships, 1,000 planes, and some 120,000 men, including a battalion of US paratroopers participating in the first airborne attack in WWII. During the whole of the Tunisian campaign, tens of thousands of sorties were flown by the Allied Forces and many thousands of bombs were dropped.

Operation Torch turned into the Tunisian Campaign, where serious major modern land and air battles took place. The biggest fight occurred in Tunisia from mid-November to January 1942, when Axis forces had raised their military presence there to 243,000 men and 856,000 tons of supplies and equipment arriving by sea and air, mainly from Italy. The urgency of both the Allied and the Axis Forces to take control of Tunisia was real, and both sides were determined to win this war, at all costs and as quickly as possible. By the end of the Tunisian Campaign in 1943, the Allied Forces had destroyed or neutralized nearly 700,000 German and Italian troops, and suffered casualties of 220,000 men (including the Torch Campaign).

A series of attacks and operations were taking place against Rommel's German and Italian forces involving mechanized and armored vehicles and bombers, and even hand-to-hand combat, as was the case in the battle of Kasserine in February 1943. By this time it was obvious that the German army was on the defensive as they pulled to the west after losing Tripoli. Hitler's orders at the time were to hold firm in Tunisia, promising more soldiers and supplies. He eventually gave considerable resources to his North African command which later proved to be disastrous to his main military objectives in Europe, especially on the Russian front.

Tunisia is strategically located on the Mediterranean Sea and foreign powers throughout the centuries have been tempted to conquer it. The country is situated only 400 km from Sicily and a few hours by ship from Malta, which was under British control during the war. Due to the proximity, the Germans were able to quickly furnish supplies and reinforcements on short notice through its fascist ally, Italy.

The Allied naval forces were weak during the initial part of the Campaign and Axis submarines could attack Allied ships in the waters of the Mediterranean with few Allied antisubmarine retaliations. Similarly, German and Italian planes were operating during the day, and went almost unchallenged at first. At night the Allied Forces were advancing west across the desert and the Atlas Mountains. Winter nights in Tunisia are rainy and cold, and this is when all allied attacked happened at the beginning of the campaign. During the day, the Axis air force patrolled the air, attacking anything that moved and ensuring almost total control of the air space.

The military confrontation between the Allied and the Axis forces was not just another battle in a series of confrontations with the Germans. It was a major campaign and to this day remains unequaled in its intensity on the African continent. Even the Yom Kippur war of 1973 between Egypt and Israel pales in intensity, number of causalities, and number of tanks, planes and navy war ships employed. The Yom Kippur war was also the last major modern war in history where armies directly confronted one another in both traditional and modern warfare. For example, the number of Israeli and Egyptian causalities combined in the Yom Kippur war was 20,000 (2,700 Israelis), compared with some 25,000 of Americans alone in the Tunisian campaign. The total casualties in all of Israeli wars since 1948 do not exceed 13,000. Total Allied casualties by May 1943 were more than 120,000 dead and tens of thousands injured. German causalities alone reached 155,000. By the end of the war, the

Allied Forces had captured more than 250,000 German and Italian prisoners of war. This discrepancy is largely a function of the length of time it took for both wars to end. The Israeli-Arab war of 1973 lasted 20 days, while the Tunisian campaign lasted seven months. In both wars, however, normal life of local citizens was completely disrupted, and in Tunisia it was not to recover again.

Tunisia was not under occupation during the campaign, though it was the site of a large-scale theater of war, which affected all life in the country. The whole of Tunisia from the south to the coast was engulfed in this war. All ports, airfields, roads and rails were under the control of the Axis Forces. All were used solely for the Axis military campaign purposes, and all were targeted by Allied bombers in many thousands of sorties, some accurately and others no so accurately inflicting tens of thousands of casualties among the local Tunisian population. The desert in the south, behind the mountains and the cities along the coast, was also a stage for massive destruction and mayhem. As shown in recently discovered archived sources, Hitler knew the importance of this war for his plan to dominate Europe, and subsequently the satellite colonies and eventually Egypt and Israel; he was determined to hold Tunisia at all costs. The other determining factor was American participation in the war. Hitler could not lose to the Americans in their first direct military confrontation in history. Thus, losing Tunisia to the Allied Forces was not just a blow to his military plans but a clear early indication of the beginning of the end of the Second World War. It was a total moral defeat for Germany, and it set the tone for the rest of the war; it also marked the beginning of a new era in Tunisia, an era of complete and total cleansing of its Jewish population.

This war was a massive operation on grand scale, difficult to imagine, in extremely harsh desert conditions, with armies directly facing off against one another. During the Tunisian campaign, more than 2,000 Axis aircraft were downed and 600 captured, compared with 800 Allied planes shot down. Here is an account of an air force participant, giving us a taste of the air operation in Tunisia: "The weight of daily attack during this period was heavier than any air force had ever delivered in collaboration with an attacking army. On May 6, during the final drive from Medjez el Bab to Tunis, we flew 2,146 sorties, the great majority of which were bomber, fighter-bomber or strafing missions on a 6,000-yard front."[15] There is nowhere to hide in the desert, which made tank warfare extremely complex and difficult. The sand and mud made it even more difficult to operate these machines, adding to the existing logistical nightmare. By the end of the Campaign Axis forces also lost some 250 war ships.

Underlying this "theater of Hell" was the complex logistical operation of supplying, feeding and maintaining the German and Italian armies in Tunisia. According to German records, some 200,000 tons of supplies had to be shipped each month to meet the basic requirements for the continued war against the Allied Forces, most of it was oil to fuel heavy tanks and other vehicles. The Italians were struggling to find ships to bring the necessary supplies by sea. This logistical operation was tough considering the lack of large ships (especially by Italy) and the increasing lack of full control of the Mediterranean Sea. Hundreds of war ships, submarines, attack boats and air bombings prevented the smooth transfer of supplies. The depths of the Mediterranean along the Sardinia-Tunisia route has its own hidden logbook of death, destruction and human remains.

During the entire campaign, Allied bombers concentrated on the supply line, starting with ports and train stations in Italy, continuing with stubborn air attacks on ships sailing to Tunisia, and ending in its harbors.

Tunisia has never really recovered since the war. Its Jewish population, as we will see, was devastated. The loss of their enthusiastic support for the French, who now sided with the Germans, was a further blow to the social and moral fabric of this community. It was the beginning of the end for them as a cohesive indigenous community in the country. And, as we will see in the next section, it was also the beginning of the end of Jewish life in the entire Arab world. The Italian and the Maltese populations also left Tunisia unable to hold their historical presence in the face of the Fascist alliance and Islamic nationalism.

It was heartbreaking for the Jewish population to see the logistical and military support Vichy officials and personnel gave to the Germans: "Vichy officials after the Torch invasion of North Africa offered to create a Légion tricolore in which French soldiers would fight with the Germans in Tunisia (November 1942)."[16a] The Germans rejected the offer. The rejection was consistent with the Nazis' reluctance to consider Vichy an ally. The French made their offer based on their calculations of how to continue to hold their colonies at all costs, even during the height of the war. Losing Tunisia to the Allied Forces, and especially to the English, was unthinkable; Tunisia was not Haiti. They were concerned not with pushing the war away from the mainland but rather about the fear of losing their God-given gift (with the blessing of the English, Germans and Italian 60 years earlier) of their Tunisian colony. Along with Algeria, Tunisia was France's playground, its backyard. This type of thinking continued well into the 1950s. Building (or rebuilding) empires was a fact of "political life" until after WWII. As Gregory Cooper states, "By 1955, the legitimacy of any colonial empire was very much in question. By 1965, the colonial game was over…and the nation-state was at last becoming the principal unit of political organization."[16] Nevertheless, the Germans were afraid of defections by the French forces and considered them an unreliable ally precisely because of their deep-rooted colonial interests. But it is curious that the French aligned itself with the Axis Forces, even more so than the Italians in Tunisia. Somehow, as the story goes, Italian Jews were spared the harsh treatment of the Nazis. The Fascists viewed them as instrumental in their own colonial aspirations in competing with the French in Tunisia, their last hope for a meaningful colonial heritage and presence. This was conveyed to the Germans and they agreed, at least in the first part of the Tunisian Campaign, to leave the Italian Jews alone. The Jewish community in this double unholy alliance found itself in an impossible situation, as both of their loyalties (Italian and French) proved to be historical mistakes for which they would later pay the ultimate price: exile and complete disappearance from the political and social maps of the world. All this had a paralyzing effect on the Jews of Tunisia. Their natural reaction of silence has lasted to this day, and in the absence of friends and supporters, their catastrophe has been of interest to no one.

The war ended with the Axis Forces collapsing like a deck of cards, and "enemy troops were surrendering in such large numbers that they clogged roads, impeding further advance." By the second week of May 1943, enemy German and Italian prisoners totaled over 275,000. Some historians (including Israelis) described all this as just another event in WWII, which misrepresents the end of the campaign. For example, as Hirschberg and his co-authors[17] write: "The evacuation of Tunisian by the Axis Forces took several weeks. They withdrew completely from Tunis on May 7 1943 and the vanguard of the British a few hours later." This distorted historical account reduces the Tunisian Campaign into a mere incident in the history of Tunisian Jews and in the history of WWII. The magnitude of the war and its disastrous effect on the Jews of Tunisia are glossed over.

Axis Generals began surrendering on May 9 1943 as the seven-month Tunisian Campaign entered its final days. The architect of the first "unconditional surrender" principle was a US General of Jewish faith (who enlisted in the military pretending to be a Christian) named Maurice Rose. All this happened while General Bradley turned his attention from fighting a "determined enemy to governing large numbers of civilians and prisoners." However, we never really found out what the Allied Forces did with the massive numbers of German prisoners. Pictures and videos showed them strolling at ease and in an organized fashion, each with his personal loads and some even with their briefcases. These Nazi and Fascist prisoners had more personal belongings going to prison camps in the days of surrender than the Jews had when they were forced to leave Tunisia for Israel and France during their exile. Also, no one from the Axis Forces was ever charged with crimes against humanity, crimes that had nothing to do with military operations. We have seen no documents of any SS soldiers arrested for their share in the horrors they instituted and initiated during their looting, raping and killing period in Tunisia. We are also unable to find out how long were they held as prisoners, nor any detailed information on Axis policies pertaining to Jews inside the country. It seems that none of the prisoners were interrogated on this question.

How were the camps maintained and supplied considering the large numbers of prisoners? Why no one was charged with war crimes? How many Tunisian Jews were killed in this Campaign by the Axis and Allied Forces?

There are many questions, very few answers and a lot of silence from Germany, France and Israel. A typical account from a Jewish perspective is the personal manuscript of Cohen-Adria,[18] a Jewish Tunisian doctor who provides a detailed account of life in the Jewish quarter and how Jews were organized. He spends many pages talking about the cultural life of Jews in the Ghettos before the war. The Second World War is mentioned in his manuscript only once; the history of this seven-month period had been completely silenced. Other publications demonstrate a similar tendency. The old generation was both silent and silenced about the ordeal because frankly, they could not possibly explain the events that took place in their country considering both their fragile existence and the magnitude of the war. It was for them both an extremely painful and shameful period at the same time. The silence of the new generation in Israel and elsewhere was inherited, and became a sort of a collective amnesia. They kept this tradition of silence, remembering nothing and knowing very little. At the same time, they could not possibly compete with the suffering of European Jews during the same period.

It is important to revisit this account of the Tunisian Campaign, because Israelis, Tunisians and Americans are still unaware of the full magnitude of what had happened in North Africa. Americans may have better sense of this war because of the high rate of causalities and the existence of a cemetery commemorating its dead in the city of Tunis. But our increasingly short collective memory has eroded this as well. Even Tunisians who lived through this period did not understand the events that were taking place before their eyes. The general view of many, including North African historians, was that the Germans came and left, leaving very little mark on the Jews of Tunisia and Tunisia as a whole. Israelis who read this will understand perfectly how devastating a war can be on a country and its people. In fact, Israelis are still trying in vain to forget the Yom Kippur war. Furthermore, Israel could not have physically, economically or morally sustained a long, drawn-out war.

The outcome of WWII was greatly determined by who wins the Tunisian Campaign. The Germans had shipped massive amounts of military equipment and hundreds of thousands of badly needed soldiers in the Russian frontier; the best-trained soldiers were sent to Tunisia. The Germans understood the importance of Tunisia in controlling the whole of the Mediterranean. Yet, military experts are often puzzled as to why Hitler invested so much of his military resources in this small country. To understand this better, we have to turn to the deeper history of Tunisia, which will be discussed in following chapters. It was also clear that the Germans underestimated the strength and resolve of the Americans who joined the British in the battle for Tunisia. Once they were involved, there was more at stake for the Germans. In a way this was also a testing ground for American military capabilities confronting the Germans in the wars ahead. The Americans and everyone else understood very well that without their involvement in Tunisia the outcome of WWII would have been dramatically different, especially for Tunisian Jews.

Not long before the end of the Tunisian Campaign, when it was clear that the Allies were winning the war, the famous German General Rommel left Tunisia with some of his staff and went back to Germany. He had lost a major war and everyone back home was aware of his failed performance. Rommel became a legend in both England and Germany in the early days of the Torch and Tunisian Campaign, each for different propaganda reasons, though each acknowledging him as a brilliant military strategist. British magazines and newspapers wrote extensively on the brilliant German General they were fighting against in Tunisia and Libya. In Germany, Rommel was the General responsible for losing Africa, but most of all he is credited to losing to the Americans. He was also responsible for losing Italy, again to the Americans. Yet this same general was posted at Normandy to offset the Allied invasion and save what was left of the German Empire. He was assigned in 1944 with convincing his forces that they could fight and win an Anglo-American invasion, which is strange, as in retrospect it looks like he was sent by Hitler into a suicide mission. He could not possibly "pull a victory out of a hat," as David Irving stated in an article about Rommel. Irving, who spent 30 years writing about Hitler, also had difficulties understanding Hitler's judgment of Rommel's military capabilities during the war.

During the First World War, Tunisia was undisturbed and participated only by sending a few thousands soldiers. By the middle of the Second World War, it had become a center stage and not just for military reasons but also because Tunisia had a major role to play within the Arab and Muslim world. While there, the Nazis planted a seed of destruction, which enhanced the already high Islamic nationalist fever. In this sense Germany has molded Tunisian nationalism. The German experience of total ethnic cleansing was replicated here to the last man. All this was done in a few short years after the war ended and without numerous concentration camps and excessive violence and torture, the Tunisian way. The Germans established the ground, and anti-colonialism provided the excuse for a complete and unapologetic system of ethnic cleansing. The Sultan watched, the French helped, and the rest of the world maintained its silence.

It is fair to say that the world's faith was dependent on the outcome of the Tunisian war. This was as clear to Hitler and Rommel as it was to Patton and Eisenhower. The opposing foreign armies of the Axis and Allied Forces were using the most modern and deadliest weapon systems, implementing the most sophisticated war strategies on the battlefield. Rommel knew this already in December of 1942 when he received an order from Mussolini, the nominal head of the Axis Forces in North Africa, to "resist to the utmost with all troops of the German-Italian Army." Soon after receiving this message, Rommel wrote a letter to his wife Lucy already admitting defeat, in which he states, "What is to happen now lie in God's hands." He did not have enough supplies to hold his positions in North Africa and therefore could not follow Mussolini's orders to resist. He knew that wars were not about resisting but about wining objectives. Rommel's African Korps were in a defensive mode throughout the war, holding Tunisia while inflicting as much damage to the country as they could. Rommel was consuming 400 tons of fuel daily but only receiving 152 tons, "most of which was used for withdrawals consumed by transport vehicles bringing the fuel to Rommel's mechanized units." Hitler had increased supply lines only after he learned that Rommel was planning an evacuation. He could not bear the idea of an evacuation and is reported to yell, "I refused to allow it. I am not going to allow it in Africa either. Hitler then made a promise to Rommel to send him 'more arms, ammunition, and troops.'"[19]

The victory in Tunisia expelling the Axis Forces from North Africa was a major step towards victory in the Mediterranean Theater of Operations and the rest of the war. A few years before Tunisia's independence, an American cemetery was built for fallen Allied soldiers. Bourguiba, Tunisia's President for life, wrote his famous memorial letter, and in it he complained that Tunisia is back to being a French colony and that they had not really gained ground as a result of the Allied victory. Here is an excerpt: "Like other peoples, the Tunisian people lived through the poignant tragedy of war and through the dark hours under the occupation of the Axis troops. The victory of the Allied troops did not bring to Tunisia immediate realization of her national aspirations. It was indeed a great frustration for a people who fought on the side of freedom and made many a sacrifice during the last two wars for the cause of peace with human justice among men, for human dignity, and recognition of the peoples' right of self-determination."

Bourguiba did not mention that Tunisia may have been under occupation, but it was Tunisian Jews who were singled out during the war, suffering great losses in life, dignity and property. He did not mention that part of its indigenous population had been abandoned by everyone, including their Islamic brothers. Tunisians lived through the "dark hours…under the occupation of the Axis troops," but it was the Jews of Tunisia alone who were completely betrayed by every segment of the population, and by every invading power. He also forgot to mention that the right for "self-determination" was directed only towards the Islamic segment of the Tunisian population. Jews were naturally excluded from this formula of future "democracy" and "self-determination." Tunisian Jews were saved from extermination by American and English forces, only to be thrown out by

Islamic nationalists a few years later. Saving the Jews of Tunisia from annihilation was not a big part of this national aspiration in Tunisia. But, this in fact was exactly the outcome of victory in Tunisia. Albert Memmi, in his "Portrait of the Colonialist," acknowledges that anti-colonialism in Tunisia prevented awareness of anything other than that issue. It was a disability which "prevented awareness" of other people and religions and it was contagious across North Africa.

The Allied Forces were badly hurt during the Tunisian campaign, with over 120,000 English, American, Australian, South African, Canadian and other casualties. The memorial plaque was the right place to say "thank you" to the liberating forces while honoring their dead. They saved the Jewish community in Tunisia from total extermination, and they saved Tunisia as whole from a German rule. What was more important to "Tunisian national aspirations" then saving its indigenous population? Bourguiba played the Jewish card for years because of the large Jewish population in the country, and he continued doing so until no Jews were left! But then, it is important to remember that Bourguiba spent most of the war in either French or German-Italian jails, and he basically had no idea of its magnitude and importance, nor was he all that familiar with the complex social fabric of Tunisian society. When the war started, he was placed under arrest by the French Vichy government and transferred to German control and later to an Italian prison. In March 1943, after five years in jail, when it was clear who was winning the war, he was allowed to go back to Tunis under pressure to cooperate with the Axis Forces. He was jailed again by the French, only to be released in 1955, a year before the limited "independence agreement" with France. He spent so many years in jail that it is hard to imagine he really understood what was going on in Tunisia (a situation similar to the present Muslim Brotherhood leader, who was in exile for years before returning during the Tunisian "Jasmine Revolution"). After taking power, Bourguiba jailed Islamists, communists and students, and got rid of anyone who could possibly be a threat to his one-man rule and his life-time presidency, a gift from him to the people of Tunisia, who were supposed to honor the time he spent in jail. Over time, as fewer Jews remained in the country, the more ruthless he and his government became.

However, there is no information explaining what Bourguiba did in Tunisia between March and May 1943. He apparently refused to cooperate with the Axis Forces, yet he was freed from a German/Italian prison and allowed to go back to Tunisia in the midst of the war. How exactly was he persuaded to cooperate with the Germans? Was Bourguiba's cooperation a desperate act for the Axis Forces in Tunisia?

Memorial Day in 2012 was held at the American Military Cemetery in Tunisia, one of 24 around Europe. One participant noted that "one gets the impression the cemetery is a historical oddity—beautiful, but strange. The memorial, unlike those in Europe, does not commemorate a shared history, a shared sacrifice."[20] This observation is indeed sad because Americans do have shared history in this land, especially through its indigenous Jewish population who now reside in Israel, France, Canada and the US. Tunisia also has the largest Jewish cemetery in North Africa, the Borgel cemetery, where tens of thousands of Tunisian Jews have been buried over the years. This cemetery is named after Borgel, chief rabbi of Tunis, who is on my mother's side of the family, dating back to the eighteenth century. Tunisia was not occupied in 1943; it was crushed and swallowed up by Germany. Tunisia was consumed by a tremendously destructive war that destroyed every hope for future coexistence between Jews, Muslims, Christians and Berbers. The Jews of Tunisia understood the direction this was taking years before the invasion, when Vichy France aligned itself willingly and enthusiastically with Hitler and Mussolini under the blessing of Islamic nationalism. Indeed, one journalist with the British Forces wrote on their drive into the town of Kairouan at the end of the war that "no Arabs came to greet us, but Jews turned out in force."

Madness or Miscalculation?

Many researchers have recently wondered about the logic of the Tunisian campaign from the perspective of both the Axis and Allied Forces. Holding Tunisia became an impossible task for Germany, and they knew this already by February 1943. Nazi Generals were aware of the impossible logistics required to sustain a fighting force, let alone win against the Allied Forces spearheaded by the Americans and English. The Americans, on the other hand, landed 1,000 miles away from their target, moving a massive force while fighting the French Vichy forces along the way, through Morocco and Algeria. The terrible terrain conditions and strict timetable made the operation risky, dangerous and some will even argue, illogical. This partly explains the high rate of causalities. It was not evident at the time that they could pull it off.

Throughout history, Tunisia has been a military target. The Romans attacked Tunisia from the sea; Hannibal attacked Rome by land, through Morocco and Spain and on through the Alps; the Arabs attacked Tunisia through Egypt and Libya; the Germans and Italians used a classic Roman invasion; and the Allied forces did so by sea, land and air, through Morocco and Algeria in the west and Libya in the east. Each invading power had used its own strategic logic to win Tunisia. Nevertheless, it still remains a mystery why Hitler continued to hold Tunisia, knowing perfectly well that he was losing the war. Either they could not stop this war machine, or too many men were eager to fight in Tunisia away from the hunger crisis in Europe and from the even more terrible battles to come in their home countries. German Generals were easily convinced to pack up and go to Tunisia and soldiers and officers easily gave up the fight in order to just stay alive as prisoners under the Americans. It could have being worse, they figured, if they had fallen prisoner to the Russians.

It seemed that Tunisia had once again "charmed" its invaders. Tunisia had a similar effect on the PLO, which was forced out of Lebanon in 1982. It's like a soldier who shoots himself in the leg in the first day of a war, ends up in a hospital injured but still alive and out of the rest of the madness of war. Were German Generals not transferring accurate, real-time war assessments to their headquarters on purpose? Were they eager to become prisoners of war? For the American Generals, the Tunisian "campaign had developed nothing (80,000 causalities) to cause them to reduce its manpower estimates, under which the US army is expected to total 8.2 million men."[21] The Americans and Canadians were very determined to move on with the rest of the war.

Nazi Anti-Jewish Propaganda

During the Tunisian Campaign the Germans desperately needed local national armies to help fight their war, as was the case in Europe as well. In Tunisia they could find neither soldiers nor support personnel to help, as no trained forces existed to help a modern conquering army. They therefore had to import support staff from other occupied Eastern European countries, including Austria, all of whom were glad to join the Tunisian Korps in whatever capacity. Axis Forces were on their own, resorting to the two things they could do: get slave workers to do the dirty work as part of their "European final solution" machine and use propaganda to hopefully engage the Muslims in the war against the Allies. The success of this propaganda machine was not really evident during the war, as propaganda takes time to sink in and work its magic. The real results of German propaganda efforts during the war came later, with Tunisian Independence; the effects can even be seen during the Jasmine Revolution 69 years later. The people behind German propaganda in the Arab world had no idea how successful their campaign would become. Dictators, revolutionaries, radical Islamists and religious preachers would all use Nazi propaganda techniques, almost word for word, disseminating it on the radio and television, and later on the internet, especially Facebook and YouTube.

There are others who claim that that there were around 14 million local Muslims in the whole of the Maghreb who were serving in the North African Algerian-Moroccan-Tunisian regiment KODAT, under German command during the seven-month Tunisian occupation. In 1942, when Rommel's army was trying to advance to Egypt, the Free Arab radio—under the control of Amin al-Husaini, Mufti of Jerusalem and leader of the Palestinian Arabs—broadcasted anti-Jewish slogans (similar to what is heard in the streets of Tunisia and Egypt today). Here is a sample of a radio broadcasted at the time: "Kill the Jews who took your valuables...According to Islam it is a duty to defend your lives. This can only be fulfilled by the liquidation of the Jews. This is your best chance to get rid of this dirty race. Kill the Jews! Set their possessions on fire! Demolish their shops! Liquidate those evil helpers of British imperialism! Your only hope for rescue is to annihilate the Jews before they do this to you."[22] This occurred long before the creation of the state of Israel, and it played a role in shaping the general Arab mood in the whole of North Africa at the time. Pushing out the Jews was already part of the political agenda among Islamist nationalists long before the war. A few years later, every country in North Africa had succeeded in doing just that, and by the late 1960s, over 1.2 million Jews had been pushed out of LCA.

The Axis Forces had invested considerable efforts in recruiting foreign nationals, including Indians and prisoners of war of different nationalities, especially those serving with the British Commonwealth forces in North Africa. Both the Italians and Germans tried to capitalize on anti-British sentiments. In May 1942, the Italian army established the Ragruppamento Centri Militari, a special unit made up of individuals of different nationalities, with the objective of using them as "Intelligence gathering and sabotage operations." Colonello di Stato consisted of a command center employing Italians from Tunisia, Palestine,

Egypt, and Arabia, as well as Muslim Sudanese ex-prisoners of war. Another center included Italians from India and Persia and Indian ex-prisoners of war. In total there were 1,200 Italians, 400 Indians and 200 Arab Muslims. All received intensive army training and were dressed in Italian fascist uniforms. This experiment however, did not go so well, mainly because of loyalty issues.

The Germans attempted to do the same thing and were much more successful, especially with Muslims. Hitler did not think much of the Indian recruits and thought that the Indian unit developed was a "joke." There was Netaji Subhas Chandra Bose, a lawyer from Calcutta and ex-president of the Indian National Congress. He was a rival of Gandhi's and decided to use the existing power balance to his advantage, towards Indian Independence from the British Empire. He traveled to Russia and ended up flying to Germany in April 1942 to meet with foreign ministry officials. Not long after that, he started broadcasting propaganda to India via a powerful transmitter at Nauen. Most of the British 3rd Indian Motorized Brigade had fallen prisoner to Rommel in El Mekili, Libya. Shortly thereafter, a Lugwaffe Major was sent to interview the prisoners to recruit them. A special camp was set up for 10,000 Indian POWs in Annaburg. All were exposed to heavy indoctrination, and 6,000 were chosen to become part of the German forces; they were called the "Legion Freies Indien of the German Army," two thirds of whom were Muslim. By 1943, the Germans selected some of the Muslim recruits to be considered for the formation of a Muslim SS division.

Among the many Nazi collaborators was the Grand Mufti of Jerusalem, Hajj Amin al-Husayni, Fawzi al-Qawuqji from Syria, and Rashid 'Ali al-Kailani who was Iraq's former prime Minister.

Al-Husayni was by far the most active collaborator and pushed his agenda as far as he could with Nazi policy makers, including Hitler himself. His anti-Jewish propaganda was as virulent as Nazi philosophy of the time and was broadcasted throughout the Middle East and North Africa. His messages were so horrific that listening to it makes one wonder about the origins of anti-Jewish hatred. He was financed and encouraged by the Nazis but was never fully trusted by them. The Nazis refused to provide him with any assurances as to how they saw the future of Arab Muslim countries; they obviously had a completely different future agenda in mind. Nazi Germany looked at the Arabs as an inferior people, and they had no intentions of being used by any Arab nationalists or Muslim fundamentalists. Their only meeting points were questions of what to do with the Jews in Palestine, in Arab lands and in Europe. Nevertheless, Al-Husayni continued on, hoping to capitalize later on German successes while at the same time enjoying a monthly salary from the Nazis and a lavish lifestyle while he could. In 1942, al-Husayni and al-Kailani sent a joint letter to the foreign ministers of Germany and Italy requesting "all conceivable assistance" to the Arab world and recognition of the independence of the Arab nations and their right to unify, and a blessing for "the removal of the Jewish national homeland in Palestine."[23] The Germans made their intentions clear by answering in a statement that "the German government was prepared to recognize the independence of Arab lands when they (the Arabs) have won this [independence]." Obviously, the Germans also dreamed of colonies in Africa and the Middle East and were not concerned with Muslims' national or colonial aspirations. The Germans did not consider instituting a new caliphate in the Arab world, far from it; their wanted to replace French and English colonial rule.

In September 1942, al-Husayani proposed the founding of another Pan-Arab center in Tunisia that would: 1) strengthen ties with Arabs in North Africa; 2) ship weapons, agents, equipment, and money to stiffen Muslim resistance in the event of an Allied landing; and 3) recruit and train Arab soldiers, who would stand prepared to defend North Africa "against any threat from the Allies, Bolshevism, and Judaism." When the Allies landed in North Africa, he made this proposal again, but apparently Hitler "wanted nothing from the Arabs." Nevertheless, Tunisia "enjoyed" around-the-clock radio hate programs from German transmitters in Greece and Italy. Al-Husayani was basically indoctrinating a new generation of Muslims, teaching them about the Jewish conspiracy and the "correct" view of the Jews in the Holy Koran, most of it borrowed from Nazi hate speech. People in North Africa listened to this kind of propaganda during the Second World War, and continue listening to the same kind of propaganda today. Nothing much has changed in this respect, only the voices and the technology, the superior transmitters and types of media. His favorite line was that the Jews were the enemies of Islam, and he did his utmost to convince his listeners of that. In one speech given in December 1942 at the newly constructed Islamic center in Berlin (Islamische Zentral-Institut), he said that the Koran judged the Jews "to be the most irreconcilable enemies of the Muslims." His speech was well covered by the mainstream Nazi media in Germany and was broadcasted to the rest of the Arab world, including Tunisia.

Despite the Allied victory in Tunisia, Nazism left the country with the long-lasting presence of Western-style anti-Semitism which has been exploited to the fullest by Islamic interests, both moderate and radical, and by the fact that the Koran can provide plenty of room for such interpretation, as in every other holy book. Jeffrey Herf has gone into detail on the magnitude and the effects of these propaganda activities.[24] His thesis stipulates that there existed a "continuity and lineages between Nazism's Arabic language propaganda on the one hand and radical Islam in the subsequent decades, on the other." European hatred of Jews received a new life in the Arab world with plenty of support from their own religious beliefs and historical backgrounds. Most of the anti-Jewish rhetoric of hate was previously unknown in the Muslim world, especially in Tunisia under the Ottoman Empire. Thousands of broadcasting hours and millions of leaflets were thrown from planes into every country in North Africa and the Middle East during a period of 4 years. Curiously, Edward Said wrote that he decided to exclude Germany from his "Orientalism" theory because Germany was not "an imperial power and had no national interest in the Orient." He thus missed an important and crucial link to understanding events in the Arab world, helping little to aid our understanding of the current Arab Spring Revolutions or the Palestinian-Israeli conflict.

The official story of Bourguiba's stand during the Tunisian Campaign was that the Nazis attempted to pressure him into helping the "Axis powers with his influence over the Tunisian independence fighters in pushing back the Allied invasion of North Africa. Bourguiba refused and was released from prison in 1943"[25] to come back to Tunisia two months before the end of the war and after five years of French, German and Italian prisons. Bourguiba was apparently walking the fine line between his belief that the Allied forces would win the war and his quest for Tunisian Independence. The Germans and Italians were fighting one of the major wars in WWII and it is inconceivable that they would let Bourguiba roam the streets of Tunisia free and in opposition to their own cause in this vicious and crucial war. But the Germans did not need Bourguiba's help in this war. The Axis Forces had of a half-million trained soldiers and support personnel; they needed fuel, food, ammunition and Jewish slaves. What could Bourguiba possibly had to offer? Tunisian independence fighters were basically nonexistent and mattered little in this war. The German propaganda machine was designed to divide and rule through hate.

In this sense Bourguiba was a pawn, used like everyone else in Tunisia at the time. There was no need for his support, but his support would not be rejected by the Nazis if offered. His refusal to cooperate with Axis forces is the accepted narrative in every publication, though none of them goes into detail as to why he was released from German and Italian prisons, or how they tried to convince him to cooperate. In March 1943, he made a noncommittal broadcast which was enough apparently for the Italians to let him go back to Tunisia, as there were many other New Destour party members who could not but admire and support the German's military might and occupation. At the end of the war the French accused him of collaboration with the Nazis and he had to flee again, this time to Egypt, to escape imprisonment. He spent so many years in jail and in exile that the whole of Tunisia including the Jews felt indebted to him. He in return accepted with humility their offer, promising to remain their president for life and above all promising that the final solution to the Jews of Tunisia would be implemented as peacefully and quickly as humanly possible.

Much has been written about the relationship between Hooker Doolittle, the American Council General in Tunisia, and the young Bourguiba, who later named a street after him. They first met immediately after the war in 1943 when Bourguiba was trying to earn American support for his nationalist movement and secure his freedom again after the French took back control of their protectorate. Doolittle sympathized with Bourguiba's nationalist aspirations, a stand which later led to his removal and reassignment to Morocco. The official American policy was not to interfere with the balance of power in the country, and he was instructed in 1942 to change course and halt involvement in any local activities. Here is the official American view at that time: "The state Department would consider any attempt to turn the Arab population against the French as dangerous to the highest degree. Our policy is directed to building up the confidence of the French authorities and the French population in general, and induces them to support the democratic cause… While the feelings of the Arab population are of some concern to us, the French position is of much greater importance. If we were implicated in a political overturn such as you suggest, it might arouse such bitter resentment on the part of the French that we might presently find ourselves ejected from North Africa altogether."[26]

It is evident that the Americans were preparing for war and wanted no surprises from unknown local population as to their war plans and intentions. It is also evident that the local population was strategically important to neither the Germans nor the Americans. Doolittle had no information on the Allied war plans and he therefore tried on his own to mingle with local politics against Vichy control in Tunisia. A week after American landings he left Tunisia for Algeria to return six months later. In any event, no written communication from him exists on the Jewish question in Tunisia because frankly, there was no such a thing as a Jewish question. The Americans were dead-set on winning the war; the French were preoccupied with keeping their protectorate no matter what; and the nationalists had their own vision of Tunisia stripped of its Jews.

General George Patton

"Attack, attack and when in doubt attack again" was Patton's trademark military strategy. Also: "Nobody ever defended anything successfully, there is only attack and attack and attack some more." These are also central fencing terms and the basis for winning fencing combats. In order to attack you must prepare yourself for winning. In order to be successful you have to practice hours each day, repeating moves, sometime the same move for months. Patton was an avid and aggressive fencer and a model sportsman. He would probably have gone wild if he had known that Muslim fencers in the Olympics and international competition settings are not permitted by their governments to fence against Israeli opponents. The rules for Islamic fencers in many of the Islamic countries are that they must refuse to combat an Israeli, even if it means losing a title. I know some athletes from Algeria and Tunisia who are praying to the highest authority, Allah, that they will not experience such a situation. They are also not allowed to speak to, let alone befriend, any Israeli athlete. In 2012, the IOC (International Olympic Committee) spokesman, Emanuelle Moreau, warned that discrimination against any athlete for any reason will not be tolerated, while Algerian NOC President Rachid Hanifi claimed that they will continue to boycott Israeli athletes. I have no doubt in my mind that Patton would have found this intolerable.

Interestingly, Patton participated in the 1912 Olympics. He was 26 years old, a 2nd lieutenant and an excellent athlete. He actually scored very well in four events of the modern pentathlon, reaching 5th place overall. He placed fourth in fencing and twenty-first in shooting. In 1913, Patton developed his own sword called the Patton Saber, and years later his own tank model. Following the Olympics, Patton traveled to Europe in search of a Fencing Master to further his knowledge on the art of the sword. He chose M. Clèry, who was a French "master of arms" and instructor of fencing at the Cavalry School at Saumur. The historic role of the Saumur School of Cavalry was to provide training to the officers and non-commissioned officers of the French cavalry. Patton went there for intense study with the master and upon his return wrote a report on his sword studies, which was later revised for the Army and Navy Journal. Many professional fencers who read Patton's instructions manual for Sabre-mounted fencing wonder why on earth he wrote this in an era where cavalry combats were over. The answer is fairly simple: fencing sharpened military instincts in modern as well as in traditional warfare. He understood that fencing is the ultimate physical chess game, proven over centuries. He analyzed each move, the timing, and above all speed and morale. From reading his manuscript it is evident that he was also extremely knowledgeable about world military history, and his war instincts were based in part on his knowledge of the art of fencing.

In March 1914, the US War Department (later renamed the Department of Defense) officially recognized the Amateur Fencers' League of America to "stimulate competitions with foil, dueling sword and saber among officers stationed at the various army posts throughout the country." One reason for such support from the army may have much to do with Patton and the Assistant Secretary of War,

Henry S. Breckenridge, who was himself a former intercollegiate fencing champion.

Why am I bringing all this fencing history, and how does it relate to Tunisia? I was the founder and Chairman of the Maccabee Tel Aviv Fencing Academy and raised a girl and boy to become fencing champions in North America. Everyone in my family was involved in the sport at the highest national and international levels possible. Our school in Tel Aviv became quite popular and included sportsmen, soldiers, combat pilots, and international participants from Malta, France and Russia. The children of an Israeli fencer and one of the only survivors of the Munich Olympic massacre were also members of our club. We have also written and published the only fencing book in Hebrew. In short, we were a fencing family that even at the dinner table we practiced arm fencing...

Paul Anspach, a Belgian Jew, won two Gold Medals in individual and team Epeé fencing at the 1912 Stockholm Olympics, the same Olympic in which General Patton participated. Anspach, who is distantly related to our Tunisian family, later became the President of the International Fencing Federation, which he helped build along with the Baron Pierre de Coubertin. Anspach is also the author of the Rules of International Fencing (in all three arms), which is still being used today as the authoritative guide for the sport. When the Germans were approaching Belgium, Anspach went into hiding until the end of the war. The Nazis in France and Germany knew he was Jewish and were determined to arrest him as they did with the majority of Belgian Jews. He continued to be the President of the Fencing Federation after the war. He married a German Jewish woman. There is no evidence that Paul Anspach and George Patton met, but it is more than likely that they did and had discussions about fencing.

Twenty-four years later, the three women fencing medalists in the 1936 Olympics held in Germany were Jewish: gold went to Ilona Schacherer-Elek of Hungary, silver to Helene Mayer of Germany, and bronze to Ellen Preis of Austria. This is perhaps also the place to mention the American Foy Draper, the fastest 400-meter runner and a Gold medalist at the 1936 Olympics, who held his world record for 20 years. He was an A-20B Bomber pilot who joined the 97th Squadron of the 47th Bomb Group at Thelepte, Tunisia. He perished or was gunned down along with his two crew members on January 1943 in the battle of Kassarine in Tunisia. His two Jewish teammates at the 1936 games were replaced at the last minute by non-Jewish athletes, a decision which was contested; the coaches and the Olympic Committee were accused of bowing to Nazi pressure. Foy's name is marked on a limestone wall in Carthage along with a long list of missing US soldiers in Tunisia.

Few generals in history have left such a decisive historical mark on the outcome of wars. Patton is one of those men. The Allied Forces were in a problematic situation during the first two months of Tunisian campaign, as casualties were extremely high. The Germans were better organized, had a better war machine and almost total air superiority. The Allies were not properly coordinated, and American infantry and mechanized armored divisions not sufficiently trained. One German officer interviewed for a documentary said that they were amazed at the low level of military strategy the Allies had demonstrated. They were "fighting like children," he said about the early part of the Tunisian Campaign. The English were controlling the campaign, trying to guard their colonies at all costs, and the French did not really participate alongside the Allied Forces for fear of losing control of their Tunisian colony. The Free French

Army later joined the Allied Forces with some 10,000 men. The Allies also made every conceivable error underestimating the enemy's military and strategic capabilities.

Patton began his European campaign in Tunisia knowing well from reading his maps and the history books that control of the country meant control of the heart of the Mediterranean, and consequently, free access to Europe, Asia and Africa. Patton's notes, letters and communiqués suggested that he understood the history of wars in Tunisia, and the Hollywood movie *Patton* was on the mark in making a historical reference to an earlier Tunisian war, 2,000 years previous. His knowledge of the military history of the region proved to be invaluable in entering this theater of war, and winning. Training his forces for combat in a short period of time proved to be his main task, without which the number of casualties would have been much greater. In this sense, Tunisia became a training ground for American and Allied Forces for the wars ahead.

Patton's military drive and strategies were legend in World War II. His ruthless approach was part of his strategy, though his political views were a whole different story, and he made no secret of them. He was a soldier and a general with a focused objective of winning the war—nothing else really mattered. He built his own image, which served his purpose of securing a victory. He obviously knew that having an image of a great warrior affected not only the morale of his men but also the morale of the enemy. And indeed, from recently released German archives we know that his image preceded him. He was feared by the Germans and Italians, and was respected by his troops. The English painted Rommel as the most brilliant and fearless German general, while the Germans had Patton to worry about, painting him as the greatest general of all time.

Jeffrey Bernard, in an article "Patton Tank Mark," suggests a long recovery for Patton's training efforts, and claims that according to the Army Researchers, it will take 1,000 years for the ecology of the California's Mojave Desert to recover as a result of the intense training Patton instituted in the 1940s in preparation for WWII.[27] Imagine what the numerous tank battles have done to Tunisia's ecology.

The web is full of conspiracy theories revolving around his death by a car accident in 1945. Many Jewish writers pointed to his anti-Semitic remarks concerning the DPs (Displaced Prisoners) who were scattered in camps after the war. At one point Patton writes, "I cannot understand who had the presumption to attribute to me anti-Semitic ideas which I certainly do not possess." He had been accused of making anti-Semitic remarks towards the Jews and of caring for German wellbeing more than those of the DPs after the war. Patton was preoccupied with the madness of war, and human and social values were according to him related to man's ability to wage war. His problem was mostly attributed to the unbearable sight of displaced people who were incapable of fighting. After experiencing so many battles and so much death, he had little respect and even less understanding for those who did not fight, irrespective of their situation. He had lost many thousands of soldiers in this war, only to find people without the will to fight and die, if necessary. Similar sentiments were developed among young Israelis who rejected the passive Ghetto mentality held by many Jews during WWII in Europe and North Africa.

Tunisian Jews under Nazi and Fascist Control

The Jewish people of Tunisia were not an ethnic group in Tunisia nor were they a small community in the margins of Tunisian society, which was how they were portrayed in Israel; in Tunisia they were totally forgotten. The Jews, who mostly lived in urban centers, *were* Tunisia. They were the forgotten holocaust survivors who lost not just their property but also their country. For centuries they were inseparable from the rest the Tunisian population. Events beyond their control have laid bare their precarious situation during WWII, which I have sketched above: The French colonialists proved to be unreliable with Vichy's new alliance with the Germans beginning in 1940; Arab Tunisian nationalists, mixed with radical Islamists, had no interest in having Jews amongst them and behaved accordingly; and the German occupation which lasted for seven months, from November 1942 to May 1943, and featured a massive military campaign between the Allied and Axis Forces.

As we have seen, the Tunisian war campaign was not just another battle in WWII. Massive forces were directly confronting one another using the best equipment available in modern warfare, and each side was completely determined to win a victory of territory and morale that would also ultimately decide the outcome of WWII. The Axis forces in Tunisia had some half a million soldiers, tons of equipment coming through all ports every day and airfields flooded with Axis bombers. All this was happening in a country of 2 million people where only 15%-20% lived in urban centers and a large percentage of those were Jewish Tunisians. The Germans were desperate for supply, especially food items. They were also in need of local manpower to help maintain their military holds. This was a major problem throughout the long lasting war. The Allied forces did not know at the time that Axis Forces were not receiving the necessary supplies of both military and basic needs. They also did not know the magnitude of the low morale of German forces once they retreated back to Tunisia from Libya. By January 1943, the Germans understood that they had to rely on locals for foodstuffs and other basic needs, including manual slave labor to maintain their military camps. It was also obvious from the behavior of POWs that most would have loved to just bask in the sun and the sand in Tunisia. This huge army needed local support to sustain itself. The Germans who looted local food supplies suddenly noticed that produce and other food items were being shipped out of Tunis in carriages, and that dollar bills were circulating in the markets. The Germans caught an American soldier who was smuggled in one of these carriages and whose mission was to purchase produce for the Allied Forces, who were also desperately in need of food and were prepared to pay handsomely for it. The locals were squeezed thin and could not have survived much longer. It can be argued that these demands for supplies resulted in the complete destruction of Tunisian economy and social order.

The Jews were the ones singled out to do the dirty work. The Germans could not ask the Muslim population for fear of alienating them, so they naturally turned to the Jews, Tunisia's urban inhabitants. It did not take long for them to build some 30 work camps around the various military bases in the country. All

Jews were forced to wear the yellow Star of David (except some Jewish-Italian elites). The Jews resisted, as they had not forgotten that for centuries they were forced to wear similar symbols distinguishing themselves from the rest of the population under various Islamic regimes. Indeed, the yellow-star identification for Jews was not a German invention. The original plan of extermination was drawn in 1942 by SS Special Forces which was led by Lieutenant Colonel Walther Rauff, who as we know was already an experienced mass murderer responsible for the construction and implementation of mobile extermination gas units. A 1977 article by *Der Spiegel* stated that Rauff and his men were empowered to "take executive measures against the civilian population," a civilized Nazi jargon for looting, robbery, murder, rape and enslavement. The original plan was to continue to Palestine after securing Libya and Egypt.

German forces were stopped by the English and retreated first to Libya and subsequently to their original Tunisian African base: "The Desert Fox campaign led by the English was in fact a major blow to Rommel's invincibility." According to Jan Freedman, the Germans had a whole network of labor camps throughout Tunisia and during the German occupation, and at least 2,500 Jews died in them. Thousands of others were forced to work in extremely harsh conditions. According to Freedman, the regular army was also involved in these executions. On the island of Djerba alone, Rauff's men forced the seizure of silver, gold, jewelry and other sacred items from the Jewish population. Apparently, the SS later disposed of "Rommel's Treasure" in the sea, attracting generations of treasure hunters; however, it has never been found. Treasure hunters these days are also very busy trying to find the 13 billion dollars in Gold bullion and cash hidden by Ben Ali and his wife Leila (President of the Arab

Women's Organization) over a period of 20 years of corruption, deceit and looting of Tunisia and Tunisian Jewish properties. This treasure has also never been found.

Little research or analysis has been done on the history of Tunisian Jews during WWII, and only during the past decade has anyone started to take notice of this situation. Information is now sketchy, as few individuals are alive to tell their story. Since 1977, some Tunisian Jewish survivors have been meeting every year on December 9 in France to remember the Nazis atrocities and hear personal accounts. It was natural that the Tunisian Council General was absent from this event since the start of Spring Revolution. But stories have emerged on how Rauff and his SS forces entered the synagogue on Paris Avenue in the middle of a prayer, shooting and destroying everything in sight, exactly as they did in Paris in July 1942, and in Warsaw. Gilbert Habib, Gilbert Taieb, Georges Smadja, Charles Zeitoun and a few others were there every year to tell their personal stories. But the rest remained silent for decades in Israel, which in turn was not interested in documenting this story at all. Next year, there may be no one around to recount anything.

For years, only a handful of Tunisians wanted to speak about this period, and even fewer people wanted to hear about it. But it is not difficult to draw important conclusions by analyzing the military situation. We do not need personal stories to say that life for Tunisian Jews came to a halt. Everything they depended on collapsed within months; their French alliance was completely destroyed, relationships with their Islamist neighbors worsened beyond recognition and their sense of security was gone forever. Tunisian Muslims could not do much to help, as their enthusiasm towards the Axis Forces was unbearable. The same goes for the French. A large part of the Jewish population had adopted the French language and culture, only to confront, 75 years later, a strange colonial beast in the form of the anti-Jewish Vichy administration, which at times was worse than the Germans. The Spanish-Portuguese Jews of the Grana (Granada), who had been playing a role for centuries by enhancing trade and cultural relations with Italy and other European countries, found out how miserable their link was as well. It did not take them long to figure out that Italy had turned to fascism. From 1940 to the end of the occupation, they invested all their energies turning to the Italian fascists for salvation from the German final solution, a last attempt to avoid extermination. The Turkish Bey monarch ruling Tunisia at the time was helpless, considering the centuries of underdevelopment in the country. All told, the Jews of Tunisia were colonized by Islam, the French, the Turkish Sultan, German Nazis and Italian Fascists—all at the same time. They were alienated completely from the economic and cultural networks with the local population, built over many centuries. It is also important to remember that the majority of Tunisian Jews were heavily taxed and very poor to begin with, and were only starting to enjoy a relative prosperity. Still, the Germans managed to levy collective fines estimated at 100 million francs, not including the Djerba lootings. They shipped to Germany anything of value, from furniture to books and jewelry, stripping the community of its wealth, and more importantly, of its ancient past.

Jan had captured the essence of the war when he writes that recent evidence proved that the North African Campaign was not "a clean one" nor was it a "legend". "Rommel himself was no racial fanaticist, but he paved the way for the machinery of destruction with his victories"… ignoring completely the consequences of his campaign.

There is one Tunisian Muslim mentioned in Yad Vashem (holocaust Memorial in Jerusalem) as helping some Jews escape from the Germans. This same person was also reported by members of his family to have hosted German soldiers who had run away from the battlefield at the end of the war. He had a large farm and was visited by a journalist who tried to get more information on the incident. The journalist was told by a member of the family not to mention the affair to workers in the farm for fear of repercussions. There are other stories told by Tunisian Jews of Muslims helping Jews in Tunisia. But in general, Muslims followed their Islamic teachings, coated with anti-colonialist sentiments, against the French and the English. Tunisian nationalists never viewed its Jews as an indigenous part of the country's population, and thus Islamic anti-colonial nationalism in the 1940s had no place for anyone who was not Muslim. By the time the war ended, Tunisia was in ruins and its people devastated. The Arabs were never taken to task for implementing "Nuremberg-style" policies that resulted in the ethnic cleansing of its Jewish people because there was no government to take to task. Some have recently called to declare the King of Morocco as a Righteous Gentile for his part in saving Jews. Apparently, he is said to have saved 200,000 Jews, all of whom were later made to leave for Israel and other countries. However, Yad Vashem (the Holocaust Memorial center in Jerusalem) does not list King Mohammed V in their database for righteous among nations. In fact, no Muslim is listed anywhere in this database. There was also a German soldier who saved a few young Tunisian Jews by releasing them from prison. This German soldier at the end of the war visited the family of one of the released prisoners asking for refuge trying to avoid becoming a prisoner of war. He was hidden by them and smuggled out of Tunisia a few years later.

He said he was not a Nazi, and the Tunisian Jewish family was the only family he had throughout the rest of his life.

It is important to remember that the Nazis and Fascists in Tunisia were busy trying to win a war that from the outset they knew they were losing. This explains why the majority of Jews were spared. It is equally important to remember that Tunisia was not really under occupation. It was a theater of war, and the country as whole was swallowed by a vicious modern military operation unequalled in history. There was really no time for the Germans to concern themselves with the details of occupation, as was the case in some European countries. There was no meaningful internal opposition whatsoever to their presence in the country; the local population basically did not count in the grand German scheme of things. However, the local population in Tunisia did not embrace the Germans and the Italians. And, it is more accurate to say that no one really understood then (as now) the magnitude of the war around them. Most Tunisian Jews had no idea what the Western world was about to do on their lands and to their lives. They were witnessing the last breath of colonial Europe.

The Germans could not break the centuries-old bonds of the people in Tunisia, at least not in the first few years after the war. Tunisia has somehow withstood every invader throughout its history, and it managed to survive the Nazis as well. But after the war, internal Islamist nationalists were able to carry out what invaders were unable to execute throughout Tunisia's history: the elimination of all minorities, including its indigenous Jewish population. Islamist nationalists in Tunisia implemented the final solution, exiling its Jews out of their lands with nearly 100 percent success.

Karin Albou has created an impossible scenario in a movie called *Le chant des mariées* dealing with friendship between poor Muslim and Jewish girls during the German occupation of Tunis. Albou has done her research and her film touches on many issues from a personal perspective, a beautiful and brilliant portrayal of the time that allows young Tunisian Jews and Muslims alike a taste of their shared history.

Towards the end of the war in May 1943, the Germans simply gave up and stopped following orders down the chain of command. They only had enough supplies and ammunition to continue fighting for a few more days. They could have stalled the enemy from their assault on Italy and Europe, but instead they just quit by the thousands. They were well trained, well fed and professional soldiers, and they just "piled into motorcycles and trucks and drove to the nearest prison stockade."[28] The Allied Forces were glad, but also completely surprised at their behavior. The might of the German army collapsed so unexpectedly and so rapidly that the Allied command was worried that their forces would become over-confident in the fights ahead. Tunisia had worked its magic once again.

Years later, after being silent all this time, a few Tunisian Jews decided that their plight during the occupation was not properly recorded in Yad Vashem (the Holocaust Memorial Center in Jerusalem). Their modest grievances toward the Israeli State revolved around their suffering during WWII at the hands of the Germans and Italians, and their life under Allied bombardment. Once again, Tunisian Jews had been drawn into a false historical narrative, adapting a European perspective within the Zionist project in order to understand their current miserable situation. Yosi Reuven, a 74-year-old from Be'er Sheva working alone in his small room, was driven by the quest to shed a bit of light and do some justice to those who were killed during this period. He was able to put together a list of 600 names of Tunisian Jews who perished during that period. The silence here screams louder, not just because history was ignored by everyone in Israel and Tunisia, but also because of the absence of numbers and statistics about how many died at the time and what their suffering meant during and after this period. The Holocaust was not just a European event.

Interestingly, Hirschberg and his co-authors in writing their famous historical account of Tunisia brought the son of Rabbi Kahlfon in Djerba as witness to what happened to the Tunisian community during the German occupation. According to him, he heard nothing and saw nothing (not unusual for a Rabbi or son of a Rabbi, even in Israel) for seven months. These Israeli historians spent two pages telling his non-story, yet they brushed aside the US Council General's account of Tunisia in the previous century as irrelevant. We will be dealing with this in the next chapter, but here we cannot but insist that a detailed and honest account of Tunisia and its Jewish population during the Second World War has yet to be written… It has not been told.

Islamic Turkish Colonialism

For those who don't know, the Souk el-Berka, in the Medina in the city of Tunis, sold only one product in the seventeenth, eighteenth and early nineteenth centuries: slaves. Blacks and whites, males and females, Christians and non-Christians who were captured by the Sultan pirates and sold to Europeans and other Islamist countries for high prices, particularly young boys and nubile girls—if they were not promptly ransomed. Forget about caravans full of spices from the East reaching Europe during the Middle-Ages; these were secondary at the Souk el-Berka. Muslim traders were as comfortable as the Europeans, if not more so, with this type of trade, and in North Africa it included not only black slaves but all types of slaves captured in raids around the Mediterranean, some waiting to be ransomed and others waiting to be shipped to various Arab destinations. It was the same story in other African countries, like Kenya, Somalia, Eritrea, Ethiopia and Sudan. There was little tolerance, only economic interests combined with religious values and holy instructions on how to put everyone under submission; the Christian and Muslim worlds celebrated in tandem. Millions of slaves were traded this way by Arab Muslim slave-traders over a period of two centuries.

The trade occurred in the market every Friday, and was forbidden by law to Jews and Christians; in Tunisia it was strictly a Muslim thing. European colonial empires were joined by the Islamic colonial powers of North Africa in the destruction of African civilizations from North to South. A big part of this slavery was the supplying of women, men and children to various Islamic countries through piracy and raids on coastal towns around the Mediterranean, and as far abroad as England. The harems of Turkish sultans and Muslim aristocrats were in constant need of a fresh supply. This practice is still a reality in some countries. A recent book by a French author reveals the dark secrets of Libya's ruling class, exposing the institutionalized rape, murder and kidnapping that occurred during the Kaddafi regime and since.

It is estimated that during the eighteenth century only five percent of the world's population were free, in the Western sense of the word. The rest were living as subjects, or as slaves. Christianity and Islam, joined in on this largest slave trade in the history of mankind. Millions of black Africans were transported from their lands to continue their existence in Europe or the "new world," or a short life of slavery in the Muslim world. Black slaves traded to the Muslim world were often castrated so no trace of them would remain once their services expired or were no longer needed. This explains in part why there are relatively very few blacks in the Arab world. The slave market in Tunisia was officially abolished in 1841, but trading in slaves continued until the end of that century. In most cases, black slaves were converted to Islam, though their practices and place of worships were separate from the general Muslim Tunisian population.

With the abolition of slavery, many found themselves in precarious living situations, and eventually turned to what now is the Muslim Brotherhood[29] for assistance. In any event, the official abolition of slavery in Tunisia (1863) happened quite early in comparison with other North African countries: Egypt (1884), Morocco (1922), Libya (1951), and Mauritania (1984). Interestingly, in 1863 the mayor of the city of Tunis wrote a letter to Amos Perry, the US Consul to Tunisia, pleading him to pressure his government to abolish slavery.[30]

Even the US government had to pay ransom money to Tunisian pirates as insurance against raids on merchant ships under control of the Sultan during the late 1700s and early 1800s. These piracy practices operated in a very similar fashion to Somali pirates today, only at that time it was institutionalized by the Bey Islamic and Turkish administration. Tunisian pirates, like those in Somalia today, had their own letterheads, translators and negotiators, who were mostly Christians and Jews. From 1801 to 1815, the US navy decided to put an end to this and began attacking Tunisian ports. With the loss of revenue from piracy, the Tunisian government was plunged into debt (to Italy, France and the UK), which eventually led to a financial crisis and later into a quasi-colonial protectorate situation with France. Previously, in 1784 the US Congress approved the sum of $80,000 to be used as ransom pay to North African piracy states; after gaining Independence, US merchants were no longer under the security umbrella of Great Britain. Thomas Jefferson sent his diplomats with money to ensure safe passage of American ships. The "no negotiating with terrorists" phase came later when Algerian pirates captured an American ship and held its passengers hostage, demanding $60,000 for their release. Jefferson argued in letters that this money should not be paid as it would lead to further attacks. His solution was the creation of a strong navy capable of fighting pirates and able to secure merchant routes at sea. He also added that "It will be easier to raise ships and men to fight these pirates into reason, than money to bribe them." But, the cash option continued, and in 1795 alone the US paid some $1,000,000 in bribery money to pirate states in North Africa, including Tunisia and especially Algeria.

The ransom money became a heavy burden on US treasury, and this ridiculous state of affairs even got Tripoli involved, as it began demanding its share of ransom money. And, when this money was not given on its target date, the Pasha (sultan, governor, Pirate) of Tripoli declared war on the US. The US attacks on Libya as a result was not a success, considering it lost its frigate *Philadelphia* to pirates in 1803, leading to a four-year naval war on North African piracy. It also did not eliminate it completely, as the US was still obliged to pay $60,000 to Algerian Islamist pirates for each American sailor captured. It was only in 1815, with the second Algerian war that bribery practices with the US ended. Interestingly, the Europeans continued to pay ransom money to these Islamic pirates under the various Deys and Beys, Pashas and Sultans, until 1830 when it was obvious that the Turkish Empire in North Africa was disintegrating.

The Ottomans in Tunisia

The last Bey of Tunisia was Muhammad VIII al-Amin, who ruled from May 1943 to May 1956. He was in fact, considered the head of state and King of Tunisia. He took over from his cousin Muhammad VII al-Amin, who in turn took over from Muhammad VI al-Amin…going back all the way to Al-Husayn I Ibn Ali at-Turki in the seventeenth century. Tunisia was ruled by the succession of Beys (Sultans, Kings, governors) as part of the Islamic Ottoman colonial Empire and was a direct descendent of Mohammed's son-in-law Husayn Ibn Ali, who was considered the first Imam and Caliph. In Libya and Morocco, there was the Idrisid dynasty and their own similar successions of Beys. I have no intention here of going through the genealogy of these dynasties, but here a sample of how the maze was built: "The Alid dynasty of Sharifs of Sousse (Tunisia) originated with Hasan Ibn Hasan, brother of Zayd Ibn Hasan. Hasan had a son named Abdallah Ibn Hasan, who had a son called Djafar ibn Abdallah. This Djafar ibn Abdallah, grandson of Hasan Ibn Hasan, began this dynasty…"[31] It is all somehow tied to the Prophet Mohammed and his extended family relationships. Even Ibn Khaldūn, a prominent Arab historian of Tunisian origin, traced his dynasty to Mohammed in order to gain respect and influence in Islamic circles. Some argue that he was a Berber or maybe even a Jewish Berber. There were also some Jews who converted and also traced their roots to Mohammed—why not? This naming tradition was clearly Biblical, and in Islam this tradition was exaggerated, designed exclusively for the religious and ruling aristocracies. The King of Jordan of the Hussein dynasty also claimed to be decedent of the prophet. In 1924, Hussein, the grandfather of the current king of Jordan, proclaimed himself the caliphate and king of all Arabs, leading to the subsequent declaration of war by the Saudis, who did not take his Caliphate idea favorably.

The point is that the religious base of the Ottoman Empire was Islam, although some Jews and Christians were allowed to take specific roles in the economy, helping to maintain these dynasties' power, wealth and collection of women. This religious and political framework was in existence for centuries. No one could verify the linkages to Mohammed and his family, and no one really had any inclination to do so anyway. As long as the ruler had enough power to sustain such a claim he would go unchallenged; it had nothing to do with Mohammed or even Islam.

Last names were only recently introduced, and everyone including the Hebrews, Muslims and Christians were using only first names, e.g. Ali Ibn (son of) Mohammed. During the eighteenth and nineteenth centuries in Eastern Europe, Jews were given a first name and then an indication of either their place of birth and or their profession to somehow distinguish them from another Isaac from another city. Eli Schumacher, for example, means Eli the shoemaker, and so on. This Biblical naming system is still popular today and presents a nightmare for every intelligence-gathering operations. Building a meaningful database of family trees under this system becomes a real challenge, and at times impossible. Because of this, the collection of taxes was (and still is) a difficult process, and a large percentage of the population simply avoided paying taxes under the Bey. Interestingly, in England and even in Belgium one of the most popular names given to babies these days is Mohammed with all its different variants. Muslims today continue using a very similar naming system to what has been used for centuries by Islam and the Turks, which had nothing to do with religion, Islam or the Prophet Muhammad.

So, using genealogy dynasty trees was a practice used only by the religious aristocracy throughout the centuries. The masses, including most Jews of Tunisia, could not trace their family tree beyond a few generations. Culture and language, names and traditions, had to be passed orally from one generation to the next.

Over the years the Beys in the Ottoman Empire were governed by their own designed rules and regulations and not necessarily under strict control from Istanbul. However, the main rules of the game were upheld by every Bey in North Africa: submission and taxes. Christians and Jews had limited participation in the political and religious system. They were left to their own at some periods, and at others, ruthlessly suppressed. They were under full submission of Islam, and as long as rules were not broken they could continue living their lives undisturbed. In many respects, the Turkish Beys were more tolerant and progressive towards minorities than the radical Islamists in control today. The Ottoman philosophy towards the Jews can be summed up by the phrase, "you don't kill the Goose that laid the golden egg." So, the Jews at some periods were protected because of their important economic role. This is obvious when talking about Tunisian Jews. Morrdecai Noah, the American Consul to Tunisia at the beginning of the nineteenth century writes about the Jews of Tunisia, recognizing the ruthless rule of the Islamists under the Bey, but was also fully aware that the Jews were permitted to operate within their own Jewish religious codes, including having their own independent religious Jewish schools and houses of worship. Tunisian Jews during the eighteenth and nineteenth centuries were alive and well—little did he know that they would disappear completely due to Islamic nationalism, radical or otherwise.

There were exceptions made for non-Muslims participating in Islamist Turkish-controlled Tunisia. Some prominent persons, including a Tunisian Prime Minister, was a slave converted by force from Christianity to Islam after the Turkish massacre on the island of Chios, which had a large and influential Jewish community. Some one hundred thousand including thousands of Jews were massacred, and tens of thousands became slaves to rich Turks around the Mediterranean. One kid who survived this event was Georgios Stravelakis, a Greek Christian turned slave and later a Muslim renamed Mustapha Khaznadar. He was the treasurer to the Bey of Tunisia, and from 1837 to 1873 became the Prime Minister. His personal history explains Tunisia's early relative anti-slavery sentiment. There were other survivors of this massacre who also became prominent financial leaders in the Ottoman Empire. Obviously, these massacres and wars were not one-sided, and during the same period the Greeks attacked a city called Tripolis (South of Greece), which had a large population of Jews and Muslims. The attack ended with the complete extermination of both groups. Recorded accounts by the Greeks of this massacre are horrific.

Hundreds of years of heavy-handed Ottoman rule and underdevelopment did not make the Jews of Tunisia disappear. They continued living their lives the best they could, by manipulating the political conditions to their benefit. Their survival as an indigenous people is the story and the history of Tunisia.

Negotiating with Pirates, First Islamist in the US

President Obama's statement on Ramadan at the White house in 2010 was completely out of context, and he should have been advised not to have mentioned a particular historical event as meaningful in terms of US-Muslim relations. He said that it "is a reminder that Islam has always been a part of America. The first Muslim ambassador to the United States, from Tunisia, was hosted by President Jefferson, who arranged a sunset dinner for his guest because it was Ramadan—making it the first known Iftar at the White House, more than 200 years ago." He did not mention that the 1805 visit by the Tunisian Sidi Soliman Mellemelli was over ransom piracy money demanded by the Bey of Tunisia, because this is what the Tunisians did for a living and had been doing this for centuries. Furthermore, Soliman was not an ambassador, and there is plenty of evidence to suggest that he was not even a Muslim.

As mentioned above, annual US payments and individual ransoms to Islamist pirates started to hurt the US treasury; this was the background and the introduction of the United States to Islam—nothing to brag about and nothing to be proud of in terms of cultural and religious exchange. Soliman Mellemelli, astonished by American hospitality and naivety, also had the hutzpah to demand—given that he was without his harem—women to comfort him while he is in Washington. Senator William Plumer stated that "our government has, on his application, provided him with one or more women, with whom he spends a portion of the night." [32a] He then pleaded that the US comply with the Bey's demands, seriously threatening otherwise that Tunisia would declare war on the US. He also stated that he would be beheaded if he were not successful in his mission. Mellimelli exploited his welcome in the US in more ways imaginable, demanding gifts for him and the Bey and a royal treatment throughout his long stay in fine hotels, paid for by the US government. Needless to say that he was surprised by the royalty treatment he was receiving.

A full account of this disgraceful visit of this conman and pirate is open to anyone wishing to know more about the first American encounter with a so-called Muslim in Julia McLeod's book.[32] In fact, it is more probable that he was not a Muslim, but a Jewish or Christian Tunisian working for the Bey, as most negotiators for the Bey of Tunisia were either Christians or Jews. Mordecai Manuel Noah, the US ambassador to Tunisia at the time, elaborated on Jewish participation in foreign expeditions commissioned by the Bey, and he was disappointed by his own government over his dismissal because of his Jewish faith. To make his point, he stated that in North Africa being Jewish did not prevent one from occupying important positions, especially in foreign affairs: "The Bey of Algiers had appointed a Jew his minister at the court of France; another consul at Marseilles; another at Leghorn. The Treasurer, the interpreter, the Commercial Agent of the Bey at Constantinople, are all Jews. In the year 1811, the British government sent Aaron Cordoza, of Gibraltar, a most intelligent and respectable Jew, with a sloop of war to Algiers to negotiate some important point connected with commerce. He was received with deference and succeeded. The first minister from Portugal to Morocco was Abraham Sasportas, a Jew, who formed a treaty and was received with open arms. Ali Bey, of Tunis, was sent as ambassador to London Moses Massias, the father of Major Massias, who is at present serving in the army of the United States. Innumerable instances could be produced where the Musselmans have preferred employing a Jew on foreign missions."[33] He therefore wondered why his government found his religion an obstacle to proper execution of consular functions. Curiously, there were more Sephardic and Berber Jewish Ambassadors in the early nineteenth century under the Bey than there have been in Israel in the decades since 1948.

Silencing Mordecai Manuel Noah

A few years after Mellimelli's visit to the US, Noah was appointed as US ambassador to Tunisia (1813). Two years later, once it was revealed that he was Jewish—a Sephardic Jew of Portuguese decent—he was relieved of his post as his religion was "an obstacle to the exercise of Consular function." He tried reasoning with his superiors, writing letters to the White House defending his post and asking for explanations. He never got a response while in office. Back in New York, he became an author, playwright and the first Jewish-American politician. He also developed a theory that some American Indians were the descendants of the lost tribes of Israel and was the first—long before Teodor Herzel, to provide a solution to European anti-Semitism on US and Canadian lands. Nevertheless, he was the first Jew in the US to encounter discrimination, not just because he was Jewish but also because he was a Sephardic Jew.

From these two events which at approximately the same time—a new Ambassador to Tunisia and the visit of a conman—we can safely conclude that the State Department at the time did not have a clue what was going on in Tunisia and North Africa, nor did they have any clear independent foreign policy in the handling of international affairs in the region. And, if they had one that made sense, it disappeared with the departure of Noah. The Americans were also in no position to influence political affairs in the region, considering the strength of European colonial interests. Mordecai apparently hid his Jewish background when serving as an Ambassador, though I'm not sure how he did that in Tunisia considering his name was Mordecai Manuel Noah, clearly of Sephardic origin. Almost one third of the Jewish community in Tunisia had Portuguese Sephardic origins. Tunisia was also the home of Abraham Zacuto, a Sephardic Jew who was expelled from Spain and later from Portugal, and became Christopher Columbus' astronomer and mathematician. In 1504, while making Tunisia his home he wrote the *Sefer Yuchasin* (Genealogy Book). Zacuto, like many others, spent his dying years in Jerusalem, and is credited with developing the almanac navigational tables, a system still in use today when GPS is not available. Zacuto is an example of a Sephardic religious scholar who was not detached from society and from the world around him. Towards the end of the sixteenth century, the whole of Tunisia entered its three-hundred-year-period of Turkish rule which was marked as an era of underdevelopment.

Noah, as a young diplomat was fascinated by the strong Jewish community in Tunisia during his stay there. He made some interesting observations about Tunisian Jews living in the beginning of the nineteenth century. Both what he said and what he avoided telling us is extremely valuable. He was planning on revealing his thinking and findings in a separate publication, but decided not to do it. He writes cautiously: "The publication of which may be dangerous to them (the Jews), while the north of Africa is in the hands of Barbarians, and I am not without hopes that the time will come, when some civilized power, capable and determined, will wrest that fine portion of the world from the hands of the assassins, and relieve an unfortunate race, who only require mildness and tolerance to make (them) useful and beneficial."[34] Obviously, there was no such "civilized" power developing, capable of delivering the Jews of the region. The "Barbarians" is used here not to describe the Barbary States but rather the Islamic Turkish Ottoman rule. The only power was the power of Islam, Arabization, radicalization and anti-Jewish sentiment, leading to the rapid and unjust redistribution of wealth. Had he known that the Jews of Tunisia and Jews of the whole of North Africa would disappear completely one day, he would have probably unilaterally had the US declare war on Tunisia and would have done away with the Bey and the Ottoman Empire in the region. In fact, he did threaten the Bey to comply with his demands to release captured American slaves and ships or face war against the US.

Communication in 1812 was very slow, and Noah was free to handle the crisis on his own. At the time, the US government was under tremendous pressure because of war with Britain in the US and Canada. In some places in the Atlantic Ocean, American ships continued fighting the English for months, not knowing that the war was over. As Consul, Noah was free to negotiate with the Bey as he saw fit. In any event, it seems that Noah and the US government took the Bey Pirates too seriously, treating them as a deserving empire when in fact they were nothing but a paper tiger based on piracy. US foreign policy at the time revolved around securing trade routes in the Mediterranean and the Atlantic, and the idea of spreading democracy and freedom was not on the table; freeing Tunisian Jews from submission was also not on the table as a policy. The US accepted that North

Africa was a Muslim Arab entity, a view held to this day. Noah was afraid that his life was in danger and in secret he boarded a midnight ship headed for Gibraltar as an escape route away from Tunisian Beylical ruthless reach.

In 1812—as in 1942, when Hooker Doolittle, the US Consul to Tunisia in 1940, received similar instructions during WWII with respect to getting involved in local affairs and politics—the US government was firmly against getting involved in Tunisian local politics for fear of alienating colonial powers of either the Bey (or the French). Colonialism, for Tunisian Jews after all, was not just French, but also Turkish, and Islamic. Jews, Christians and Muslims knew the difference between French and Turkish colonialism, and it was evident that underdevelopment was the defining feature of the latter. But they obviously did not have any choice in selecting their colonial power. At the beginning of the nineteenth century, the Bey was already losing his power and grip over Tunisia. The rapid developments in science and technology in Europe had already made his rule obsolete. France, England and other colonial powers were already establishing Tunisia's economic role in the world as a provider of agricultural food products and natural resources, and an importer of finished goods, including guns, canons, powder and other military items, a role typical for all African colonies. Even the ships used during this era of piracy, in the ports of Tunisia, were built elsewhere.

It would have been easy for the US to get involved both times, in 1815 and 1943. No one would have stopped them, especially not in 1943. In fact, a US occupation of Tunisia after the tremendous number of lives lost in the region would have perhaps been a blessing to the long-oppressed indigenous populations in the country. Allied forces probably had every right to change the course of history in Tunisia at that time and taking sides would have resulted in such a change.

Noah never did publish the full account of his encounter with the Jews of Tunisia, but judging from his other publications it is obvious he was quite knowledgeable about their history and their participation in society—he had a very similar history and customs. Upon his arrival in Tunisia he immediately noticed that all commerce was concentrated in the hands of the Jews. According to his reports he estimated the Jewish population at that time at 60,000 in Tunis and the surrounding cities alone. Many others were living in distant villages, and many more had converted to Islam or were not counted because of their remote locations. According to Noah, the Jewish population in North Africa was estimated at around 700,000. None of the numbers he presented pleased historians in Israel or Tunisia. Neither Jews nor Islamist nationalists viewed his reports as serious historical documents. He was also fully aware of their power and influence in Tunisia: "With all the apparent oppression, the Jews are the leading men; they are in Barbary the principal mechanics, they are at the head of the custom-house, they farm the revenues; the exportation of various articles, and the monopoly of various merchandise, are secured to them by purchase, they control the mint and regulate the coinage of money, they keep the bey's jewels and valuable articles, and are his treasurers, secretaries, and interpreters; the little known of arts, science, and medicine is confined to the Jews…These people, then, whatever may be said of their oppression, possess a very controlling influence, their friendship is worthy of being preserved by public functionaries, and their opposition is to be dreaded."[35] This extremely powerful description of Tunisian Jews is not exaggerated. Every account from travelers to this region of the world said the same thing.

Their central role continued unhindered and was even intensified when the French took Tunisia as a protectorate.

Noah's contact with the Jews of Tunisia was a natural one as he was a descendent of a Spanish Portuguese Jewish community, many of whom emigrated to North Africa. Noah's own family was wealthy and was able to buy their way out of Portugal to England and from there with his family to the Southern US and Cuba where they bought agricultural land.

Noah grew up to become the first national Jewish politician in the United States, and I urge all readers to further examine his life and writings. It is quite amazing that a Jew of Sephardic Portuguese decent became a US consul to Tunisia at such an important historical juncture in the region, marked by complex relations between the US and the countries of the Mediterranean and North Africa. His political views and his detailed accounts of Tunisian Jews are equally fascinating.

Berber and Jews of Tunisia

A heated debate was recently held in Arabic on Iranian TV between the Berber writer Yahya Abu Zakariya and Ahmed Adghirni on the origins of North African Berber and the links between them and Berber Jews of the region. It was a curious discussion, and I cannot recall ever seeing a similar discussion on Israeli TV or other media in Israel. The Arab view goes as follows: The Berbers have contributed to Islamic and Arab culture in North Africa since the seventh century and have done a great service to Islamic civilization. The Jews, on the other hand, were "utterly foreign to the region, only arriving from Andalusia following the Reconquista. Moreover, they were the eyes of the French colonialist movement. When the French army came to the Maghreb, it was the Jews who led them to the mujahideen, and when the French left, the Jews quite naturally went with them."[36] In fact, the whole Berber movement is viewed by many Arabs as a plot designed to disrupt Arab and Islamic rule in North Africa.

The term Berber was given in colonial times by colonial powers to the indigenous population of North Africa. They call themselves *Amazigh*, meaning "free men" (in Hebrew *Benei*

Horin, as opposed to slaves in Egypt), and there were other tribes with different names scattered everywhere in North Africa. The Romans and Greeks referred to them as "Barbar," or Barbarians, and the name was kept exactly the same in the Arabic language to this day. The Muslims, since the invasion of North Africa, had a condescending colonial mentality toward these indigenous populations; their business was conquest and conversion of infidels, and everyone who was not Muslim was an infidel. The name Barbar had been changed by the British sometime in the eighteenth century, to Berber. The only people who still refer to them as Barbar are the Germans and the Arabs. (Hegel, writing on the history of the world, would give us insight into how little European intellectuals knew or cared to know about North Africa or Black Africa). We are yet to see the name change from Berber to something more in line with their own languages and history; the English word Berber stuck, and everyone uses it, including the indigenous population themselves. They have their own distinct languages and dialects, their own customs and cultures. That they kept their identity throughout the centuries, even in the face of Arab conquest, is an amazing story in itself. Even more amazing is that even today Jews and Algerian Berber are trying to figure out the details of their common ancestry—tribe names, names of villages, of people, oral tales and myths. Thirty million Berbers are searching for their unique identity in North Africa and elsewhere, mainly to distinguish themselves from the Arabs of the region. The subject could provide ample research material for hundreds of curious university students.

Ibn Khaldûn is one of the most famous Arab scholars in history and social sciences. He was born in Tunisia in 1334 and as we will see, his story is important in discussing North Africa and its people, including its Jewish heritage. He travelled extensively throughout this part of the African continent. His parents were from Yemen and moved to Spain before he was born. (For some reason, many Yemenite Jews and Muslims were traveling back and forth, and Yemenite names keep appearing in different manuscripts and books throughout the Middle Ages). With events in Seville turning against them, they migrated to Tunisia along with many other Spanish Jews. A century earlier, Yemen went through a period of revolt against Saladin, and some Jews embarked on developing a new religion combining Judaism and Islam. At the time a large and vibrant Jewish community existed in Yemen. Jacob Ben Nathanael, a prominent Jewish leader in Yemen, wrote to Rabbi Moshe ben Maimon—better known as Maimonides—in Spain and got a letter back with an explanation as to why this religious movement should be stopped. (This incredibly efficient line of communication is intriguing at that era and over such long distances.) Both Ibn Khaldûn and Maimonides followed similar professional routes, including travelling to Egypt for fame and recognition; the former became a teacher and a well-known historian, and the latter became a teacher, a doctor and a philosopher.

Ibn Khaldûn spent a good part of his time trying to understand the origins of the Berbers. His purpose, it seems, was to figure out a way to convince them to convert to Islam. He tried all kinds of theories to make this happen and settled on an interesting account of history, mostly to either please his Islamic audience or to make history happen through manipulation, still a common practice even today. According to Ibn Khaldûn, the Muslims, upon their invasion of North Africa, found many Berber tribes all around the area, from Alexandria (Egypt) to Tangier (Morocco). Some were Jewish, others were Christian, and others pagans who worshipped the sun and the moon. They had kings and chiefs, and often fought back against the Muslims.[37] Khaldûn rejected many hypotheses regarding the origin of the Berbers and reached his own, not-so-original conclusion, based on the Bible that the Berbers were the descendent of Canaan, son of Ham. Ham is the same fellow who had been cursed by Noah, along with his forth Son. The problem with this hypothesis is that centuries earlier it was also accepted that because Ham disgraced his father he was cursed through his son, Canaan, and that this curse was used to describe many people in the lower classes of society, such as serfs, the uneducated, black slaves, etc. Khaldûn, in fact, adopted a traditional scenario, first turning to the Bible for answers and then adopting the cursed son as the father of the Berber people. In other words, Khaldûn sees them as those who refused to toe the line and become Arabs and Muslims, primitives with a long way to go to be saved.

On another front of Islamic expansionism, there is the Turkic Jewish population, East European Jews, also known as the Ashkanzi (German) Jews. These ethnic groups today account for 80 percent of world Jewry, and according to Arthur Koestler, these Jews are descendants of the Kahazr people who adopted Judaism somewhere in the eighth century. Both the Kahazr and the Berber people were fighting the expansion of Islam into Europe during the same period. And when Joseph, King of the Kahazre, received a letter from the Sephardic Jew Hasdai in Spain inquiring about their religion and asking to which of the 12 tribes they belong, he replied that according to their legends his people are decedents of Japhet (Yefet), son of Noah, and that they are not part of any of the Twelve Tribes of Israel.[38] Hasdai was intrigued by this new Jewish community coming out of nowhere. Koestler, a secular writer and journalist, backed up his thesis by turning to Biblical and Koranic sources, myths and legends. Koestler was a Hungarian Jew living in London and had published numerous books and articles; this book, *The Thirteenth Tribe*, was his last work before his death. In 1983 Koestler (age 77) and his wife committed suicide. His theory continues to be extremely controversial among Jews and various anti-Semites groups, including some Palestinian intellectuals who find his theory appealing, as it provides another layer to justify their political and historical grievances.

There is obviously no conclusive evidence supporting this theory, but evidence of this conversion was widely known by North African and Spanish Jews. This may or may not explain the rapid population growth of this Eastern European Jewish population. But, we will leave the quest for purity of race to others, since this is the least interesting part of human history in general, and Jewish history in particular. Nevertheless, adopting Noah's story was a convenient scenario for religious historians. The story of Biblical Noah was being adopted in various ways over the centuries: "The idea that serfs were the descendants of Ham soon became widely promoted in Europe. An example of this is Dame Juliana Berners (c. 1388), who, in a treatise on hawks, claimed that the "churlish" descendants of Ham had settled in Europe, those of the temperate Shem in Africa, and those of the noble Japheth in Asia—a departure from normal arrangements, which placed Shem in Asia, Japheth in Europe and Ham in Africa—because she considered Europe to be the "country of churls," Asia of gentility, and Africa of temperance. As serfdom waned in the late medieval era, the interpretation of serfs being descendants of Ham decreased as well."[39] Interestingly, during the eighteenth and nineteenth centuries, the curse of Ham became a justification for slavery of Black Africans. The sins of Ham were translated as a curse for darkness or blackness, hence the curse of the entire continent. Some churches in the US and elsewhere, including Mormon ones, refused entry to blacks as a result of this interpretation of the Bible. Nevertheless, this interpretation was rejected later by many theologians who argue that the whole curse story had nothing to do with Africa, north or south of the Sahara.

According to Ibn Khaldûn, the Berbers were not the Canaanites expelled by King David after he defeated Goliath. He obviously did not have the current Palestinian problem in mind, but in providing such a refutation he related the Muslim Biblical account to counter Jewish history in the Middle East and North Africa, and at the same time has provided a readymade story for the Berbers who fiercely resisted conversion to Islam and Arab colonialism—they were the cursed people. Nevertheless, turning to the Bible (or the Koran) for answers to everything was a common practice, used as a political justification for Islamic and Christian expansion, and later by nationalist Jews in Israel as well. It is all a matter of interpreting the Holy Scriptures, and as we have seen throughout history, anything goes.

A genetic study was recently done by a young Israeli scientist, Eran Elhaik,[40] who decided to test the Kazahr hypothesis on the origin of Eastern European Jews. (Missing Link of Jewish European Ancestry) Like Kostler, Elhaik concluded in favor of this hypothesis, and his findings clearly supported the theory that Jews of Eastern Europe are in large part the Kazahrs. Interestingly, at the beginning of his study, Elhaik points out that he had not analyzed the genetic makeup of the Sephardim or North African Jewry. Indeed, his whole genetic study relied heavily on Spanish and North African Jewish historical publications. His genetic study revealed nothing that was not already known from reading the history books, including the erroneous conclusions reached with respect to Yemenite and Ethiopian Jews. These genetic studies are not crystal balls and are to be treated very cautiously and with suspicion. In other words, they are very heavily manipulated by the ideologies and the finances behind the analysis.

Ibn Khaldûn is considered one of the greatest philosophers of the Arab world. His "History of the World" manuscript, was mostly written while he was in hiding, living among the Berbers in Algeria. He traced his ancestors to noble Arabs in Yemen, and even back to Muhammad. This stretch of the imagination was not part of any delusion, but necessary for establishing respect from his peers and colleagues. Anyone who could write was called a scholar, and anyone in a position of power built his own genealogical tree connecting him to Muhammad. Some scholars today dispute his ancestral claim, and many have suggested that he really was a Berber and not an Arab. After all, Ibn Khaldûn was preoccupied and fascinated by Berber history. He spent years with Berber tribes enjoying their full hospitality and in essence became one of them. Bourguiba had a portrait of Ibn Khaldûn on the wall of his palace, one of the four men he most admired: "Hannibal, perhaps the greatest of military commanders, St. Augustine, who was born in what is now Algeria, Jugurtha, a king who stood up to the Romans, and Ibn Khaldûn, who changed the way of writing history."[41]

Ibn Khaldûn made a very curious statement which even today makes the history of North Africa seem confusing if not chaotic, with far-reaching implications as to the future of the political and social history of the region. His writings on the Berber have already changed Algeria and Morocco, while Tunisia is still on hold with its present Jasmine Revolution, refusing to acknowledge its own history and origins. The current leadership believes the country to be unique in the Arab Muslim world, and is on route to make Tunisia more fanatic and religious than it ever has been in history.

Khaldûn claimed that many of the Berber in North Africa were of Jewish decent and acknowledged the existence of large Jewish Berber tribes. Did the Hebrew people come from the west, from Egypt? Were the Hebrews the indigenous population of North Africa? During the Arab conquest, Khaldûn writes about a Jewish Queen named Cohena (female Cohen) who roamed throughout North Africa supported by the local population along the coast, all the way to Tangier and further south towards the Sahara desert. The Arabs were defeated in their first attempt of conquest by this Queen. It is a curious story and history and if it were written by anyone else no one would have taken notice. Most Arab intellectuals decided not to take this statement about the Berbers being Jewish too seriously, for obvious reasons, as acceptance of this claim would throw Arab historians into unknown and undesirable territory.

His other works on history and sociology, though, are taken very seriously by Arab scholars. In one instance an Arab scholar discarded the findings of Jewish heritage in Berber society to the point of striping Khaldûn of his position in world Arab history. For Arab philosophers and historians, this part of Khaldûn's writings is very disturbing. However, every Berber in North Africa is aware of this history, and it is an important part of what holds their ancient tradition to this day. It has also somewhat inspired centuries of anti-Arab colonialism and conquest. Al-Qaida's presence in Libya and Mali today are one consequence of the deeply entrenched confusion surrounding North African history. Libya and Mali, like Tunisia, Algeria and Morocco, are also searching for their histories.

Berber struggles for rights and recognition in Algeria and Morocco today are also part of this story. What is certain and undisputable is that the Berber and the people of the book, the Hebrew people, shared a lot in common in terms of survival, stubbornness and a particular sense of uniqueness in identity and culture. Historical records tell us that they might even be one and the same. No one knows for certain, and even geneticists cannot help much because of the power of ideologies and biases. Many of the Moroccan, Tunisians and Algerian Jews coming to Israel in the 1940s could not be distinguished from other indigenous Berber populations in North Africa. But, today, in order to become a Jew in Israel, you have to pass an exam and a year or two of intense (and meaningless) Biblical study, including bribery money along the way, for the rabbi's coffer. This was obviously not the case in North Africa in recent nor in ancient history because the religious establishment was dependent on the Jewish community and always held in check by them, not the other way around. Religious fanaticism became a way of life and pillar of Judaism in Israel only recently. In any case, no individual of Berber origin will tell you he is an Arab, even if he had adopted the Arabic language or Islam. Recently, Berbers have been consolidating their identity everywhere in North Africa, searching for historical clues to help them survive as a people, but always refusing to become Arabs. It is not difficult to see radical changes happening in North Africa which will put into question the adopted history and religion, a process which is fit for Free People.

We will now turn to the main contradictions which lie at the heart of the political confusion in North Africa and which may help explain in part the recent and current Arab Spring revolutions. The Berber struggle is manifested in their refusal to become Arabs. They have adopted the Arabic language and to various degrees Islam, but refuse to go any further. After adopting all things Arab, they are still trying to distinguish themselves from the Arabs, which is not an easy thing to do. Still, their demands and claims to uniqueness are being questioned by the Islamic states of Morocco and Algeria. They are gaining grounds in both countries, and major changes to the Maghreb are taking place and will continue in the future, with Islamic fundamentalism either taking total control towards creating even further extremism, or a shift occurring towards pluralism and openness toward cultures and religions. The new Berber movement looks at the examples of Australians or Americans who speak English but are not British, to show that this can be done also in North Africa. At present, however, the Berbers are still in a situation somewhat similar to what North African Jews are undergoing in Israel, trying hard to belong, and often becoming more fanatic than their religious masters. Religious fanaticism on all sides in the Holy Land, as we know, is out of control. Some Berbers are doing the same thing, trying to become more Muslim than their Muslim Arab masters.

In Morocco, a Berber manifesto was written in 1996 as part of the new constitutional reforms which reads: "There is a national question that commands high attention. It has to do with the denial—conscious or unconscious—of the 'Amazighity' of Morocco (i.e. its Berberity)."[42]   More than 60 percent of Moroccans are of Berber origin with their own distinct language and culture. Like the Jews of North Africa they too have a history dating back more than 3,000 years. The history of both the Jews in North Africa and the Berbers[43] overlap, and it is impossible at times to distinguish between the two. The Moroccan Berber Manifesto acknowledges that "[t]his Berberity has a great importance for our Moroccan and Maghrebian identity, and its continued denial will, very likely, have dire consequences." This extremely important paper goes on to state that in order to understand current political problems they must go back to history from centuries ago, not just from the colonial era. This phrase is a key to national maturity, and demonstrates an advance in thinking that third-world theorists like Edward Said and Frantz Fanon could not have dreamed of.

The Moroccan government diffused this time bomb by acknowledging their distant history and accepting that their country is more than just Arab. Some Berbers have even argued that the whole of the Arab culture and civilization was adopted from them. The Berbers refused for centuries to send their kids to schools afraid they would be forced to learn Arabic; as a result, they paid the heavy price of remaining poor and uneducated, with a majority of Berbers living on the margins of society. Centuries of Arab domination and underdevelopment did not lead to their integration, nor were they viewed as equal. The call for complete Arabization before and after independence was a constant theme throughout Arab colonialism: "The complete Arabization action must aim not only to eliminate the French language as a language of civilization, culture and social intercourse, but also—and this is very important—to see to it that the local dialects (be they Berber or Arabic) become defunct…and that the use of any language or dialect—in the school, radio and television—other than standard Arabic be prohibited."[44] Berbers have often been "forced to become Arabized in order to earn their living" since independence. (It was the same situation during the early era of Tunisian nationalism.) Furthermore, they were forbidden from holding public office and thus had no part of official Moroccan society. The manifesto also states that Arab Moroccans during the Pan-Arabic nationalist era were busy accumulating wealth and never really cared about the poor indigenous population. In other words, they demanded submission to Allah for everyone else, while they themselves amassed power and wealth.

This important manifesto was not written by some obscure revolutionary group but by state officials and intellectuals; everyone should read this document aimed at soothing the pain of nationalism and preventing future collapse of the Moroccan Kingdom under religious control. Here is another interesting quote: "Whoever claims that the Islamization of a Moslem becomes valid only through his Arabization has excluded, in his ethnic computation, nine tenths of the Moslems from the Islamic community world-wide." This clear attempt to separate Islam from the Arabs says, in effect, "as long as you are a Muslim, your language does not necessarily have to be Arabic," as is the case in most of the Muslim world. This theory obviously shies away from mentioning any other religious groups, such as the Jews, for example, who made up more than 10 percent of the Moroccan population in the 1900, not to mention Tunisian Jews. This part of the story is much more complex, and it is not mentioned anywhere in the manifesto, as virtually no Jews remain in Morocco to force a debate. But even in Israel, where the majority of Moroccan Jews live, the debate is also nonexistent. And finally, here is the thing that does away with Said's theory of Orientalism, the fifth request in the Berber Manifesto: "In the last 40 years, the political trends that have adopted a fanatical stand about Arabism have exploited their effective hegemony and used their authority to orient 'research' and teaching. Thus they have oriented historical studies on the Maghreb and the teaching of History in accordance with their wishes and ideological inclinations." It is important to remember that the "Mohammedan conquest of Africa was only achieved after 70 years of murderous warfare"[45] and by the end of it "[t]here remained not a single Berber in the provinces of Ifrikiya (what is now Tunisia) who had not become Muslim." (Ibn Abd El Hakim 710AD). This was obviously part of Arab wishful thinking. It was simply not true. Until 1948, Tunisia still had a predominant Berber culture.

Moroccan Jews in Israel were undergoing similar systematic discrimination and marginalization at all levels of society, from culture and politics to science and research. The oppressors in this case were not a Muslim Arabs but European Jews. Their religion was more or less the same, but the culture was very different, and their oppression illustrates the darker side of Zionism and modern Israel. For example, the 2012 Nobel Prize in Physics, which was awarded to Serge Haroche could not have come from the Israeli Moroccan population. Mr. Haroche was born in 1944 in Casablanca and studied in France, and is always referred to as "French." He studied under Claude Cohen-Tannoudji, an Algerian Jewish physicist who also received a Nobel Prize in physics in 1997. But discrimination is only one part of the North African Jewish tragedy in Israel. The other part is the complete and total ignorance exhibited by Israelis from all social classes towards any Jew who did not come from Eastern Europe. This sentiment transcends all segments of society, including the State, and has shaped the character of all ethnic groups in Israel. Their history does not even exist in the Israeli education system to this day. Eastern European Jews control the state apparatus, and in a sense they are no different from the Arab Moroccans controlling the Berbers. Jews from LCA have been under shock treatment therapy in Israel, forced to renounce the languages and cultures they practiced for thousands of years. They have been made to feel ashamed of their origins. Obviously, Israel has a long way to go in order reach maturity and publish a similar manifesto admitting its historical errors to new generations of Israelis thus letting history take its natural course. What we get instead is the continuous ignorance and deep silence of the population itself, not to mention 65 years of war and violence in the Middle East.

In Algeria, the Berber situation is quite similar. There, some 5 million indigenous Berbers who are struggling with the Arabs for control of the state with all of its bureaucratic machinery. The Berber largely kept to themselves for centuries and most were converted to Islam, though always refusing to become Arabs, whatever that meant.

The further east we go, the tighter the Islamic control becomes. Tunisia, being in the middle of North Africa, finally fell into the hands of Arab Islamists, with no meaningful Berber or Jewish population to keep them in check. Tunisia had been invaded and reinvaded throughout its history by the Phoenicians, the Romans, Vandals, Byzantines, the Arabs, Ottomans, Spanish and French, the German and the Arabs again, and each invasion brought with it destruction and poverty—seldom reconstruction and development. The Arab invasion and the Ottoman colonial occupation and its disastrous presence resulted in the pushing the indigenous population to the margins of civilization, often behind mountains or far inland into the desert. Indeed, the move by the Berbers to the south was basically a defense mechanism against invaders and various religious convertors, both Christian and Muslim. The hostile desert environment prevented invaders from approaching and controlling their affairs and lives; it was the only way for them to remain relatively free. When the Germans invaded Tunisia in WWII, quite a few Jews fled 400 kilometers south into the deep desert. This method, which worked for centuries, was no longer a viable way to survive, so the grand exile was their story throughout the twentieth century—especially with the introduction of Islamic nationalism disguised as anti-colonialism.

At a recent festival in the Tunisian town of Tamazret, a Berber activist stated: "Amazigh (Berber) culture has always been a taboo topic in Tunisia throughout our history, since the days of the Ottomans. It continued under the French, after independence with Bourguiba and Ben Ali, and still exists today with the current Islamist-led government." Similarly, another Tunisian Amazigh activist Nouri Nemri said: "The main challenge is with the authorities, who often try to hamper the free expression of Amazigh culture in Tunisia."[46] Nouri knows his history and the history of the Berbers in neighboring countries. The 100,000 people still holding on to Amazigh culture in Tunisia, and the millions who are supporters and practice the culture worldwide, will continue to pose a challenge to all present and future Islamic governments in Tunisia. They too are waiting to be counted in the next revolution. It is therefore no accident that a recent movie about Egyptian Jews by an Egyptian director was banned and forbidden to be aired on Egyptian TV.

A young documentary maker by the name of Kamal Hachkar has revealed his Berber roots in Southern Morocco by producing a stunning documentary called *Tinghir, Echoes from the Mellah*. According to the *Moroccan World News*, "The story of the film revolves around a young man who lived almost his entire life in France. He thought all Amazigh of Morocco were Muslims,"[47] and was amazed to find so many Jewish Berbers from the same village where he himself was born. His documentary was attacked violently by Moroccan Islamists, and hundreds of demonstrators demanded a ban of the movie. It did not take long for Amazigh activists to counter these demonstrations, claiming that this is part of their history and were against banning the film. A Muslim, Hachkar traveled to Israel in search for Moroccans Jews who still kept their Berber language and customs. He even used Skype to establish video communication between a Jewish family in Jerusalem and his own Berber Muslim family in Tinghir. Years ago they were neighbors, spoke the same Berber language and had centuries of shared history. The synagogue was situated right beside the mosque. They go in, pray and meet outside to discuss other issues. There was little friction, as both were Berber in language, history and culture. Indeed, 400,000 Jews once lived in Morocco…

Kahena, A Common Legend

2,100 years ago, long before Muslims conquered the area, Tunisia, then called Carthage, embarked on a daring war campaign attacking the Roman Empire not by sea but by land, through Iberia, over the Pyrenees and the Alps into northern Roman territory; they ended up occupying most of the Roman peninsula for over 15 years. The Carthaginian civilization dates back 3,000 years, and its origin is disputed by historians; they could have been Canaanites or Phoenicians. But they also could have been Africans or Hebrew tribes scattered eastward from Egypt. Most accounts about the Carthaginians come from Roman sources, and after so many invasions by various empires, it is difficult to accurately know their origin. And it seems that the more archeologists dig up, the more complex the story becomes. The quest for answers on questions of racial purity has even the gene scientists involved. As mentioned elswhere in this book, ideology is also involved: opposing groups of scientists, each with their own biases and prior historical knowledge, present disputed findings to specific target audiences. There is a lot at stake, as ethnic and religious groups are funding scientists to try to discredit ancient claims to territories and history.

Suffice it to say that evidence of a Jewish presence in Carthage was found not just in Tunisia, but also in Spain and Morocco. Geneticist Harry Ostrer of Yeshiva University in New York embarked on a research study of the "biological basis for Jewishness" among North African Jews. The apparent intent behind this "pure Jewish race" study is to "help reveal genetic predispositions to heart disease, cancer, diabetes and other widespread diseases, which helps treat them at an earlier stage."[48] But, this is only a part of the story, as I suspect that geneticists are heavily relying on history books and ideologies to back up their theories—Professor Ostrer is no different. The question remains, which history books is he using, and what are the political and religious ideologies behind them? According to Ostrer, "the latest research revealed that the North African Jewish community displays a high rate of marriage within their immediate community." But what is a "high rate of marriage"? Or how is it different from the Ashkanzi communities in Eastern Europe? What is the hidden historical agenda? Why are Jewish scientists so heavily involved in the gene business? Are they trying to prove that the questionable purity of the Jewish race is not just an Ashkanzi thing, but also applies to all of North African Jews as well? An interesting study was done on how German Jewish geneticists in Israel were thinking during the 1950s and how data even on blood samples were politically and ideologically manipulated.[49] If anything, it begs the question of why purity of race was so important in the early 1950s.[50] Apparently, most publications during that time were of a historical, sociological and anthropological nature; very little real scientific research was done at that time.

History has inspirational individuals who have captured the imagination of many, justifiably or unjustifiably, and Tunisia has given the world two such military personalities: Hannibal and Kahena. The world-famous male generals Patton (an American fighting in Tunisia) and Hannibal, have their female counterpart in Kahena, who according to an Arab historian in the fourteenth century was a Jewish Queen who led a brilliant military campaign against the Arabs in North Africa. Her Hebrew and Berber name was Cahina (a female Cohen), and she ruled a territory spanning Algeria, Tunisia and parts of Morocco. Algeria, with its large Berber population, is more aware of this history, and today this story still captures the imagination of Berbers who struggle for recognition, and for social and political rights in Algeria—especially women's rights. In Tunisia, the Berber population has been almost completely converted to the Arab-Islamic world, so this story plays a much lesser symbolic role. Her presumably Jewish background does not help in this respect, but it does spark the imagination of many Berber in North Africa. Islamists of the Jasmine Revolution will never allow this part of history to be accepted, and Arab historians since the fourteenth century have tried to downplay her Jewish background. Cahina led a series of attacks and counter-attacks against invading Arab armies. Her successes and military strategies to win the battlefields are legend. In Hebrew, her name is derived from the word Cohen, a Jewish Priest. The Cohen or Cohanim are believed to be direct decedent of the Jewish Kohanim who "halachically required being of direct patrilineal descent from the Biblical Aaron."

Hasan Ibn al-Nu'man of the Umayyad Dynasty heard of the legendary powers of Kahina and led his troops into Numidia to confront her, only to be defeated and forced to flee. In an attempt to prevent retaliation by Hasan, Kahina employed a "scorched earth" campaign, burning and destroying anything which may be useful to her enemies, thereby creating a type of barrier between them. A rather similar and effective scorched-earth campaign was used by the Russians during the various Nazi invasions in WWII. It seems that this state of destruction and underdevelopment continued for centuries under the control of the Arabs, who for centuries did not build anything in Tunisia besides mosques. The Arab conquerors had no interest in reversing the trend and rebuilding Tunisia, nor the whole of North of Africa for that matter. This apparently had little effect on the mountain-dwelling Berbers, but desert-dwellers withdrew their support from Kahina, thus creating a weakness that Hasan used to his advantage.

In the early 700s, Hasan's forces defeated Kahina, and conflicting accounts say that she was either killed in battle, sword in hand, or committed suicide by swallowing poison. Since then, various tribes have laid claim to her legend. Berber, Arabs and Maghrebian nationalists, as well as North African feminists, all use aspects of her life story to support their own agendas and to teach moral lessons. The Algerians have adopted Kahina not only as a military chief, but also as a religious leader, hanging on to the little history that remained, and trying in the process to bridge the contradictions between their acquired Islamic faith and their past, which may have everything to do with the Jewish people of North Africa.

Unfortunately, Tunisian Muslims have done much to deny the Jewish elements in their history and culture. (The new female heroine is now Amina, who stripped for the cause of freedom and got arrested for insulting the Islamic nation.) And the Israelis are also so far uninterested in this part of Jewish history. Nevertheless, the story of Kahena remains controversial. What we do know for certain is that she was not an Arab, nor was she a Muslim. Her stance and the myth developed among the Berber population lasted for centuries and helped them withstand Arab influences to some degree. The whole story, passed on from generation to generation with added twists and myths, was alive in every North African family. After all, the Berbers had to have an internal and meaningful cultural and religious code which united them throughout the Arab conquest and occupation. So, the story of her being Jewish is really not implausible. However, it does require genuine scholars ready and able to tackle the very complex parts of this unknown history, if this is at all possible. I know from friends and colleagues that even today Muslim Berber are proud to have Kahena associated even remotely with the Hebrews. It's unbelievable but it is true. Islamic invasion, Turkish and French Colonialism, as well as the struggle for independence, have triggered more awareness of these historical connections, and they are not about to disappear, not in Algeria or Morocco—and hopefully not in Tunisia as well. The people of the Maghreb, especially the elderly, know that Jews were an important part of their history and culture. The young, however, have no idea even what Jews look like, since there are none around in Tunisia today. They are now faced with powerful, and at the same time meaningless, religious propaganda. Religious fanatics are so far exploiting every situation to do just that, fueling hate, and in the process leading to violence.

Jewish Tunisia

In 1900: "Tunis is Jewish that, but for the French hatred of the Jews, it would be the ideal place for Mr. Zangwill to establish his New Jerusalem. The climate is near enough to that of Palestine; and in much a very Oriental place, the ancient customs and ceremonies of the Jews would not look ridiculous."[51] Under the nose and not so much the blessings of the Bey, the Tunisian Jewish community was controlling Tunisia, especially the city of Tunis. Two parallel Jewish communities developed according to the restrictions imposed on them over the centuries: the visibly poor Jews who could not be distinguished from the Berber tribes and the merchants, traders and bankers mostly of Sephardic origin. All cultural aspects of both groups are Berber to this day. One could not have survived without the other. The poor, or Jewish Berber, or Tunes were a living proof for the Bey and the Islamic authorities that Jews were living under strict submission to Islam, which meant that their social position was lower than the Arab Muslims. Their existence thus provided the necessary cover for the merchant class to prosper and advance their affairs. Their elimination would have necessarily led to upheavals from Arab Islamists, which was why rich Tunisian Jews felt obliged to hand out charity to the poor sections of town. Every Friday, food would be distributed to celebrate the Sabbath, an act that was a necessary obligation required for the survival of the entire Jewish community in Tunisia. The existence of the poor Jews were a daily reminder to the Bey that the system of Islamic submission was alive and well, and that Jews were at the bottom of the social hierarchy. This was an old tradition and even Christopher Columbus, who recent studies suggest was a crypto Jew, left one tenth of his wealth to the poor, some to the Jews scattered at the entrance of the Lisbon Jewish Ghetto. In addition, every so often, some rich Jews would pretend to be poor just to appease the current social order.

Their Jewishness was visible and not just by the clothing Jews were forced to wear, but also by their physical appearance. In the older days, Jews were made to "wear black and blue. A black fez was obligatory for Tunisian Jews and a white chechia for Livornesi. Green was absolutely forbidden to them." These dress codes changed according to the Bey's moods. But despite their unequal position due to Islamic laws and hundreds of years of oppression, the Chevalier Hesse-Wartegg wrote in 1882[52] that they were "only inferior to the Arabs in number." This English traveler wrote extensively about the workings of society, offering a lengthy and detailed description of the customs and everyday life of Tunisians and Tunisian Jews. He compared the customs and social hierarchies in Tunisian society to that of Japan, indicating the many similarities that existed between the two. A centuries-old social system existed, and a balance was struck and maintained at all times between what was permitted and what was forbidden, between ancient religious codes to be observed and the Bey's requirements and regulations (which changed quite often), between the ruling religious aristocracy and the masses.

And, as long as everyone knew their place all was relatively well, stability was kept and communities were left to their own. Towards end of the nineteenth century, neither the Jews nor the Arabs carried arms because "they are not necessary in Tunis, which is safer than most European towns."[53] Our English observer also provided a lengthy description of Jewish women and their role in the survival of the community, stating that "the great idea the Tunisian Jew had in marrying is that of perpetuating his race." Divorce was permitted but not an easy thing to do for a man because of the signed contract and money he had to pay. Also, women made sure that these attempts did not go unchallenged, and divorce contracts had to be followed to the letter. They, along with their extended family, would make sure these procedures were enacted. Indeed, Bourguiba's laws on woman's rights 60 years later, unheard of in the Arab world, can be largely attributed to how Jewish women traditionally lived in Tunisia. Marriage, for example, was for Tunisian Jews a community as well as a religious affair, unlike Muslims in Tunisia, for whom a marriage contract was an exchange done between two families. There was no imam and no visit to a mosque by the newlywed couple and their families and friends. In the Jewish tradition, the marriage ceremony was a long affair involving the rabbi and his entourage, the synagogue, the Hammam (Mikve or bath), celebrations with families and friends, very similar to the way it is celebrated today everywhere, with amazing Jewish Tunisian unique cultural twists and delicious foods. These ceremonies were of course much longer, lasting more than a week and involved complex series of celebrations. It is within the first few days of marriage that the newlywed woman had to make clear to her husband who runs the show in the family, clearly indicating that oppression of women was not part of their culture.

However, Jewish Tunisian women at the time did not have the "dream of returning to Jerusalem,"[54] as Rahel R. Wasserfall claimed after interviewing old Tunisian women in a Moshav (Agricultural Settlement) in Israel as part of a study for a book. The Return to Jerusalem became a dream only after their nightmare situation in Israel, materially, spiritually, historically and morally. Once in Israel, all was taken away. The Return to Jerusalem dream became their only escape to comfort their miserable situation; many of the young are doing the same thing today. All historical evidence tells us that no one in Tunisia dreamt about returning to Jerusalem at any time during their long history, not even the very religious people of the community. At most, religious scholars would travel to Jerusalem to further their studies, develop personal relationships, or simply to die there, as was the case with Nathan Borgel (a scholar and chief rabbi of Tunis), who left for Israel at the end of the eighteenth century. (The same was also true for Ethiopian Jews and many other Jewish communities as well.) During their 3,000-year history, Tunisia was their home—not to be replaced or confused with any other place on earth.

Jews and Muslims in Tunisia were feeding and learning from each other's custom and culture, as both were under Turkish Islamic colonial control. Many customs were shared by all inhabitants, and were uniquely Berber in character. Even the Bey's administration was part of this cultural system. Religious fanaticism as we know it today was non-existent. A very old Tunisian Jew whom I interviewed said that today's Islamic rage is a thousand times more severe than what he endured during his lifetime in Tunisia. Muslims did not pray in the streets towards Mecca as they do in the streets of Paris, and you could see many of them drinking and smoking in local cafes and restaurants—

even during Ramadan—very much like the old Ethiopian Jewish women sitting in Be'er Sheva's cafes in the early days of emigration to Israel. Nor was pilgrimage (*hajj*) to Mecca part of the Tunisian culture in any shape or form. Very few if any joined the Egyptian caravan to Mecca, not because it was expensive and dangerous to do so, but because Tunisia had its own Islamic religious tradition. Those who were determined to celebrate *hajj* had to endure a long and miserable voyage, which for a poor person could last years. The irony is that modern technology in transport made *hajj* what it is today, and not as part of a sacred religious tradition.

On the Sabbath, the markets were closed, and during Ramadan, society entered different kind of existence. Many of those forced to follow the strict tradition were sleeping or in hiding during the day, and special announcers went house to house at night reminding everybody that they must get up and eat. Essentially no one worked during Ramadan. Years later, Bourguiba decided to help break this tradition by purposefully drinking orange juice on live TV during Ramadan. He knew then where all this religious fanaticism was heading. Even today, in 2013, people are pretending to follow the strict, illogical one-month fast. A large segment of the population goes into hiding so they can drink and eat to their heart's content without the watchful eyes of the Islamic government and its informers. The Berber population never really understood the religious logic of Ramadan. They had a hard enough time consuming enough food throughout the year as it was and this Ramadan business was not going well for them.

Outdated Islamic codes for women's place in society, both today and historically, have their mirror in the Jewish tradition in Israel. It is a religious fanaticism resulting from the misinterpretation of history, the Scriptures, the Koran and of man's relationship to God in our modern society, combined with contagious religious nationalism. In Beit Shemesh, a city near Jerusalem, you could still see road signs asking women not to enter, or move to another sidewalk. In some places women are asked to sit at the back of public buses, even today in 2013. In comparison, the Jewish women of Tunisia at the beginning of the twentieth century were light years ahead of their Muslim sisters in the Islamic world. Within the ultra-religious Hasidic communities the situation is even more extreme, as women are made to follow a very strict lifestyle of total religious submission, which amounts to Hassidic women not venturing out of their houses. These religious ghettos in Israel are all part of new modesty regulations to be enforced at all times by specially formed units. Of course, the internet is forbidden, and having a computer at home is still under discussion by our "super intelligent" rabbis from the Abraham, Isaacic tradition. These fanatical codes were designed by fanatical men from another era and enforced by the Islamic or Jewish traditions. Tunisians can take comfort that religious fanaticism is very much alive in the Holy Land among Jews as well. The Muslim Brotherhood of Tunisia can be comforted that their calls to take away a gold medal from a Tunisian Olympiads athlete in 2012 will not sound strange to a segment of Israel's population. Oussama Mellouli, who won the gold in a 10km swim, was seeing drinking just before the race, held during Ramadan, which upset Muslims in Tunisia who claimed he should have competed while fasting. But such illogical demands could have easily come from fanatic ultra-religious Jews in Jerusalem. Fundamentalism and religious fanaticism is certainly not exclusive to Muslims.

Our nineteenth-century English observer noticed very early that North African Jews had no friends anywhere, and were politically, ideologically and culturally isolated. This was also observed by the Sephardic council general Noah in 1815. Yet these same communities have survived centuries of oppression and submission, largely dependent on their ability to amass wealth and infiltrate colonial administrations, Turkish or French, in whatever capacity, just to survive. This was not an easy task considering the number of colonial invasions that occurred throughout Tunisia's history.

Israeli Zionist historians, like their Muslim counterparts, have no interest in presenting the Jewish community in Tunisia as having had any meaningful existence. Ben-Gurion called them the "dust of the earth" and others referred to them as primitive, backward, centuries behind civilization, etc. Both Zionist and Muslim historians were ideologically biased bent on uncovering a small, oppressed and primitive Jewish community. The Zionists had their own interpretation that Tunisian Jews were poor and miserable and were in need of emancipation—they needed to be saved. In his analysis of the Ottoman conquest, Zeev Hirschberg discarded not just the tremendous influence Jews had in Tunisia, but also misrepresented their population numbers during the 1800s. Hirschberg could not accept the population count published by the US consul general in Tunisia at the time, and writes: "We must of course remember that Noah only knew Tunisia by personal observation." Who else was in Tunisia at the time able to report anything? Surely the observation of the consul of the United States was not just personal information? Hirschberg discards Noah's accounts yet he goes into lengthy description of strange and unreliable account of Tunis during WWII by a rabbi's son. (See chapter above on Tunisian Jews under Nazism.) Similarly, David Biale, in *Cultures of the Jews*, also provides curious population numbers for Jews in Tunisia, Algeria, Libya and Morocco.[55] The same goes for Muslim historians who have their own agenda in making sure that the history of Tunisian Jews is merely one of useful, temporary residents having little influence on Tunisian culture, politics, economy or history. Even the Bey of Tunisia throughout the Ottoman occupation regarded them as such, a view adopted by all subsequent Islamic nationalist governments.

At the beginning of the nineteenth century, long before the French "adopted" Tunisia as a protectorate, Tunisian Jews ran Tunisia's trade and commerce, and retail shops in the various bazars and markets. They were what we call today small-business owners in all sectors of the economy. As such, they were the engine of Tunisia's economy. They played well their role of introducing goods and services of the new colonial economy in Tunisia. This was a natural role for them, considering their trading experience over the centuries. The American Consul Noah knew about their role in the economy; it was evident to him that Tunisian Jews were basically running the country. Many accounts from this period in history point to the same Jewish influence in all aspects of Tunisian life. What is certain is that one could not speak of Tunisia without describing its unique and large Jewish community. This was also the case long before Islam and Mohammed. It is only today that both Israelis and Muslims have discarded Jewish Tunisian contributions to the history of the country.

Literary history and archeological digs have given us ample evidence of this rich Jewish community, dating back 3,000 years. The Talmud mentions Tunisia a few times; Josephus give us testimony of the transportation of 30,000 Jews from Israel to Tunisia by the Romans under Emperor Titus. Near the ruined city of Carthage lies a site known as Gammarth, where excavations have revealed a third-century Jewish cemetery. At a place called Hamman Lif, the remains of a well-preserved third-century CE synagogue have been discovered containing a mosaic displaying the words "Sancta Sinagoga." Many of the archeological discoveries from this era were found decorating Ben Ali's (the dictator ousted in 2011) and his wife Leila's summer house in Hamammet. The chief archeologist of Tunisia visited the house after the 2011 revolution and burst into tears seeing the ancient archeological treasures in the house of the former dictator, similar to what Moshe Dayan did in Israel. No Muslim ever shed tears at the ethnic cleansing of Jews in Tunisia.

The Jews brought prosperity to the country and to North Africa as a whole, orchestrating trade in a number of products such as hides and skins and African silk, olive oil, and other foods and spices. Seizing the opportunities in Tunisia were also Christians and Jews from Italy, Sicily, Portugal and Spain, as well as Malta, and they formed new communities in coastal cities such as Sousse, Monastir, Sfax and Gabes. England exiled its Jewish community in 1290, France in 1394 and Spain in 1492. Most of those expelled settled in countries of North Africa, and Tunisia was always a favorable place to resettle. Many of the Muslims in Tunisia were also descendent from Spain (Moriscos) and came to the country during the fifteenth and sixteenth centuries. The Muslim dynasties of the twelfth century, the Almoravids and the Almohads, harshly persecuted the Jews, who were given the choice of conversion or death, and in many instances were sold into slavery. By the thirteenth century a more tolerant dynasty, the Hafsids, had assumed control of the country, and Jews were allowed to resume the practice of their religion, though much of the discriminating legislations remained, including the *jizyah* (a poll-tax for non-Muslims), the requirement to wear distinctive clothing and segregation into special quarters of the cities known as the Harat-al-Yahud.[56]

As can been seen, history had not been kind to the Jewish people of North Africa, nor to the rest of the Muslim world, or for that matter to Jews of the Christian world as well. Tunisia is but an example of this sad saga of Islamic expansionism, imperialism, feudalism, colonialism and underdevelopment all at the same time. Before 1948, the Jewish population of Tunisia reached a peak of 140,000, not including the many who converted to Islam. As in Spain, many Muslims in Tunisia were Jewish converts hiding their identity and in Spain they were called *marranos*. In the 1950s, half of the Jewish population left for Israel, the other half to France and other countries. By 2011, only 700 Jews were living in Tunis and 1,000 on the island of Djerba. It is therefore not difficult to comprehend that the exodus of Jews was not an accident of history, nor was it just a Zionist plot.

The arguments that Tunisian Jews left due to Zionist propaganda (the Arab Tunisian view), Muslim persecution (the Zionist view) and/or messianic Jewish promises (both the Zionist and Arab Tunisian views) were the acceptable cover stories. These views, however, cannot completely explain the total disappearance of the Jewish community from Tunisia. A different kind of analysis is warranted to break the silence and ignorance. The same phenomenon occurred in almost every Islamic state, under almost exact circumstances, with varying degrees of submission and terror. The Jews of Yemen were also viewed through the same lens, and so were Iraqi Jews, and so on…. Over the centuries Jews of the region moved from one place to another due to Christian or Muslim persecution, or for economic reasons. For centuries they remained in LCA until Islamic nationalists took over the agenda and the State and began to institute new types of political organization and terror—all with the blessing of the international community.

S.D. Goitein has provided an interesting account of the living conditions of the Jewish population in North Africa during the tenth and eleventh centuries, using documents and letters from the Cairo Geniza.[57] Most of the writers were Jewish, and 80 percent of these documents were written in Arabic, the dominant language in the region at the time. Goitein paints a rather interesting picture of the movement of people and goods, including a regular mail service that existed throughout the Middle East and North Africa. There are documents listing in detail the types of Jewish-owned boats and warships used in that period, a fascinating read for boat builders, sailors and insurance companies. It was also evident that people could move freely from one area to the next without confronting serious obstacles. According to documents analyzed, Jews moved as much as other communities, and did so within an amazingly efficient system of travel and communication. One traveler writes of his journey from Bagdad to Tunisia, and from there to Spain. Jewish religious scholars traveled to Jerusalem for internships, while donations and gifts were sent to help the local learning centers cope with economic hardships. As I mentioned before, many Yemenites, both Muslims and Jews, founded new homes in Tunisia, and traces of Yemenite culture can be found in some remote Berber tribes. The author speaks of the unity of the Middle Eastern world during the Middle Ages: "This is all the more remarkable, since the European shore of the Mediterranean, including Spain as well as the African and the Asian sides, were split up into many separate political units, often at war with one another."[58] He finds this amazing because the preserved documents and records demonstrate "life as it really was, especially of the middle and lower strata of society, uncensored by literary selection and presentation." Thousands of such letters and documents are preserved, waiting to be analyzed; hopefully will not be burned by the new nationalist Islamic regime in Egypt.

Tunisian Jews have roots in the region dating back into antiquity. According to Flavius Josephus, Julius Caesar granted a special status and rights to the Jews of the newly created Roman province of Africa (now Tunisia), adding to an already existing Jewish community there. The fall of the Roman Empire and the rise of Islam and its rapid conquest and expansionism saw the Jews struggling to choose between conversion and submission. No one has statistics on how many chose to convert to Islam (or to Christianity), but those who converted did not have to live under such strict and rigid social rules and specially defined tax system as *dhimmas* had to. This system continued for centuries, and gradually collapsed over time; the relative protection they received has disappeared completely from most North African countries. The *dhimma* has outdone its usefulness and it was replaced by North African nationalism, as well as by policies of ethnic cleansing, leading to the total destruction of all Jewish communities in the region.

This traveler goes on analyzing the situation: "As dhimmis, Tunisian Jews flourished. But of course flourishing is relative: When confined to the bottom rung of the social ladder, one is happy not to be groveling in the mud just below."[59] The convivencia—the term coined by Spanish historians to depict the ostensibly harmonious ties among Muslims, Christians, and Jews in the medieval Islamic world—requires a very large asterisk. This age, according to Princeton historian Mark Cohen, was "marked by a legally-prescribed regime of discrimination and even witnessed periodic outbursts of violence." Yet, at the same time, historical records are clear: Jews played a significant role in the culture and politics of the country, and the Jewish community as a whole lived in substantial security. The occasional eruptions of violence signaled a temporary failure of the deal struck between Muslims and Jews, and not—as their Ashkenazi brethren attest—a way of life (and death)."[60]

The concepts of imperialism, colonialism, and globalization are being redefined here in light of the fact that Islam is now a dominant political religious power in the world. Islam is not an oppressed minority, since it started expanding 14 centuries ago. The expansionist side of Islam has led to the destruction of societies and cultures in countries all over the world. In Africa, thousand-year-old tribes and customs have disappeared due to Islamist nationalists who tolerated nothing but the total submission to their rigid political religious structure. What was not destroyed by European colonialism was destroyed by radical or political Islam.

In the mid-1900s, radical and not-so-radical Islam began aligning itself ideologically with the liberal ideology of the West through its adaptation of third-world anti-colonial theories and ideology. In essence, they pretended to be the oppressed people of the world, like sub-Saharan Africans. This alliance worked well, and in some countries one could not distinguish between radical Islamist students and Liberals or Leftists. Islamists were also able to use the Palestinian cause in order to integrate themselves into the mainstream ideology of the Left. They cried foul and pretended that they were the oppressed people of the world while at the same time promoting an extreme Islamist agenda, avoiding all inherit contradictions in the process. The first to fall in this false rhetoric were the Africans. North African anti-colonialist theories were easily exported to the south of the continent. Those who have adopted Islam as their religion reached a point of no return and are devoted to the idea of religious expansionism. The whole of the African continent is threatened, and with it the complete disappearance of African traditions and ancient histories. This underground religious war was taking place in Africa throughout the Cold War, unchecked and undetected, while oppressed people of the world were voicing their anger through radical Islam as the religion of the oppressed, as the voice of the "wretched of the earth." The rich oil nations of Islam supported this, laughing all the way to their own banks. And, in the process they bought as much fertile land as they could in Africa, especially East Africa, where the land is cheap and workers are plenty.

North Africans and black Africans read Frantz Fanon in order to enhance their radical Islamic ideology. But, there was nothing revolutionary in his world-vision besides his grand design of anti-white anti-colonialism and its replacement with an Islamic nationalism. What is curious from our point of view is that he is the single biggest contributor to Islamic Africa, which may soon encompass the whole continent. In a way, Fanon's writings were also the destructive force behind the race confusion among blacks in the US who now called themselves "African Americans." This identity mismatch is both ridiculous and damaging at the same time, almost as much as the Ashkenazim and Sephardim division of the Jewish people. Millions of Americans as a result were stripped of their national identity. What's wrong with having Americans with different skin colors? Who cares what the color of their skin is? It is easy to cross over to the fake world of

Fanon, Said and even Albert Memmi, of the oppressed Muslims and their brand of anti-colonialist struggle. This is why we see so many black Americans turning to Islam as their newly adopted religion, as they believe it to be the religion of the oppressed.

Fanon, who took up residence in Tunisia after being expelled from Algeria in 1957, did not care much about the Jewish communities oppressed for centuries, or the Berbers struggling to maintain their identities. The hundreds of thousands of Moroccan Jews who found it impossible to remain in their country did not fit his theory—these issues were not important. He "despised" the white bourgeoisie and with them all the Jews living in North Africa just because some of them adopted French culture as an alternative to the Turkish Bey and Ottoman Islamism. He after all, adopted the French culture quite naturally. He never uttered or wrote a word about the masses exiled from North Africa. The white Jewish intelligentsia of the West did not criticize him because they too were misled, believing the thesis of "Arab" Jews of North Africa and the Middle East. In a way, Fanon had carte blanche to voice his pro-Islamic, anti-colonialist thesis and he for years went completely unchecked and unquestioned.

I argue that "the peasant's spontaneity" on which Fanon built his revolutionary theory was not that spontaneous after all. A careful reading of the famous chapter "Spontaneity: Its Strength and Weakness" shows that all the examples he gives of peasant spontaneity belong to a distinctly Islamic, anti-colonial tradition that, by the time Fanon was writing, had been in existence less than a century. It is only by remaining silent about the Islamic sources of this tradition that Fanon managed to present it as a spontaneous and visceral peasant outburst. In the Algerian context, the categories of spontaneity and organization emerged only after all references to Islam were erased. Rather than spontaneity and organization, what *The Wretched of the Earth* actually describes is the combination of two systems of organization: one Marxist, and the other Islamic.[61]

Let us now return to population statistics of the Jewish communities in North Africa. The table below is but an indication to how such figures have been distorted. These numbers reflect the French population count based on the Bey's tax lists. In reality, the numbers were much larger in each North African country. In Morocco alone, the Jewish population in the 1900 was estimated at 200,000 and doubled in size by 1948. The Jewish population in Tunisia was estimated at 60,000 in 1815; by 1900 it grew to 90,000, and to 140,000 by 1948.

Jewish population in 1900[62]

	1900	%
Africa	**372,659**	**0.28%**
Algeria	51,044	1.07%
Egypt	30,678	0.31%
Ethiopia	50,000	1.00%
Libya	18,680	2.33%
Morocco	109,712	2.11%
S. Africa	50,000	4.54%
Tunisia	62,545	4.16%

This population count is interesting when we analyze the Jewish population of the city of Tunis. The total population of the city of Tunis in 1946 was 364,593 and 449,820 in greater Tunis. The Jewish population in the city during the same year was close to 100,000. Almost one third of the city's population was Jewish, much like Bagdad, which also had a large Jewish population. Libyan Jews, too, formed a significant urban minority in Tripoli and Benghazi. The rest of the population in Tunisia was scattered in smaller towns and villages. Today the city of Tunis exceeds two million, and it is for all purposes 100 percent Muslim.

This situation of Jewish dominance in the urban centers existed for centuries in spite of tough discriminatory property laws enacted by Islamist governments and the French during WWII. Accordingly, "The Vichy regime also sought to 'Aryanize' all Jewish property."[63] In July 1941, a law mandated the confiscation of all Jewish property except for personal residences. Vichy authorities awarded Jewish-owned businesses to "trustees," who were allowed to pay themselves from the profits of their businesses. Although the trustees were supposed to sell the enterprises under their control to suitable European settlers, they often postponed this step in order to take more money out of the business. (Because of this greed, many of the businesses were not sold by the time the Allies landed in North Africa, and would eventually be returned to their original owners.) Vichy officials handled the "Aryanization" campaign differently in each colony. As in other areas, enforcement in Algeria was most systematic under the newly established Office of Economic Aryanization. French anti-Semitism at the time was not just a follow up of German policies. It had a life of its own, and Paul Baudoin, the Vichy Minister of Foreign Affairs agreed that, "The present evolution has been freely chosen and is not in the least aimed at pleasing our victors." Anti-Jewish laws were rigorously implemented in North Africa, eliminating the little progress that was achieved in this respect.

In 1938, 70 percent of Tunisia's export was destined for France, and included olive oil, wheat, barley, wine and maize, in return for manufactured products and sugar. Ninety percent of Algerian exports went to France. Phosphates and ore also a large part of North African exports to the mother colony. In fact, Tunisia was the largest exporter of phosphates to France, with a shipment of 2,000 tons in 1938 alone. Most of Tunisia's imports came from France. North Africa as a whole supplied more than a million tons of wool. Very few manufactured goods were produced in Tunisia before WWII. However, many French businessmen set up shop in Tunisia, producing soaps and textiles, and building distilleries, fruit-drying plants and sugar refineries. In fact, most of the manufacturing sector was held by French colonialists, and the bulk of finished manufactured goods were imported. Jews were involved in all of these industries, mainly on the wholesale, retail and service levels. This situation created a total reliance on manufactured goods, coal and petrol, and led to an alarming government deficit until the German invasion. Still, from an economic perspective, Tunisian Jews had no incentive to flee the country before 1940. Economic activities were at their peak before the war as many French companies enjoyed the benefit of cheap labor and excellent living conditions for their families.

Statistical data about the demography of Tunisia up to WWII helps give us insight on the living conditions in the country. Apart from the Jewish population of Tunisia, there was also a large segment of French nationals living there. Their population grew from 19,000 in 1881 to 240,000 in 1946, with most living in Tunis and Bizerte. During the same period, a large Italian community flourished in Tunis, reaching 100,000 in the years before the war. All existing statistics on Tunisia come from French Protectorate archives, but the numbers are often inaccurate as they are derived and interpreted from tax records. Accurate numbers are also hard to come by when estimating the Muslim population. The French made a distinction between the indigenous Muslim population and Arab foreigners residing in the country. Thus the foreign population of Tunisia—including Italians, French, Arabs and Maltese—reached a staggering number of almost half a million people in the years before the war. Only a small percentage of them lived in rural areas; in a way, Tunis was highly European in character, though Jewish Tunisian-Berber in soul.

According to the census, 60 percent of Tunisian Jews lived in Tunis and were concentrated in the old Hara Quarter (a Tunisian style of a Jewish Ghetto). By 1956, their numbers had fallen dramatically to 57,000, and by 1964 to 5,000. By 1967, following the Six-Day War between Israel and its neighbors, the Jewish population had basically disappeared from Tunisia. In 1966, the Hara quarter was completely razed to make room for urban development, thus virtually no traces remain to visit, and no real-estate demands of any kind can be made in the future, forming a sort of religious black hole.

The exile of Jews, French, Italian, Maltese and Libyans since 1966 made Tunisia a "homogenous" society, probably for the first time in its Muslim history and in its longer pre-Muslim past. Tunisian independence meant that Tunisia now belongs to Muslims and to Muslims only. The nationalism and socialism of post-colonial Tunisia was mixed with a complete process of ethnic cleansing disguised as anti-colonial sentiment, a strict black-and-white mentality and the narrative of Muslim oppression. However, the Islamic nationalist movement also meant the complete redistribution of captured and abandoned wealth left by everyone who ran away from the new, oppressive reality.

The fertility rate among Muslims continued to be high, and improving mortality rates led to a doubling of the population. At the beginning of the twentieth century, there were two main hospitals concentrated in Tunis, and by 1965, there were 16 hospitals, 33 beds per 10,000 people (ranked 73rd in the world), as well as 666 doctors, one doctor for 7,000 people, or 0.13 per 1,000. To put this in perspective, in Israel the numbers for the same period were 2.5 doctors per 1,000 people (ranked 1st in the world) and 9 hospital beds per 1,000 (ranked 5th). Fertility was uncontrolled, and was left to the religious and cultural beliefs of its people and its religious leaders. Like Jews, Muslims stressed the virtue of large families, and Tunisia was no different in this respect. If Jews had remained in Tunisia, they would make up 15-20 percent of the population, as the Palestinians do in Israel today.

These and other statistics on health and the economy paint alarming pictures of neglect and poverty raising the question: what on earth was the government doing after Independence? A country that had never gone to war and had a thriving economy until Independence had poor health and economic statistics. No underdevelopment theory can excuse the numbers, nor could any anti-colonial theory remedy it. The same goes for unemployment rates and other statistics. What the two countries did have in common was the number of smokers, although the reasons for the high numbers of smokers were different.

In 1956, immediately after independence, anticipating Sharia, Bourguiba abolished Koranic law in favor of Personal

Status Code in family planning, raising the marriage age for women to 17, prohibiting polygamy, modifying divorce codes, giving the right to vote to women, and condemning the veil as a "dust rug." Girl's attendance in primary school went up five-fold in just ten years. During the same period, women occupied one fifth of the non-agricultural workforce.

Louis Frank, a French traveler wrote a book in 1811 with some remarkable descriptions of North Africa and Tunisia. He writes: "Tunis entière pour l'Afrique ce que sont pour l'Europe les Bourse de Marseille, d'Amsterdam, de Londres et de Paris." This economic boom was a result of trans-Saharan trade, as well as trade with the whole of North Africa. By this time, the slave trade was a small fraction of all trade activities. Napoleon was also eyeing Tunisia, seeing the opportunities in occupying the country very early, but opted instead for an occupation of Egypt in 1798, and then Malta. It is important to remember that France viewed Tunisia as an important trading partner long before its colonial takeover, as it supplied vital food products, from wheat to olive oil. The need for food and raw materials was particularly important during the 1788 famine in France, and later equally important to feed Napoleon's growing army. At the end of the eighteenth century, pirate activities continued to flourish providing major sources of income for the Tunisian Beylical government. At the beginning of the nineteenth century, hundreds of Tunisian vessels were moored in Malta and Marseille. In Egypt, it was recorded that one third of all merchants were Tunisians. Tunisian trade in the Mediterranean was unhindered and permitted in part because of French and English fighting for control of Africa and the Mediterranean.

In April 1880, a land dispute took place (eventually leading to the French colonization of Tunisia), whereby General Kahyar

Edin tried to sell 250,000 acres of agricultural land in Sahel (between Tunis and Susse) to a Marseille company for two million francs. The Bey of Tunis objected, claiming that the land was property of the General for personal use and could not be transferred to foreigners. Also objecting was Youssef Levi, a naturalized English Jew who claimed he owned the land adjacent to the property, and that he wished to buy the land in dispute. The English, who up to now stayed out of the issue, had decided to send battleships to uphold Levy's rights. The French withdrew their support, not wanting to confront the English over this land deal. Levy remained in control of the disputed land until 1882, when it was purchased by the French soon after the Treaty of Bardo, by which Tunisia became a French protectorate.

Some argue that this real estate deal to a non-Muslim was what triggered the colonization of Tunisia. Land in Tunisia at that era was under Koranic law, and so it theoretically belonged no one. Only God owned the land and claims to private property could be done to individuals who proved their connections to the land and accordingly only to Muslims. The Koranic law and customs in Tunisia permitted the ownership of private property for those who could prove they worked the land and produced the "fruits of their labor." But in 1887 the laws were changed when the Bey was forced to accept, under pressure by the French and the English, the fundamental premise that land can be owned by anyone. The question of land has always been important in both the old and new worlds, and in Tunisia during the nineteenth century the question was highly complex, especially in the less-populated south of the country. People could claim their ownership by submitting proof to a committee who then registered the land in his name at the *conservation fonciére*. From 1885 to 1925, only 10 percent of all arable land in Tunisia was registered this way because one had to pay hefty sums for this registration. Many locals basically lived without ever registering their houses or agricultural plots. Until the French showed up, there were no official deeds, nor even any roads throughout most of the country. The Berbers liked this situation, as it made it hard for the Sultan's tax collectors to harass them; the less contact there was with the Sultan's administration, the better off their lives were. But gradually, the grand scale of ruthless exploitation by the Sultan led to a situation whereby poverty became an instrument of survival. This was an acceptable method, and a reality in every region of North Africa. It even helped the Jews survive the Nazis.

The Beys and their extended families at the time favored this arrangement and acquired large estates for themselves as part of their contract with French colonialists. By 1898, another Islamic land rule called *Habous* was abolished, freeing up to one third of Tunisian land to private or protectorate hands. *Habous* was a way to hold ownership of large plots of land through titles given to mosques, thus avoiding taxes as they were considered charities. This was also the way in which Muslim religious institutions became wealthy, similar to the method used by the Catholic Church in the Christian world.

The Berbers in the south were viewed by the French (and supported by the Bey) as nomads having no title to the land since they moved north and south depending on seasons and other factors. It was thus agreed that they should hold only grazing rights, and no actual titles to the vast desert territory. In 1901, these tribes were given certain rights of use, and only with government permissions. In this way, the Bey's regime exploited the native population without giving back anything in return in terms of development and services. The corrupt land and economic system was designed to guard the fortunes of the elites under the umbrella of Islam. Change occurred only when an uprising was about to take place. When the indigenous population could no longer tolerate the injustices or tax burdens, the Bey eased the hold to let off steam, gaining valuable time in the process and a temporarily mollified population. The French exploited Tunisia in a very different ways. They had built an extensive modern infrastructure for the exploitation of resources as well as an efficient system of transportation for the delivery of goods to the motherland. This meant modernizing the ports, building railroad tracks from the mines, as well as refineries, textile mills, government buildings, schools, hospitals and leisure facilities such as sports clubs. This was not part of a planned system of modernization, but rather a natural extension of France's own economic interests and technological development.

Social and economic inequalities widened during this time, affecting not just the elites but also the indigenous population who provided the cheap labor needed in construction, the textile and mining industries and agriculture. However, the mechanized and modern agricultural methods introduced by the French led to a different kind of economic crisis, primarily affecting those who lived on the margins of society. The Franco-Tunisian company, for example, employed some 100,000 Tunisians in the early twentieth century, with a few foreigners employed in management positions.[64] Apparently, too few Frenchmen chose Tunisia, in spite of the incentives given to anyone willing to come and participate in the process of colonization. By 1940, 50-60 cargo ships a month were arriving at the port of Marseille, mainly from North Africa, full of merchandise and food products.

Again, France was a favorable trading partner long before it became Tunisia's colonial master. One-hundred years before colonization, trade between Tunisia was expanding; in spite of economic depression in Europe, and custom taxes on French goods was 2 percent, compared to 10 percent for all other nations. The English and Dutch, as well as independent Tunisian Jewish merchants, and those trading with Italy, complained about this preferential arrangement, as they found it extremely difficult to compete.

Until WWII, Tunisians were under an extremely complex system of exploitation, between the French colonial power, the Islamist nationalists, and the Bey and his extended family and aristocracy. Jews, Muslims, Maltese, Libyans and Italians all operated within this complex social and economic system. The same system only intensified when the Nazis and Italian Fascists began participating in this mass exploitation. Indeed, these new exploiters were an unknown beast to Tunisians, in terms of their intensity, ruthlessness, resolve and objectives.

The end of the war witnessed the total destruction of the country's infra-structure built over a period of 60 to 70 years. The ports in Tunis and Bizerte were completely destroyed. The train tracks and electricity infrastructure were totally damaged. The whole of Tunisia was greatly affected by the six months of Nazis occupation. German military camps were scattered across the country, at over 40 locations in and around the cities, and all were destroyed by the Allied Forces. This massive destruction in material and infrastructures led Tunisia into a complete social and political turmoil.

Tunisian history provides us a window into the inherent nature of Islamic nationalism and to Islam's relations to other religions and other people. Tunisian Jewish history also shows us the colonial imperialistic nature of Islam over the centuries as Jews and also Christians were continuously told to convert.

The "five hundred years of relief given to the Jews were over," as Mohammed instructed that if after 500 years Jews were not completely converted to Islam, then they should be forced to do so, and we all can imagine what that meant. People of the book were protected for brief periods over the centuries, but the general trend was conversion or death and extreme poverty. Some of the Jews living in Tunisia had not forgotten the same process they endured in Spain. That was the history of Islamic nationalism in Tunisia, and that was the history of Islam in almost every country in Africa, from Eritrea to Nigeria. It was the history of Jews in every Islamic country in the Middle East as well. It was indeed no accident that Tunisian Jews chose to flee when given a chance; they knew what future awaited them. This story of exile and exodus was repeated with local variations in almost every Muslim country: Egypt, Iraq, Yemen, Iran, Morocco, Algeria, and Libya.

The history of Jews in LCA has been largely ignored by both the established Eastern European elites in Israel, as well as by the Islamists in and outside the Tunisian government. Neither group had an interest in reviewing or analyzing the history of these people, nor did they have the ability to recount this story of survival dating back thousands of years. Both had much to lose in doing so. The Islamists risked losing their complete hold over the history of their conquered lands, the riches of this land and the religion that holds it all together. The Zionist establishment risked losing its complete ideological and economic control of the holy land. Both the Islamists and the Zionists viewed the Jews of Arab lands as inferior people, to be used, ruled and converted (assimilated in the case of Israel) sooner or later.

In a way, North African Jews were not even refugees in terms of class, mentality or status. They do not exist in the history books and our schools mentions them only briefly to appease the ruling class's own conscience (in both Israel and Arab countries). This has much to do with the Palestinian cause. It seemed that the more motivated the Palestinians were, building their national identity and inventing their history along the way, the less the grievances of North African Jews were noticed or taken seriously. Jews of North Africa knew that they had no choice but to leave their ancient homeland. Every single individual we talked to knew that staying in Tunisia was risky and absolutely unbearable according to their belief system and cultural heritage, which was necessarily not just Jewish. Tunisia for them was lost and, with it thousands of years of history.

When Sheikh Abdul Aziz bin Abdullah, the Grand Mufti of Saudi Arabia said in 2012 (the year of the Tunisian Jasmine Revolution) that all churches must be destroyed because Muhammad said that there is no place for two religions, he meant it. The Grand Mufti takes this seriously, and he is not the only one who believes this. Almost every Islamist nationalist today agrees with him, they have to. It's part of the nationalistic religion and part of centuries of teaching. The Mufti's Fatwa was uttered not in ancient times but in the year 2012. The media in the West do not usually question any of this, nor do they report on the persecution of Christians in Egypt after the so-called "revolution." The Christians in many Muslim countries have been clamoring for support for a very long time, and their only available action was to resort to emigration and exile, the traditional activities of minorities in the so called Muslim countries.

In Saudi Arabia, there are a million and half Christians, mostly foreign workers, who are asking for some recognition of their human rights. State officials usually claim that it's too bad, since these foreigners knew the conditions before arriving. Elliot Abrams wrote in 2001 that this was exactly the same reaction given by religious officials: "Well, we noted there are churches in every other country on the Arabian Peninsula: Kuwait, Oman, Yemen, Bahrain, Qatar, and the UAE. You (Saudi Arabia) are the only exception. Are you suggesting that all those churches should be closed?" "Yes," he then replied. "Every one of them!" He also added that "The Grand Mufti's statement ought to be widely denounced around the world, and won't be—a scandal and a shame."[65] And in Tunisia the call for Sharia law by thousands of people, after the so-called Jasmine Revolution, is classified under the same umbrella of strict and extreme form of Islam. They too should take note of what the Grand Mufti says. Why shouldn't they if they want Sharia law? The demonstration which took place only days after the Mufti's Fatwa showed different kinds of banners, such as "No constitution without Sharia," and "The Koran is our Constitution." An engineer, who refused to give his name, added in one interview that, "a Muslim should live under the tenets of Islamic law. The secularists would have one believe that Islam chops off the hands of thieves, but one must study Islam. The West has failed."[66] He thinks he is a moderate, educated Muslim.

Tunisian Islamists want Sharia by convincing the population that this is the right way to go, the right thing to do. Everyone must want and love to have Sharia. There is no need for violence or force to make this happen. Large numbers of women took part in this demonstration, all covered according to Islamic dress codes, and some wearing the full Niqab. The ultra-conservative Salafists who sprung out of nowhere in 2012 demanded full-face veils for female university students, castigated a TV channel for allegedly blasphemous coverage, and beat up journalists at a protest.[67] Where on earth was the revolution?

Even international organizations have been infiltrated with unreasonable religious demands, disguised as Palestinian activism. For example, UNESCO's International Scientific Committee for the Drafting of a General History of Africa made a comparison between Israel and Cuba in the years before and after independence: "To summarize the comparison between Cuba and the Jewish state, while Israel had been a de facto ally of white supremacy, Castro's Cuba had been involved in black liberation."[68] This was presumably a very scientific statement written in 1993. Is there any wonder that funding was cut by US and Canada? In 2011, the US reduced its funding for the organization by 22 percent, and Canada decided not to increase its share totaling some $10 million a year. This was a result of UNESCO unilaterally granting full membership to the Palestinian Authority, where only states can be members, thus recognizing a de facto Palestinian State.

France was not the only link to Tunisia. Italy had a strong presence in Tunisia through Tunisian Jews of Sephardic-Portuguese origin who maintained close links with Italy, in terms of both trade and culture. Unlike the accepted view, this community was not a separated Jewish community from the indigenous Tounes, Jewish Tunisian Berbers. The complexities of dealing with the Bey and his Islamic base led to some interesting and intriguing strategies, all of which were aimed at keeping the community alive. The Jewish community had to complicate its presence, and in the process multiplying its power and influence. They had to be divided in order to survive as a Jewish community. The Livorno Jews living in Tunisia for hundreds of years maintained their social structure and controlled trade with

Italy and other European countries. The Bey viewed this part of the population differently, and encouraged their trade activities. It did not take them long to form their own Jewish council, synagogues and ritual centers. This was part of what Tunisia represented throughout the centuries—a multicultural entity.

Tunisian Kristallnacht

Long before the 1938 Kristallnacht in Germany, Tunisia had its own version of rampage and violence against the indigenous Jewish population by Muslim Arabs. The event was sparked by a soccer match. In 1917, the *Union Sportive Tunisienne* was created out of a desire to increase leisure activities. Four sports clubs were formed: The Pères Blancs (White Fathers), a Latin club made up of Christians and financed by the Tunisian Catholic Church; The Club Tunisois were mostly Jewish Tunisian athletes; The French Club; and the African Club, which was made up of Tunisian Arabs and Muslims. For centuries Tunisian Jews were called Touansa, the Tunisians, no one else was named as such. The association organized its national tournament which became a national battleground resulting in the creation of a "true" single Arab-Muslim sport association. The final match between the African club and the Tunisois (Jewish) club led to total chaos and violence by Arab spectators. The official Tunisian narrative was that the terrible atmosphere leading to violence was a result of Tunisian soldiers arriving after WWI upset that Tunisian Jews were exempt from participating. There was also the Balfour Declaration, which apparently affected the mood among Muslims. This obviously was not true, and was indeed nothing but an excuse for this early show of Muslim Arab nationalism. No one in the street, Jews and Muslims alike, knew about the Balfour Declaration in the same way that no one in the Arab world has seen the movie *Innocence of Muslims*, which presumably led to outrage in the Arab world, the death of the US Consul in Libya, and terrible violence leading to the burning of the American School in Tunis and looting of hundreds of school computers.[69] A teacher at the school for 20 years described the event: "It was completely inhumane," said Kouki, who could not comprehend that such an event, could happen to "a place of tolerance and open-mindedness."

Back to 1917, the final match was held at the Chedly Zouiten Stadium and the Jewish Club won 2–1, leading to an incredible show of violence everywhere in Tunisia. Hundreds of Jewish and Muslim spectators of the game were fighting each other as though in a mass boxing fight. Apparently, even Muslim and Jewish boxers, such as Tunisian heavyweight champion Hassen Karroche and Cohen Judas, were among the spectators fighting each other. The Jewish and the Muslim communities collided like never before. Tunisian Muslims rushed to the street and were joined by other Muslims, breaking windows of Jewish shops and looting everywhere in Tunis and other cities. The Islamists could not tolerate that people under submission would fight back. The cultural balance held for centuries was broken, and Tunisia was on the verge of a civil war. There are no statistics on injuries or deaths, but many ended in hospitals, some with life-threatening injuries. In a government inquiry, Judah Cohen, a Jewish boxer, was found responsible for inciting the violence and was sentenced by the Sultan. Cohen had no intention of taking punches without reprisal and landed a few too many individuals in a hospital. Julie Chaouia, a famous Jewish dancer intervened on Cohen's behalf and pleaded with the Sultan for his release. Her reputation and influence, as well as her romantic relationships with Ismail Bey (the Sultan), led to Cohen's acquittal.

But the release of Yehuda Cohen led to even more riots in the streets of Tunis against the Tunisian Jewish population. The Muslims were furious and Arab emotions were out of control. Tunisia was plunged again into total chaos. Tunisian Jews were not taking this violence as a one way fight like they used to and fought back, resulting in total chaos never seen before in Tunisia or elsewhere in the LCA. The French Minister of War, General Lignolet, decided to adopt extreme measures to calm the situation, banning all demonstrations and mass gatherings, and suspending all sporting activities for one year. These riots are not to be confused with crazy fans going wild in the streets of London, Berlin, or even the recent hooliganism in Jerusalem (Beitar). These riots had nothing to do with soccer and everything to do with Islamic nationalism in its early years. Annie Robbins, a human rights activist, wrote about the political aspects of a recent riot against Arabs in Jerusalem following a soccer match in 2012. She describes at length the Jewish fans chanting anti-Arab slogans in the street of Jerusalem, concluding that hate of Arabs, apartheid and right-wing politics led to this shameful demonstration, forgetting to mention that this event was quickly confronted by Israeli police.[70] Hooligans exist in every country, and they are dealt with by sports federations, national sport policies and state security. In recent soccer riots in Egypt, hundreds of people were killed and many more injured as pro-Mubarak supporters clashed with Islamists. This event and the Tunisian soccer game, which almost led to a civil war, are completely different from what happened in Jerusalem in March 2012. Confusing hooliganism, which can easily be dealt with, and political radical agendas in the Islamic world, does not help our understanding of either the Israel-Palestinian conflict or the historical situation of Jews in Tunisia.

Tunisians, as a result of these rampages, were forbidden by the French General to play soccer in tournaments. After many discussions between Tunisian Muslims and Jews it was decided that a new association would be formed, called the *Union de State Tunisien* (UST). The only problem with that was that the UST was a name associated with Jewish Tunisian athletes, but everyone agreed for the love of the sport that UST would be the new name. At the last minute, a young Muslim named Mohamed Zouaoui objected and opted for the creation of a purely Arab-Muslim Sports Association. In line with the Islamic nationalist movement, a new organization was set up and was called *Espérance Sportive* (Sports of Hope), "hoping for the end of tyranny, hate and exploitation by the French Colonialists," and furthering the injection of politics and religion into all layers of society. Football was central to life in Tunisia during the 1920s. All cafes in the center of Tunis were meeting places for organizers and fans; all conversations ended up talking about sports and soccer matches, and politics and football became one. *Espérance Sportive* was also formed in this spirit, only without Jews or Christians. A young Habib Bourguiba, who later became President-for-life, was heavily involved in the decision-making process of this organization. It was given a green light a year after their initial request, and it is still the major sporting organization in the country today.

Jewish sport clubs sprouted like mushrooms soon after the French Protectorate came into effect in 1881. Jews could not take Muslims to court, and often had to suffer in silence when confronted by Muslim violence. Under the French Protectorate, Jews looked at sports as a way to defend themselves, and as a way to express their excitement at their newly found leisure time and relative freedom. With the formation of sport clubs, Jews were no longer easy targets but instead became the envy of nationalists and Muslim activists. In many ways, anti-colonialism was a cover for taking Tunisia from Jewish control and sporting incidents was a way to do this. It is interesting to note that Noah, the US consul, estimated in 1815 that there were some 700,000 Jews in North Africa, of which 100,000 were able to hold and use arms. He did not elaborate on this statement, but I guess he could not help but think about the various possible ways of getting rid of the Bey administration and its piracy practices—without resorting to all-out war between Tunisia and the US. The 100,000 individuals able to hold arms were enough to overthrow the Bey's corrupt rule in the whole of North Africa, similar to the consular activities by Stevens in recent events in Libya. By 1920, Tunisian Muslims felt threatened indeed by the Jewish population and its hold on life and culture in the country.

During the same period other sports clubs were formed in boxing, horseback riding, horse racing, swimming, volleyball, fencing and even flying. In all of these sports Jews and Berber, Maltese, Italians, French and Arabs participated with equal enthusiasm. In boxing, enthusiasm was translated into real achievements, with Jewish Tunisian boxer Victor Perez becoming a world Champion in 1931. He captured Europe and America by storm, winning rounds everywhere he went. His last official boxing match was in 1938 in Berlin, where he wore his famous

Star of David trunks and was booed by German spectators throughout the fight. In 1943, he was captured by the Nazis in France and sent to Auschwitz, never to return. He died on January 22, 1945 on the "death march" from Monowitz to Gleiwitz.[71] According to archival accounts, Perez lived through Auschwitz by being forced to entertain the Germans in boxing matches. Two other Jewish boxers were with him in the camp, the Greek Champion Salamo Arouch and Jacko Razon. Perez started boxing at an early age and the club where he trained already existed in 1920. I know this from bits and pieces I gathered from my own father, who was heavily involved in Tunis in both boxing and soccer during the same period. We still have pictures passed on from this era, taken in 1925 showing the athletes in full uniform, very organized and very determined. The great Jewish Tunisian boxer Chiche said in the 1950s, "To have a great boxing reunion, you need a Muslim, a Christian and a Jew." Now, Tunisians can only have reunions among themselves, behind closed doors, with a sign at the entrance that reads "for Muslims only" or "Touansa (Tunisians) not allowed."

On Albert Memmi

In a recent interview, Albert Memmi claimed: "Look at the relationship between the Jewish and Muslim communities in France today. It's ironic: there are six million Muslims [10 million now]. I say to Jews, you wanted to escape the Arab influence, but now there are more Arabs in Paris than there were in Tunisia, in Tunisia there were 3 million Arabs."[72] Jewish

North African neighborhoods in Paris are now almost empty of Jewish businesses. One merchant interviewed said that "the neighborhood is changing. Up until the early 1990s there were more than 200 Jewish-owned businesses, most of them by Tunisians. Today there are only about 15." These businesses were mostly owned by Jews of Algerian and Tunisian decent. Memmi's statement is problematic because Jews did not want to escape Arab influence. They were pushed out of Tunisia in the same sense as most Palestinians were pushed out of Israel. Furthermore, and equally important, Tunisians are not Arabs. They are of Berber, Jewish Sephardic, Italian and Maltese origin. Tunisians (including Muslims) rarely admit to being Arab anywhere in the world. They usually say they are Tunisians first, and when not among Arabs, they will say Berber, not to be confused with Arabs, as many Algerians do. By the beginning of WWII there were two million Tunisians, living mostly in rural areas as nomads and farmers. Only 7 percent lived in urban areas. The Jews were a central minority of this urban population. The other problematic point in his statement is that he takes for granted that this is the way history had developed and that it has taken its normal course. He sees no problem with the development of a homogenous Tunisian population of just Muslims, something that did not exist during the 3,000 years of Tunisian history. There is also a total omission of the role and an objective of Islam within the State.

This misunderstanding of history is common in all anti-colonial and post-colonial theories that started and ended their paradigm by examining the relationship between the colonizer and the colonized; black and white, oppressed and oppressor. There was no room for other types of political and historic considerations to be taken into account, especially those that stem from Jewish participation. Memmi is equally confusing when he states: "We would have liked to be Arab Jews. If we abandoned the idea, it is because over the centuries the Moslem Arabs systematically prevented its realization by their contempt and cruelty. It is now too late for us to become Arab Jews. Not only were the homes of Jews in Germany and Poland torn down, scattered to the four winds, demolished, but our homes as well. Objectively speaking, there are no longer any Jewish communities in any Arab country, and you will not find a single Arab Jew who will agree to return to his native land." Memmi is obviously not completely naïve. But it is curious that he does not point to the simple historical fact that Tunisians are not Arabs. They were never Arabs, and they also never wanted to become Arabs—all historical evidence points to this. The current history of Tunisia, and throughout the Maghreb, is a continuous struggle of many who do not want to be defined as Arabs, not on personal, historical or cultural levels. The Jews in this history had no choice but convert or be heavily oppressed. Tunisian Islamic nationalism determined their faith long before Independence. They either chose to become Arab Jews or leave Tunisia altogether. That was the only choice given to them during the anti-colonialist Islamic nationalistic period.

The silence of this story has not been broken yet by political theorists or by the general media. For example, a recent article in the *New York Times*[73] discussing the 1948 Palestinian Naqba forgets to take note, as Leo Rennert states, that "there were two 'naqbas' in 1948, not just a Palestinian one. Starting with the 1947 UN partition plan and then Israel's birth in May 1948, about 850,000 Jews who had roots in Arab lands dating back a couple of thousand years were summarily persecuted, deprived of all legal rights, stripped of their property and forced to flee from Iraq, Syria, Egypt, Algeria, Tunisia, Morocco and other parts of the Arab world. Their synagogues were torched and many were lynched by their Arab neighbors. The number of Jewish refugees from Arab lands was greater than the number of Palestinian refugees."[74] Rennert recognizes that any discussion of peace talks with the Palestinians must take into account the history of Jews of LCA for the sake of resolving the conflict. Jews of LCA are demanding the opening of the history books and to be counted in all future negotiations. It would indeed be interesting to see whether Memmi changed his political opinions in light of the Islamic takeover of Tunisia and the rest of LCA.

Ethnic Cleansing

Bourguiba's legacy in Tunisian history is unquestionably extensive and complex. After all, he singlehandedly expelled the Jews from Tunisia, jailed as many Islamists as he could, and brought Palestinian politics to Tunisian dining room table discussions. At the same time, in his early years, as leader of the New Destour party, he introduced social policies unheard of in a Muslim country, even by today's moral and political standards. He was ahead of his time in trying to make Tunisia a moderate and progressive society, which is consistent with the country's own cultural identity and history—only without the Jews and the Berbers. Did he really try to separate Islam from State business? Tunisian Jews really believed that he was their guardian angel. No other Muslim country took this "liberal" direction, and this made Tunisia unique in this respect. More than a year after the famous failed revolution in January 2011 many still argue for and against the reforms taken by Bourguiba. Some even blame him for the crisis situation Tunisia was in. The controversy is not going away. Islamists of all walks of life can still remember how their freedom was ruthlessly curtailed during the 30 years when the country was ruled by Bourguiba and later by Ben Ali. Some were imprisoned for their Islamic or Jewish faith, and others, like communists, for their political views. Bourguiba did not have to worry about Jewish discontent because by the time Tunisia achieved independence, one-third of the Jewish population was already gone. The rest waited for Bourguiba to save them from radical Islamists or modern Islam. To this day, many cannot believe that he subscribed to the Islamic narrative of wanting Tunisia only for Muslims. Tunisian Islamist extremists who control the State basically wanted a return to a never-existing strict Islamic rule, rejecting any and all progress made by Bourguiba. They particularly wish to strip women of their gradually acquired rights.

The reforms Bourguiba instituted were natural considering the fabric of Tunisian society. Before independence, close to 140,000 Jews were living in the country and many were educated in in French, Italian, Hebrew and Arabic (Judeo Arabic). Bourguiba had a Jewish candidate who was elected to his National Legislative Assembly, Alber Bessi, who was a loyal member of the Neo-Destour party headed by the President. But these kinds of associations and alliances were short-lived and limited in scope. My basic argument is that the liberal tradition of Tunisia has its roots in Jewish Tunisia, from ideas of open economy and competition with colonial powers to the moral fabric of Tunisia, its culture and traditional music and even its culinary habits. This is the legacy left by Tunisian Jews who are now gone forever.

Like all other post-colonial dictators of the Arab world, Bourguiba's policies centered on short-term economic and political objectives and long-term policies guaranteeing his continuous hold to power. In retrospect the outcome of his policies on minority rights and religious and economic freedom were not much different from his colleagues in other countries in North Africa. Anti-colonial struggles made him forget that he was not the Bey of Tunisia. He had adopted the Bey's absolute rule and mixed it with Arab and Islamic nationalism and anti-colonialism, which eventually led him to the total ethnic cleansing of Tunisia, or "ethnic cleansing Bourguiba-style." It was politically initiated by the Bourguiba regime with the welcoming support of the Jewish Agency and other Aliyah organizations who apparently thought they were helping emancipate Tunisian Jews. Bourguiba believed in a non-alignment, third-world ideology leaning towards the West, especially France and the US for economic support. Thus, his policies towards the Jews were carefully considered in order not to upset the balance of power inside the country, while at the same time appeasing donor countries and his own Islamic interests. This explains in part why Jews moved out in waves every five to ten years, as he did not want them all to leave at the same time. Essential jobs held by Tunisian Jews were filled by Muslim Tunisians. But it was all a gradual and controlled process, and those holding essential positions were not permitted to leave, creating an atmosphere of fear and panic. Wealth was also being gradually transferred (the proper word is looting) to the Muslim population. His policies were intended to prevent all Jews from leaving together, as was the case in Yemen in 1951.

Andre Nahum sums up this policy well: "The powers-that-be artfully got rid of their Jews while trying to make people believe that they were doing everything possible to keep them. Officially, they said they wanted to keep us while they ushered us towards the exit. In fact everything conspired to make us leave."[75] He summarizes the politics of the Tunisian government, but obviously does not tell the whole story. Journalist Jean-Pierre Allali believed that "Bourguiba pursued a strategy of deception, stringing the Jews along as long as Tunisia needed their skills, yet all the while intending to get rid of them."[76] This theory fits well, but Bourguiba's understanding, at least in the beginning of his administration, was no different in fundamental ways from what the Israeli government through the Labor party believed. Third-world socialists in the post-colonial era often took control of governments and resources, reorganizing the distribution of wealth according to their views, aspiring to build "classless societies." In Tunisia, as in Israel, the looting of property and redistribution of wealth to party affiliates were the acceptable norms. North African Jews in Israel thought it was part of the Zionist ideology, but the idea of modernization and the building of a monocultural society were central to their rule. Almost all political writers and thinkers in the post-colonial era were guilty of the same misrepresentation of what was really occurring in these newly formed countries.

This total disregard for the needs of the indigenous populations was still the prominent ideology at universities even during the 1970s. In order to understand the politics of Bourguiba's deception it is important to understand the acceptable political theories of the time, and more specifically, how Islamic nationalists saw the world and understood history. Bourguiba, like Nasser of Egypt, held national socialist ideology of nation-building and reconstruction, mixed with their Islamic views. North African Jews were an obstacle in this grand objective. Socialist and nationalist ideologies mixed with Islam naturally led them to target the Jews. (The same was done to every minority in the country.) The nation-building under Islamist socialism did not go well with the rich Jewish history of Tunisia. After independence, Tunisians had a hard time accepting that Jews were not simply an ethnic group, but a large part of the indigenous population in all of its plurality and cultural richness. To ease their guilt today, the handful of Tunisia Jews remaining are viewed as a small comforting ethnic group, a tourist attraction and part of a guided tours to the Synagogues and Jewish cemeteries. Ethnicity in this sense is nothing but an illusion fit for the Western tourist industry and anthropologists.

What Bourguiba and his ministers were afraid of was the creation of a state within state if Jewish Tunisians were left to grow and prosper as they had done over the centuries. Tunisian Jews were basically a threat to the nationalist Islamist movement. The massive Jewish (and European) presence, along with the hundreds of foreign organizations operating in the country, had Islamist nationalists feeling very insecure. The result was that all non-Muslims paid the price for Tunisian independence. Prior to that, colonialists also felt insecure with the presence of Jewish merchants and traders who could easily compete with them. Jews historically spearheaded the Tunisian economy, confronting the colonial power almost as equals, a result of centuries of trade in and around the Mediterranean. Their trade links with France, Italy and other countries were solid until WWII. The French had no problem with the ethnic cleansing policy in Tunisia because it was good for French business and aided colonial control. Thus, Jews of Tunisia were confronting three powerful forces determined to see them gone: Islamist nationalists, the French (and the Italians) with their colonial interests, and the Zionists. None of these powerful interests wanted a strong Jewish community, and each contributed to ethnic cleansing. In this axis Tunisian Jews did not stand a chance.

The French integrated part of this population into its own country, benefitting from their contributions in all areas of society. Indeed, no one doubts the positive contribution of Tunisian Jews to French society. In fact, it was part of their calculation as a long-term colonial investment. They targeted the communities that linked North Africa to the rest of Europe, thus opening the door wide open to a total and complete exploitation of an impoverished local population who later screamed of oppression and demanded independence. Colonialism had nothing to do with ideas of modernization as a guiding force. Even the Beys during the long Ottoman rule knew its value. But the Jewish presence limited the free and unchecked exploitation of Tunisia by colonial powers. This role continued even after WWII when Tunisian Jews successfully competed with French colonialists, to the point of blurring the lines between colonialism and a protectorate. In short, the Jews of Tunisia were not afraid of dealing with France and Italy on equal footing and had no psychological barriers of a colonized people. There was no inferiority complex dealing with traders in other European countries, who in many instances were also Jewish.

It was Islamism that built barriers by linking national aspirations to radical Islam, leading indigenous communities to hopelessness and despair. In this sense, Bourguiba never understood the intricacies and complexities of Tunisia, its culture and its trade links, its history and Berber heritage. In a way, he tried to rebuild Tunisia by destroying it first, an old, uninspired tactic. It is difficult to understand why and how Tunisian Jews relied on him for safety and support. They were hoping for a Tunisian leadership that never came, and as a result their situation deteriorated daily while their options for survival in place narrowed. There was no Jewish problem in North Africa

SILENCING THE PAST:

in general, and in Tunisia in particular. There was an Islamic nationalist problem, a colonial problem and a Zionist problem. Short of taking up arms there was nothing the Jews Tunisia could have done.

As mentioned above, third-world socialist dictators in almost every North Africa country and Middle East followed the same ideological and religious route, resulting in the cleansing of its Jewish and Christian populations. The table below will give us a sense of this. Today there are only a handful of Jews in every country listed:

	1948	**1976**
Morocco	265,000	17,000
Algeria	140,000	500
Tunisia	140,000	1,700
Libya	38,000	20
Egypt	100,000	200
Iraq	135,000	400
Syria	30,000	4,350
Lebanon	5,000	150
Yemen	55,000	1,000
Aden	8,000	0
Total[77]	916,000	25,620

More than 600,000 of these exiled people arrived in Israel, and 300,000 left for France, England, America and Australia. This population of LCA now comprises just over half of Israel's Jewish population. Over a million people have been displaced from their homes in Arab Muslim countries.[78] This process of total ethnic cleansing in Tunisia was completed by 1967.

It is not generally known that the number of Palestinians who fled the newly formed State of Israel was surpassed by the numbers of Jews who were forced out from LCA. During the 1947 United Nations debates over the establishment of the State of Israel, the head of the Egyptian delegation warned that "the lives of a million Jews in Moslem countries will be jeopardized by the establishment of the Jewish State." Haj Amin el-Husseini, chairman of the Palestine Arab Higher Executive, told that UN body, "If a Jewish State were established in Palestine, the position of the Jews in the Arab countries would become very precarious." "Governments," he added ominously, "have always been unable to prevent mob excitement and violence."[79] Unfortunately, this is also true in 2012, a year after the Jasmine Revolution, when thugs and mobs demonstrated against a handful of Jews (and imaginary Jews). Freedom of expression for such thugs is now permitted and encouraged under the law of Tunisian land. The Palestinian cause became an excuse for rampant anti-Jewish sentiment and savage indoctrination. When the State of Israel was established, the Jews in Arab countries became hated outcasts in their own lands, terrorized, imprisoned and often banished. This led to the mass exodus of Jews who sadly realized there was no future for them in the lands of their ancestors. These Jews were not just robbed of their property and their houses; they were robbed of their own countries, as most of them were descendants of indigenous people living there for thousands of years.

In 1992, during a debate in the UN Security Council on the situation in the former Yugoslavia, Tunisia stated that it was essential to "put an end to the reprehensible practice of 'ethnic cleansing'." It was not Israel's creation which resulted in a Jewish exodus—it was the Arab response to Israel's creation, scapegoating their innocent Jewish citizens. It was not Tunisian independence, per se; it was the deliberate policy of Arabization and marginalization of the Jews. In almost all Arab and Muslim countries from the late 1940s Jews had to have Muslim business partners, by law. Presumably the Jewish partner in the Kosher butcher's business departed Tunisia leaving his Muslim partner in charge.[80] As Shabi writes: "According to Islamic law, all non-Muslims in Islamic Lands should be subdued and be treated as dhimmis (second class citizens)."[81] They are often forced to convert to Islam, through humiliating taxes imposed on them. This has been happening in the Islamic World for 1,300 years. Muslims have demanded concessions in non-Muslim countries, but non-Muslims have been systematically persecuted, terrorized and ethnically cleansed in Islamic lands.

With the recent rise of the Muslim population in the traditionally Christian/Secular West came the noticeable rise of Islamic violence and terrorist activities aimed towards non-Muslims. However, Tunisia was probably the only Islamic conquered country where Jews could actually survive and withstand the upheavals of hate in the Muslim world. The Jews in other countries had tougher experiences of persecution, such as in Egypt, Iraq, Syria, Libya, Algeria and others. Tunisia's mild nationalism under Bourguiba rule gave some assurance to Jews that the situation in Tunisia was different, more enlightened, at least in the beginning of his rule. By 1967, there were no Jews left to find out how tolerant and peaceful Tunisia was. Everyone had had enough of living under submission to Islamic laws, perpetual oppression, underdevelopment and poverty.

Grand Exile of Tunisian Jews

Every Muslim will tell you that Jews were not really persecuted in LCA (Lands Conquered by Arabs), at least not in the European sense of the word. Tunisia was no different. According to this narrative, Muslim and Jews got along just fine throughout the history of the Maghreb. The submission system worked fine, and Jews were content living with them. Jews left their native homelands because they wanted to do so. Muslims did not force them, they say. One million Jews decided all at the same time that they must exile themselves from their countries of origins where they lived for centuries. Unfortunately, this is also part of a great historical deception.

Jews of the Arab world were pragmatic in their views as to the future of their families, culture and wellbeing. This pragmatism led to their total disappearance. Today's events everywhere in the Arab world prove that they did not have any other choice but leave. The Jewish population knew that they could not defeat Islamic nationalism, nor could they successfully fight for their own religious, political and cultural freedom. They were not prepared to fight as the Palestinians do. They knew better than anybody that Islam as it emerged after the war would not tolerate another religion regardless of how "peaceful" Islam can be. The tolerance and pluralism Islam had in various periods in history was gone. Imams and anti-colonialists had joined forces, fighting for independence alongside the politics of ethnic and religious purity. Islamists were disguised as socialists and progressives committed to economic equality for everyone. And, this worked very well with the masses of Arabs and Berbers living in poverty.

The Jasmine Revolution exposed this backward ideology, which displaced millions and forced endless wars and many conversions. Israel and the Jewish people are no longer the focal point in this debate, at least not directly. Sure, Islamists try to insert the Palestinian question everywhere they can in order to stir or subdue the ignorant masses. They tried this recently in Egypt, Iran, Lebanon and Tunisia but it does not work anymore. Amidst the current Syrian massacre of its own people, Islamist students in the West disguised as progressives are trying to bring to the front the Palestinian question again. But the universities, especially in the US and Canada, are already tired of this type of aggressive Islam and their quest for Sharia heavens. These Islamist elements in the West can no longer agitate and spread their message of Islamist expansionism disguised as Palestinian struggle. The Palestinians will do just fine without their help. To prove this we need only to turn to the fact that there are no Islamists in the West demonstrating against the massacres in Syria, where over 140,000 people have been killed. According to them, this is an internal Islamic war and has to be handled by Islamic forces or countries in the region. Syria tried to get Israel somehow involved in the conflict. Bashar al-Assad is still trying to figure out a way to unify Syria again under the umbrella of hatred towards Israel. But, for the first time since the creation of Israel this is not working. Israelis were very careful not to be dragged into the Syrian conflict, and the opposition forces could not figure out how, theoretically or ideologically, they can insert the Israel-Palestinian conflict in order to avert attention from the real crisis around them.

The recent demonstrations against Jews in Tunisia where only one thousand Jews are now living were a pathetic demonstration of hate, which can only be understood on a social- psychoanalysis level. Thousands of Tunisians shouting "death to the Jews" was not a pretty sight even for the enlightened radical Islamists; it was shameful, and Islamists will have to figure out fast a different agenda to stir the masses. One can measure the level of oppression just by looking at the pro-Palestinian rhetoric. The more they speak against Israel and the Jews the more ruthless the regime will be towards its own population. The question remains: can they succeed in getting Israel to play its traditional role again?

Tunisian Jews' only alternative was to pack up their meager allowed belongings and leave. Some were begging in French ports for money for bus or train fares to reach the centers where their families and friends ended up. This small community knew their limitations and they could not be expected to stand up to Islamism when the West, as it is evident today, is also unable to do so. They lasted as a community for 3,000 years in Tunisia because Mohammed's words and teachings were never taken literally by anybody. After all, Mohammed was a prophet, not God. Both Jews and Muslims regarded the prophets, all of them, as regular men with vices and imperfections like the rest of us. Also, Muslims needed the Jews to be able to relate to Mohammed's words and to relate to their own ancient history. They needed the Jews to relate to the religious world around them. The Jews were the living proof of Mohammed's teachings and to the Koran itself, like Christianity is. In a way his teachings are meaningless without Judaism. Mohammed also understood that Jews would help the Arabs amass wealth and power. Now, the question is: how long it will take Tunisians to understand that radical Islam has nothing to offer to any of them? How long will it take Tunisians to understand that they too are guilty of ethnic cleansing?

Ha'artez reported early in 2011, at the beginning of the Jasmine Revolution, that 10 Tunisian Jews landed in Ben Gurion airport requesting Israeli citizenship. They were brought by the

Jewish Agency, which is a quasi-government office responsible for bringing Jews to Israel. The Tunisians were afraid for their lives and could not see any stability coming any time soon, so they left. The interesting part, as usual, was the comments people made on this bizarre story. Tunisia, once the light of sanity in the world of Islamic radicalism everywhere had just made a great leap into darkness.

Let me simplify the argument by comparing ethnic cleansing by Israel to that of Tunisia and all of the Muslim states combined. Israel is often accused of ethnically cleansing its Palestinian residents, yet today close to 20% of its population is Palestinian, and millions more live in the West Bank and Gaza. In contrast, very few Jews are left in Muslim countries. It is a simple yet a powerful argument. But no one is demonstrating in the streets of New York and Paris to contest these historical injustices. Muslim countries have instituted a total population cleansing policy for decades without opposition from anybody, and with the blessing of all international bodies and governments.

In fact, it is impossible to compare what Israelis have done to the Palestinian population and what was done to Jews of LCA. Israel never had a policy of ethnic cleansing, and if they had one it did not work, and there is a proof attesting to that effect. But it worked very efficiently in Muslim countries. Whole indigenous populations were forced out forever. Thousands of years of existence, of civilizations were extinguished in 65 years. The story becomes even more complex as history teaches us that these communities were not ethnic groups but indigenous population existing, as in the case of Tunisia, long before Islam became a religion, a thousand years before Mohammed.

Jews of LCA became ethnic groups in Israel and remained as such for decades, holding little political input even though they were the natural historical justification for the existence of Israel in the Middle East. Very soon they will disappear completely, and with them the stories and parts of the essential puzzle of the history of Jews in the Islamic and Arab world. But uncovering this history will necessarily lead to uncovering the Palestinian history and that group's quest for justice.

Landau, a professor of political science at the Hebrew University sums up an acceptable perception of how Jews of LCA viewed their situation in published works, claiming, in an article entitled "Bittersweet Nostalgia- Memoires of Jews from Arab Countries": "They vary in their usefulness as well as in their literary quality. In most, nostalgia reigns supreme."[82] Jews were nostalgic because their social and political situations were not favorable. They were nostalgic because apart from memories they had nothing. This book, however, has nothing to do with nostalgia. This book deals with the politics behind the ethnic cleansing in LCA, recognizing the precarious situation of these communities. Personal stories from Tunisian friends and families were transformed into political expressions, which are reflected throughout the book. Those who are feeling too nostalgic may be allowed to tour Tunisia. The Tourism Minister, Elyes Fakhfakh, of the newly elected Islamist party in Tunisia, made a statement to a Middle Eastern tourism conference in 2011 that the pilgrimage to the Island of Djerba should be commended: "Celebrated for hundreds of years, this religious rite is an achievement that should not change because it illustrates the openness of Tunisia to the world. [...] It is an achievement of the revolution, which established freedom of worship."[83] But the same Jewish ritual was cancelled a year before because of post-revolution unrest. Mr. Fakhfakh is nostalgic for a non-existent period in Tunisian history.

Many of the Jews lived in specially constructed Ghetto called El Hara. This area was destroyed in 1956 to make room for urban development. The living conditions in this Ghetto were horrific, in keeping with tradition of making life hard for the Jews. Only the rich Jews could afford to live outside of the Ghetto. Italian Jews were also permitted to reside elsewhere. As Fakhfakh writes: "No sanitary public services were offered, water comes once in a while from a public fountain and the sewer runs in the open in the middle of the street, source of epidemics and multiple hygiene problems." The Jewish community in this Islamic country was reaching its rock bottom and was in total decay entering the twentieth century. In El Hara Jews were basically in captivity, not just by the Islamists but also by backward Jewish religious interests. When the first Alliance Française Universelle School opened in Tunis, the various rabbis were reluctant, to say the least, to let this happen. They would not let the community slip through their fingers to colonialism and modernity. I guess this is what Rabbis and Imams have in common. The Tunisian community was religious in so far as it helped them survive. But, the majority was far from fanatical in the practice of their religion. Religion was the foundation, but tradition and customs were what kept them alive. Religion was culturally based, and not the other way around. Colonialism for Tunisian Jews meant modernization, freedom of association and again regaining a certain dignity absent for centuries under the Sultan's Islamic form of colonialism.

Some Jews integrated quite well into the French colonial situation economically and culturally. Many adopted the language and the French culture at the beginning of the twentieth century. French Colonialism worked its charms and succeeded beyond expectations, —until WWII. With the Nazi invasion and the French Vichy government the Jewish community simply disintegrated morally and culturally. The war period unmasked the real interests of French colonial power, as well as the Islamic quest for independence and its own ethnic purity policies. Evidently, one cannot blame the Jews for adapting to French Protectorate life, as years later Muslims by the millions also chose France as their homeland.

In 1962, The *Canadian Jewish Chronicle* published an article by Edwin Eytan, interviewing a few Tunisian Jewish families as they were embarking from ships in Marseille. Thousands were arriving, most with 4 dinars (2 dollars) in their pockets, a few pieces of silver jewelry and some winter clothing. Most were professionals, shop keepers, workers in French Corporations and government workers. They looked well fed and even well dressed, not your typical refugees, more like orphans. The poor and the well-to-do were still in Tunisia figuring how to get out. One of them was an economist who for years worked as the head of the Tunisian Government Investment Authority. He was asked a direct question by Eytan: "Why did you leave Tunisia?" He answers "For long we relied on Bourguiba, but with the start of the Bizerte crisis we felt that he was losing his grip. The Destour Young Turks are taking over. We believe them to be xenophobic and anti-Jewish." Another woman added, "Bourguiba is mortal like all of us. And after him there is nothing left for us." Similar answers were given by other Jews who were determined to continue on to Israel and France via ships moored not far from the French-Tunisian shipping lines.

Jews were escaping Tunisia in a hurry believing that if they wait it might be too late. Rumors were circulating that Tunisia was planning to close its doors. The economic situation deteriorated as the job market shifted with Bourguiba's socialist measures and the rise of cooperatives, most of which destroyed their livelihoods. Jews were lining up to get Visas at the French embassy in Tunis, where it took 2-3 weeks to get the necessary documents. People, whose professions were deemed indispensable, such as teachers and some government workers, were not allowed to leave. Everyone had to pay exit taxes and get special permission to take more than basic personal belongings. The economic shift against the self-employed, the nationalization of industries, increasing Arab control of schools and other anti-Jewish incidents all led to an overwhelming sense of insecurity and a sense that this was really the end of the road for Tunisian Jews.

But personal stories tell us only a small part of what happened in 1956. Jews were now preparing the third wave of exile. By 1967, the Jewish people of Tunisia had nearly disappeared completely, as the community witnessed a greatly reduction in size and the breakup of families and friends. In 1956 the Information Secretary, Bechir Ben Yemmed stated that "we the government are interested in our Jews remaining in Tunisia, but it is clear that all citizens are free to leave the country." He added the next day that the Government is worried that "their bodies are here but their hearts are elsewhere (Israel)." These and other statements made by state Islamic nationalist officials immediately after Independence made Jewish Tunisians extremely suspicious. The problem with these kinds of statements was that Jews felt they were an indigenous population, more so than the nationalists calling for homogenous society. Tunisian Jews were an integral part of Tunisia, and anyone speaking this brand of nationalism was promoting the politics of ethnic cleansing. Under the Tunisian brand of Islamic nationalism, Jews were asked again for full submission. They were equal before the law in this new Islamic state, so long as their hearts and minds were only in Tunisia. They had to adapt to nationalism within Islam, or else leave—without packing their belongings and without taking the keys to their houses, as the Palestinians did and as Spanish Jews did centuries ago, many of whom ended up in Tunisia. Thus began one of the periods of looting the property of close to 140,000 people who generally were better off than the rest of the Tunisian population.

The Jews of Tunisia were not a minority; they were Tunisia. On the eve of the WWII there were a few towns which were 100 percent Jewish Berber and non-religious. The historical narrative accepted by both the Islamic and the Jewish establishments gave an erroneous perspective on history. Tom Bowden,[84] like many others, called the Muslim population the native population of North Africa and the Jews there as (temporary) residents, for 3,000 years mind you. The young Turks, third-world socialists, pseudo-communists, and Islamists of all kinds in and out of Tunisia had no business setting the conditions as to how the Jews should behave, organize and worship. None had the historical or religious right to demand that Jews should conform or leave. Let us remind our leaders that even today only 5 percent of Tunisians identify themselves as Arabs.

Tunisian Islamic nationalism combined with a third-world anti-colonialist ideology were set to create a homogenous society where everyone had to be Muslim, spoke Arabic, worshipped Muhammad and submit to Islamic law. This has formed the basis of the Tunisian state, post-Independence all the way to the current Jasmine Revolution.

Demographic calculations were very much on the mind of the Islamic nationalist politicians. The Tunisian Jewish birth rate was not different than the birth rate of everyone else in the country, and were they allowed to stay they would have comprised between 15-20 percent of the Tunisian population today, mostly in urban centers, which would have made them even stronger politically and economically. The nationalists were torn between the economic benefits of having the Jews stay and the ramifications for the Tunisian Islamic state if they stayed. (Similar calculations were done by state officials in France and other countries with relation to the massive Islamic influx of immigrants.) The short-term benefits of ousting the Jews won the upper hand in this struggle. Next in line in the creation of a homogenous society were all the other Tunisians: the Italians, the French the Maltese and the Berbers. The first two groups left for mostly the same reasons Jews were exiled. The Berbers, on the other hand, were completely integrated, converted and assimilated into the ideals of nation building, Islam and Tunisian unity.

In August 1956, a government decree was implemented, designed to eliminate religious courts including rabbinical and Sharia courts. The nationalists instituted a civil court to curtail radicalism of all religions in order to bring the country forward and modernize the state of Tunisia. For most Jews of Tunisia this was painful on more than just a symbolic level. The decree did not really affect the everyday life of Tunisian Jews, as most of them were not even religious and seldom needed these rabbinic courts. But the existence of these courts for Jews played a major role in assuring their existence even if most were alien to them; it was an old tradition related to the very survival of Jews in Tunisia. The rabbinical role was to be cherished, left alone, even if it was not needed or taken seriously most of the time by the general Jewish community; a similar situation exists in New York and Tel Aviv and other major cities. The government was afraid of radical Islam and of Sharia law, so in order to sound moderate (to themselves and to the rest of the world) they had sacrificed this Jewish institution which presumably, according to them, was equal to Sharia. They obviously knew that both were not equal. Radical Islamists wanted and still want state Sharia law to be implemented, while the Jewish rabbinical courts were symbolic and nonpolitical—even the Bey knew this. This old institution was catering to a small minority within the Jewish population, but historically it was an important part of it. Bourguiba also had a modern Islamic state in mind in 1957 when he proclaimed his famous Personal Status Code designed to liberate women in Islamic Tunisia. This was indeed unheard of, in any Islamic state, to this day.

Tunisian Jews understood the 1956 constitution and the contradictions inherent in it; its main point was that Tunisia was an Islamic state, but would tolerate and protect the exercise of all religions. The constitution was adopted in 1959, but its content and its spirit were already known immediately after Independence. Tunisian Jews were obviously naïve to believe that a secular Tunisia was even a possibility. Being a large Tunisian community may have led them to be hopeful that nationalism and anti-colonialism as an ideology would be enough to sustain a modern state. For the Jews of Tunisia living in an Islamic state was difficult then as it is for anyone now, including Tunisian Muslims. We are all aware of the massive exodus of Muslims who cannot live under Islamic rule in their own countries. What happens to their Islamic beliefs once they settled in Western democracies is a whole different story, and I suspect that here too, Islam needs the Christian and Jewish worlds to survive.

The constitution of 2012 after the Jasmine Revolution was basically the same as the one drawn in 1959, with two major differences: first, freedom to exercise all religions was still there, even if there are no other religions to speak of in the country, and second, they have added the Palestinian cause as a central clause. Every Tunisian Jew living in France, Israel and elsewhere had seen this creeping radical Islamism coming. It was present since the Arab invasion in various forms and degrees, and the new nationalists had simply implemented a long-sought dream. No one now has the right to ask: Who needs another radical Islamic state in North Africa?

Two years after Independence, Bourguiba's government abolished the Jewish council of Tunisia headed by Charles Haddad de Paz. This was a major setback for everyone, including the most naïve segment of the Jewish population who up to then believed that the new nationalism might work in favor of the Jews. The government had its reasons for doing this. It was done under the banner of the need for centralizing government control to lead Tunisia forward into a modern post-colonial era. The move, in fact, was a show of force to bring this large segment of the Tunisian population under control. Bourguiba, as we have stated elsewhere, was torn with this Jewish question, whether to embrace, control or let go of that group. My argument is that all these options were implemented at the same time, Bourguiba-style of ethnic cleansing. This politics was not new in Tunisia; the Bey used the same tactic under Ottoman control.

Here is a quote concerning the rationale behind the dissolution of the Jewish council in Tunisia, uttered in a meeting in between the Justice Minister Ahmed Mestiri and members of the council: "If, despite this, there are still people who keep a certain nostalgia for the Protectorate [...] who are considering leaving because they feel more French than Tunisian or more French than the French themselves, who are also staying here but transfer their capital and enterprises abroad, if there are other people who dream of the Promised Land living in the country but turn their attention towards Israel, consciously or unconsciously playing the game of Zionism [...] well, we tell each other that it is better—for themselves and Tunisia—that they leave and we don't prevent them from leaving to any destination."[85] Members of the Jewish council were again shocked at the language, and the intent behind it. Nothing was more clear as to where all this was heading.

A thesis called "Seeking a Place in a Nation: The Exodus of the Tunisian Jewish Population 1954-1967," was presented at the American University of Cairo in 2011, and it concluded that: "The persistence of the Jews within the country indicates that there are those who did feel significantly 'Tunisian' enough to want to remain and also of there remaining a place for them within the Tunisian nation. For this group, 'Arab,' 'Tunisian' and 'Jewish are all part of their identity, and as they have not left during the 2011 Revolution, they are significantly invested in and secure of their places within the Tunisian nation, thus indicating the individuality and fluidity of identity." This presents us with the irony of how history is twisted and distorted, silencing the most important elements of Tunisian history and the Jewish indigenous population. If we accept that the Jewish population of Tunisia is both ancient and indigenou, we can also conclude the opposite: that the Islamist nationalists were not Tunisian enough in their identity to be able to accept an indigenous population that is not Muslim, or nationalist for that matter. Furthermore, the conclusion of this Egyptian thesis sees "Arab" as part of the identity of Jews of Tunisia, which is historically false. No Jewish Tunisian feels that "Arab" is part of their identity, not today, nor in the past 1,300 years. Considering that the Jews preceded the Arabs in North Africa by some one thousand years, they never felt like they were part of the Arab identity. In fact, as mentioned above, the majority of Muslim Tunisians today also do not view themselves as Arabs.

This thesis sums up one of the saddest stories of a displaced people who vanished as a result of an Islamic nationalist regime. Almost the entire population left Tunisia in a short period of time. The thesis does not turn to those who left for explanations as to why; instead, it relies on a handful of people who remained, presumably as models for adopting a perfect triple identity of Arab, Tunisian and Jewish.

Silence, or simply ignorance, became synonymous in every interpretation of the event, in almost every country. The US foreign department published a Tunisian handbook claiming that, "the issue of Tunisification (replacement of foreign by Tunisians in the civil service and the education system) and Arabization (replacement of foreign languages by Arabic as the official tongue) lacked the emotional and dysfunctional impact that had accompanied similar actions in newly independent neighboring states."[86] In fact, nothing was further than the truth. This nationalist process was a process of Islamization, and it had a devastating effects on the significant minority population segment of Tunisia.

The results of the 2012 presidential election in Egypt and the subsequent Muslim Brotherhood government of Morsi were not just based on votes, but also on discussions as to what would be best for Egypt's political stability in the streets. A win for the former Prime Minister would have had a devastating effect on mood of the Egyptian people. The religious groups such as the Muslim Brotherhood were known for raising threats and using intimidation and violence. It was thus not a surprise to learn that even the losing candidate agreed to such the outcome, for the "sake of Egypt." However, 50 percent of the population did not vote because there was no democratic choice to be made, and among those who voted, the split was right down the middle. Once elected, Morsi was pressured to respect the rights of minorities and respect Egypt's international peace treaty with Israel. It remains to be seen if both will be honored by whoever wins in the end, given the current instability in that country.

The rights of minorities within Islamic constitutions were historically entangled in unresolved contradictions, and the only way out was to leave, which is exactly what many Tunisian Jews did years ago, and what the Coptic Christians are doing today in Egypt. The process in Egypt will be complete when no minorities are left in the country. Edward Said, a Christian who grew up in Egypt, also left in search of his identity elsewhere, as did Albert Memmi, who left Tunisia in search of a better "learning environment." Tunisia completed this process of "ethnic purification" and is now doomed to enjoy the fruits of Islam, nothing but Islam.

The Jewish presence in Tunisia disappeared like it never existed. André Nahum, author and medical doctor, wrote: "Curieusement tout était oublié, effacé, gommé. Comme si ça n'avait jamais existé! [...] Que les gens et même les lieux aient changé, cela pouvait se comprendre, le vent de l'Histoire étant passé par-là, mais disparaître ainsi 'sans sépulture' m'était intolérable et soulevait en moi une immense impression d'injustice." History and culture are always changing, so it is understandable that we forget some aspects of our past, but to disappear completely, to become a small footnote in the history books cannot but invoke our total sense of injustice—far greater than what the Palestinians are going through, I may add.

Nahum also writes of the complete ignorance of the new generation of Tunisians, the young ones who cannot believe that there was ever such a thing as a Tunisian Jew. He tells the story of a recent encounter in Tunisia with a young man who simply refused to believe that he was a Tunisian Jew, a Berber who spoke Tunisian. The young man is but an example of how easy it is for Tunisia to hide its past. The injustice Nahum speaks of is the silence of the world as to what had happened to Tunisian Jews, people who had no tools to voice their frustration towards historical injustice. Is it possible for a community 140,000 strong to just disappear like it never existed? Apparently yes. It is the same story in the whole of North Africa and the Middle East. Nahum, like many Tunisian Jews, expresses frustration towards the incomprehensible situation that occurred to an ancient people who have simply vanished from their territories and from history. Since the beginning, Tunisia was never without this part of the indigenous population, and it could never throughout its history be defined without them. This is why the Jasmine Revolution is failing miserably. Tunisia without its Jewish past is a different country. The ousting of the previous government and its replacement with a Muslim Brotherhood political party reinforced the reasons as to the origins of those injustices. The reawakening of radical Islam in Tunisia was an inevitable process, and Tunisian Jews were fully aware of it; unlike everyone else, they are not surprised at what is happening in the Middle East and North Africa. What was painful was the silence that came after the grand exile in Tunisia, Israel and maybe even France.

Here is a quote describing the spirit of Tunisian Jews in exile, written in 1997 by Emile Tubiana, trying hard to ignore reality, out of fear or maybe naivity: "Ya sidi, n'ouvrez pas ce sujet, c'est une 'Gomma,' il n'est pas dans l'intérêt ni de la Tunisie ni de son peuple, ni dans l'esprit du Juif tunisien. Il faut le reconnaître que nous sommes les seuls, malgré tout, à aimer notre pays et à ne parler que du bien de la Tunisie et nous nous efforçons à passer la culture judéo-tunisienne à la nouvelle génération." Tunisian Jews, even in exile, are still proud of their origins. Tubiana begs us all not to open this Pandora Box for the sake of Tunisia which we love (the only ones to really love Tunisia), so we may always say positive things about the country and this way we can pass Judo-Tunisian culture to the new generation. What he says is important because it reflects a total misunderstanding of why Tunisian Jews left and ended up in all corners of the world. It also reflects a total confusion as to what, if anything, can be passed on to a new Tunisian Jewish generation. The quest to remain positive, no matter what, about Tunisia is nothing but a vestige of centuries of submission to Islamic Tunisia. Or maybe, it expresses a wish that one day Tunisian Muslims will be kind enough to let Jews come back, or at least recognize them in their history books along with the harm that was done to them.

Tunisian Jews in Israel and elsewhere were tormented for years about the reasons for their exile from Tunisia. Most left the question unanswered, afraid of the implications resulting from such inquiries, afraid that no one would believe them. Others, for reasons of pride, would claim that they left of their own free will, Messianic reasons, or Zionism. It is the same story for many Moroccan Jews who cannot but accept that they decided to come to the Holy Land for Messianic reasons alone. But the Jews of Tunisia were pushed out by a variety of planned government policies within a specific international political climates and during the rise of Islamic radicalism and nationalism. Tunisian Jews had no choice in the matter, in the same sense that Palestinians in 1948 also had no choice. Let us imagine a scenario whereby Islamic Tunisian nationalists headed by Bourguiba had instituted Hebrew or French, or both, as official languages besides Arabic. Let us imagine that they would have also included Italian as a third language. Bourguiba was good at imitating others, so he could have permitted a Tunisian Hebrew radio station and a television channel. This is not a far-fetched scenario; after all, Arabic is an official language in Israel, and so is Russian these days. Such a second-language policy would have resulted in much less emigration by Tunisian Jews; most would have remained in Tunisia. But pluralism was only given lip service during Bourguiba's time, as Islamist nationalists could not perceive that it was healthy for the country's economy, nor for the dynamic cultural evolution of their society. Tunisia had done everything possible to reject an important part of its cultural and social history, before and after independence: allowing its ancient population to live and prosper. Also, the removal of the Jews was done under the watch of all Western democracies, and in silence.

It is for these very reasons that Tunisian politicians and intellectuals only pay lip-service to the Palestinian cause, a leftover from Nazi propaganda. Historical records of its own minorities paints a sad picture of ethnic cleansing far more serious than what the Zionists did to the Palestinians. Even the word minority is inadequate to describe the Jewish population in Tunisian society. Together with the Berbers, Christian Italians, the French and the Maltese they would have been the majority of the population, especially in urban centers. Intolerance of Judeo-Tunisian history runs deep in the Tunisian psyche today, and the only place where it is acknowledged is in the highly controlled Jewish tourist industry (Golda Meir prophecy).

Like the Palestinians, Tunisian Jews have been searching for relatives and friends and some connections to the places where they used to live, study and thrive. The internet has been flooded with search requests of relatives and classmates. For a few years, forums were flooded with information trying to put the pieces of our historical puzzle together. Those who were able to use a computer had no coherent memory of past events, and the old generation was disappearing fast and unable to provide full account of what had happened. The internet became a useless tool for spreading tragedy—it cannot reflect history.

ITALIANS IN TUNIS

In the 1926 census of the Tunisian colony, there were 173,281 Europeans, of which 89,216 were Italians, 71,020 French and 8,396 Maltese, They mostly lived in Tunis, Biserta, La Goulette, Sfax, but even in small cities like Zaghouan, Bouficha, Kelibia, Ferryville.[87] In the 1946 census, the Italians were numbered at 84,935, but in 1959 (three years after many Italian settlers left to Italy or France after Independence) they were only 51,702, and in 1969 less than 10,000. Today they are only 900, mainly concentrated in the metropolitan area of Tunis. Another 2,000 Italians, according to the Italian Embassy in Tunis, are "temporary" residents, working as professionals and technicians for Italian companies operating in Tunisia.

North African Christians have experienced a similar dwindling of population, and their number in Egypt may shrink even further, with recent events clearly pointing to what the future holds for them. According to the Middle East analyst Aidan Clay, some 200,000 Coptic Christians have already left Egypt as a result of the 2011 revolution. The anti-Christian sentiment even reached Canadians of Egyptian origin that left Egypt to settle in Canada. Some had their names published on hate web sites, accused of defaming Islam and were called "dogs in diaspora." The brutal persecution of Copts in Egypt has the international community alarmed: Christians are fleeing Muslim nations for the freedom of the West. But now relocation is not enough, as Jihadists try to silence the voices of their victims with death threats."[88] In Gaza, Christians are also demonstrating against kidnapping of family members in a bid to forcefully convert them to Islam.[89]

Canadian Prime Minister Stephen Harper has gone further than any Western leader in trying to inject some sanity into the systematic persecution of minorities, especially Christians in Muslim countries. In Mississauga, on April 23 2012, Harper told a diverse crowd that included many Canadians who had fled religious persecution that he would establish an Office of Religious Freedom to ensure defense of persecuted religious minorities, and that this would remain a foreign policy priority.[90] He said: "When you see in Egypt peaceful members of the Coptic community being attacked, when you see Baha'is being persecuted in Iran, when you see Jews being persecuted, when you see Christians unable to practice their religion freely in China, I think all Canadians believe in the importance of both defending religious freedom at home but also defending religious freedom abroad."

No other country has shown an interest in this issue so far, and the Prime Minister's stand on this is a step towards solving an enormous problem. Harper understands that the question is not simply a religious one, but has to do with the survival of very old, distinct and indigenous communities in mostly Muslim countries.

The Jasmine Islamic Revolution

"I voted for the first time as a Tunisian citizen. It was the first election of the Arab Spring. Pictures of smiling, proud voters flooded the Internet. The world watched, surprised and hopeful. Moderate political Islam in the Arab world was touted as a possibility rather than an oxymoron. A year later, we have no democracy, no trust in elected officials, and no improved constitution. Human rights and women's rights are threatened. The economy is tanking."[91] (Souhir Stephenson)

Tunisians took to the streets on Land Day in March 2012 in support of the Palestinian cause. Many professional associations, unions, student and others joined in because the Palestinian issue is "close to the heart of every Tunisian," as one of the demonstrators claimed at that time. The Palestinians have obviously done a good job at controlling the conversation in the streets and homes in Tunisia. The demonstration took place at exactly the same time when Rashid Ghannushi called Roger Bismuth, leader of Tunisia's small Jewish community, to show his concern over the faith of Tunisian Jews. Bismuth heard the demonstration while talking to Ghannushi, believing it to be a demonstration by a handful of Salafists. He later learned that this was a massive demonstration of support for Haniyeh Ismail, the Palestinian leader in Gaza. Apparently, the newly elected Muslim Brotherhood leader of Tunisia apologized to Bismuth that indeed Tunisian sons are involved in this despicable demonstration.[92] Tunisian leaders still believe that they could reconcile their religious Islamic beliefs with human rights and democracy. Bismuth's argument when he turned to the courts was that many Jewish families cancelled their Passover stay in Tunisia as a result of threats from Islamic demonstrators. He also claimed that Tunisia has an economic interest in keeping stability and peace. Obviously, many in the new Tunisian leadership agreed with him. Bourguiba, we remember, converted the "Zaytuna mosque into a western-style university, eliminated sharia courts, and alienated Muslims by maligning the hijab and appearing on TV during Ramadan drinking orange juice."[93] In 1981, he arrested some 3,000 Islamists for speaking out in mosques without state permission. One of those arrested was Ghannushi, who today heads the largest Islamic organization in Tunisia and is the acting head of Ennahda, which took power during the revolution.

Is Hate fuelling the Tunisian Revolution?

I forget who said that "Hatred is like darkness: the more there is, the less you can see."[94] The Muslim Brotherhood believes that widespread hunger and poverty will strengthen its political position—and it is probably true. As the central government's corrupt and trickery system of subsidies collapses, local Islamist organizations are taking control of food distribution, and have establishing a virtual local dictatorship on the streets.[95]

The Jews of Tunisia were always careful not to offend Muslim sentiments, seldom questioning the Islamic rules of Pashas and Deys (Turkish governors) and Beys (upgraded title of a Dey) out of fear of reprisals. They also learned how to distinguish between the Islamic faith and the hateful rhetoric of men professing to hold this faith. So, they tolerated and at times even respected Islam as a religion; they could not accept the politics behind the religion. But it would be naive to suppose that Muslims and Jews lived in harmony in the region. The history, ideologies and religions at play do not support such an ideal coexistence. Yet we continue to find people using this theory to advance a Palestinian/Islamic agenda. But the harmony everyone talks about existed between the Jewish communities and the Berbers; it was seldom with the Muslim Arabs. There is no evidence that Islam has ever coexisted in harmony in the region of North Africa. Today, the only place on earth where this is actually working somehow is in Israel, in Jerusalem, Nazareth, and Acre. Accepting this historical fact is both frightening and depressing because the future looks grim. However, 60 years after the Holocaust, European Jews have no problem buying German goods, visiting Germany or making friends with Germans. The new generation cannot be blamed for what their fathers and grandfathers did. The rationale helping to justify this has the Israelis repeating: "you must not forgive and you must never forget," but the rest is just fine.

But can anyone imagine a similar situation occurring in the Arab world? There was a short-lived euphoria regarding this possibility when in 1991 Yitzhak Rabin decided to change strategies and recognize the Palestinian right to build their own state. The euphoria lasted a week at the most. It felt good but did not feel right. Half the Jewish population of Israel (from LCA) was not mentioned in the grand design of how the future would look in the Middle East. European countries emerged from WWI and WWII acknowledging the need to rebuild their States, economies and political relations with each other, assuring that past wars belonged to the nightmares of older generations, and different historical eras. Then the Berlin Wall came down, and Russia opened its borders to trade and influences. Most border disputes in Europe were resolved, yet in Israel wars and hatred continue with no end in sight. How can this be suppressed? How can we move on?

In Palestine, these reprisals expressed themselves in violence as early as April 1920, when the San Remo Conference took place, which gave England the Mandate for Palestine. Led by the Grand Mufti Haj Amin el-Husseini, and during the Muslim Nebi Musa festivities that month, Arabs in Jerusalem rioted, and their primary objective was to attack Jews."[96] A year later, major attacks by Palestinians resulted in many more deaths. In 1929, el-Husseini wasted no time in making clear that the whole struggle is about the honor of Islam: "The Jews have violated the honor of Islam, and the eyes of your brothers in Palestine are upon you and they awaken your religious feelings and national zealotry to rise up against the Jewish enemy who violated the honor of Islam and raped the women and murdered widows and babies." Thirteen-hundred years of constant identical rhetoric by Islamists everywhere.

Hundreds were killed during those 1921 riots, and many other similar events were happening elsewhere at the same time. The Arab population of the West Bank and Gaza frequently employed violence to express their frustration and anger. The members of the UN did not take seriously the words of the Egyptian delegate to the UN in 1947 that "the lives of one million Jews in Muslim countries will be jeopardized by the partition" of Palestine. By 1948, another warning was delivered, this time by the President of the Jewish Congress, Dr. Stephen Wise, to the US Secretary of State. The magnitude of the catastrophe was being revealed, that "between 800,000 and a million Jews in the

Middle East and North Africa, exclusive of Palestine, are in 'the greatest danger of destruction' at the hands of Moslems being incited to holy war over the Partition of Palestine. [...] Acts of violence already perpetrated, together with those contemplated, being clearly aimed at the total destruction of the Jews, constitute genocide, which under the resolutions of the General Assembly is a crime against humanity." His plea was also published a few months later in a *New York Times* in an article entitled "Jews in Grave Danger in all Muslim Lands: Nine Hundred Thousand in Africa and Asia Face Wrath of Their Foes."[97]

As the previous chapters demonstrated, during this time radical Islamists were increasingly making inroads in the Arab world's most advanced, liberal, and tolerant country—Tunisia. Tunisian secularists in the streets were confused to learn that radical Islamists in power are being portrayed as moderate and democratic. Thousands took to the streets of Tunis in May 2012 to celebrate the end of French colonial rule in 1956. As one might expect on Independence Day, most were in an anti-imperialist mood. Even Google had contributed a "doodle" in their search engine celebrating Tunisian Independence and the Jasmine Revolution. But who are the "imperialists" in the Tunisian imagination today? Not the French, not anymore! The "imperialists" today, according to secular forces in Tunisia, are the United States and, oddly enough, Qatar. Both are seen, fairly or not, as the backers of Tunisia's radical Islamists. This was really an odd situation. "No to America, no to Qatar, the people of Tunisia will always be free."[98] "People here are against the United States helping Ennahda," Ayadi continued. "All Americans who come here are against the Islamists, but the American government is supporting them. I wish we had a good, modern, respectful Islamic party. I'm a Muslim and I'm proud of it, but I'm not proud of this party."[99]

Israelis keep asking "why do Arabs hate us so much?" and their question is justified. Underneath it all, there is tremendous hatred accumulating and erupting every few years for all kinds of reasons. It has nothing to do with the Palestinians; it is State-controlled hate. Their leaders probably know this, but they are too busy accumulating personal wealth and power, just in case they are ousted by popular uprisings again. Lee Smith, in his book *Strong Horse*, makes the case that "violence is a central factor in Arab political life, and it is impossible to understand the region without taking this into account."[100] His point is an interesting one. Violence and hate is an Arab "thing" and not necessarily Islamic. For example, Indonesia is a Muslim country and does not have the same culture of violence as countries of the Middle East and Africa. According to him Arab states should take serious steps to curtail violence and hate. It a State responsibility, as only governments are capable of taking the necessary steps to calm the mood in the streets.

This is not the place to discuss philosophy of religion, but it is the place to question certain aspects of Judaism, Islam and Christianity. It may comfort Tunisians to know that Israel also has many fundamentalists, religious sects, cults from Europe and from the Arab world. They may not be as violent as some radical Islamist sects, but they will certainly become ones if we let them, or if they somehow take over the Israeli government and its institutions. But in Israel, few take everything written in the scriptures literally, including the words of the prophets; they already said what they had to say in their historical moment. And they are all dead and cannot contribute to the current discussion on any level. But the need to strip all religions of hate

SILENCING THE PAST:

is real and it affects every country in the world. Those who insist on waking up our dead prophets often do not have religion, but rather economic and political, interests in mind. Needless to say, neither the Old and New Testament nor the Koran carry with them objective truths affecting our earthy survival today, except the belief in one God. Almost everything else is negotiable.

Since the Jasmine Revolution, not many Jews have been visiting Djerba Island on Lag BaOmer. For the second consecutive year, Jews and Israelis were warned not to travel to Tunisia to visit Djerba's ancient synagogues. The Tunisian tourist company in Israel stated that as a result of the less-than-welcoming atmosphere in the country, Israelis were encouraged to visit Germany, Poland, France or other European countries. Islamists in Tunisia, as in everywhere else, need the Jews, especially if they are just in the background, in small numbers. Ancient Judaism was very much part of the Koran and Mohammed mentions them and their habits, religions, customs and above all their prophets. The Jews as traders, craftsmen, professionals and advisors had to continue to play their historic role in order to survive. They were permitted to survive for both religious and economic reasons. Thus, Tunisian Jews have been an intricate part of the history of Tunisia, all the way back to Carthage and the invasion of Islam; it is impossible to separate them from the rest of the Tunisian population. It is impossible to understand Tunisian society without them, even today. Tunisian Islamists may tremble at the thought that here too Jews played a major historical role. In one recent incident, a Jewish property purchase took place in Djerba, and the Islamists cried foul, claiming that the Jews are trying to "Palestinize" Tunisia. The outcry was real, and the new government decided to reevaluate real estate laws in relation to Jews. It is interesting to note that most Tunisians are familiar with land purchases by Jews in Palestine, but are completely ignorant of the land and property confiscated from Tunisian Jews during WWII and since.

Tunisia has joined the nation of Islam by getting rid of their Jewish population. It has joined the world of intolerance towards anyone who was not a Muslim. It has rejected the pluralism of faiths and ideas in favor of an all-encompassing religion, radical Islam. In fact, it has renounced the very character and soul which made Tunisia unique among nations. Let's face it; living in a monocultural country with one religion must be very depressing, whether Muslim or Jewish. Tunisia is following that path today with the election of a radical Islamist party, even though they keep telling us that there is no contradiction between Islam and democracy. We cannot even imagine what Israel would look like if it were run by religious radical conservative elements. They currently influence the State but they do not run it. These religious elements are trying to control and impose their outdated and distorted ancient beliefs system on the rest of the population, but so far have not succeeded. Unfortunately, it is not difficult to believe that they will in the very near future. The important thing to remember is that Israel is made up of mostly Jews from LCA, Palestinian Israelis (20 percent), Russian Jews, Ethiopian Jews, Indian Jews, Druze, Christians, Baha'i people, and of course, Jews from every European country, including Holocaust survivors and their offspring. People speak their mind freely even if or especially when they are not asked to. Palestinians in and around Israel know the virtues of Israel's pluralism, and most would not prefer to live elsewhere, especially not in a 100 percent Muslim country; recent polls proved this to be true. However, it seems that the period of pluralism in Israel will also not survive for too long.

The Egyptian Philosopher Murad Wahba captured the essence of what the Jasmine Revolution meant in Tunisia and the Spring Revolution in Egypt. He stated that the Muslim Brotherhood has no interest in resolving the social and political issues of the twenty-first century. In fact, he says, they have developed "anti-bodies" to any meaningful change. Wahba sees troubles ahead because the Muslim Brotherhood are using the same mentality used in the thirteenth century, acting on words of the Koran without any critical thinking; according to him, this is leading the Egyptian people into an international war or internal civil war in the near future. Egypt is in a real crisis, as is Tunisia, and soon Israel will be too. Countries under these beliefs systems are guilty of ethnic cleansing of minorities, and especially of Jews. All have executed unthinkable historical wrongs, as Islam never existed without its Jewish population. It was one of the pillars holding Islam together, especially in Tunisia. Essam al-Erian, deputy head of the Muslim Brotherhood's Freedom and Justice Party in Egypt joined the call for the return of Egyptians Jews to Egypt, forgetting that today Egyptian Jews do not exist. They were ousted from Egypt and have disappeared completely, exactly like Iraqi Jews and Tunisian Jews.

Religious activists of all religions operate in all societies, converting whoever they can along the way. Islamist activists, however, have raised such activism to another level. Chabad (ultra-religious Jewish) activists are amateurs in comparison. In Tunisia, Islamic activists appear with sweet words and sometimes with colorful sweets, along with black and white pamphlets telling shop owners and various hotels that alcohol is against the Koran. They will nicely make suggestions, the Tunisian way, that maybe the shop owner should not serve alcoholic beverages, not even Boukha. For those who don't know the Boukha is, the

Jewish Tunisian fig vodka which moved its manufacturing plant to France after being burnt down in anti-Jewish riots in 1958. Business owners often comply because they know that the sweeter the words the harsher the consequences. Many in Tunisia have received these Mafia-like friendly visits. This is now on headline news in Tunisia after the Jasmine so-called revolution. This type activism has been there for decades and was historically directed against Jewish Tunisians.

Tunisian Military

Tunisia started to build its army in 1956, immediately after Independence, enlisting the 1,500 Beylical guards and an additional 3,000 newly enlisted men. Fewer than 10 years later, Tunisia under Bourguiba found itself providing soldiers to the Arab front in the Middle East Israel-Arab conflict. Bourguiba was unable to grasp what happened in Tunisia during the Second World War. His lack of military knowledge continued when he decided to send some 2,000 Tunisian soldiers to Egypt to help with the war efforts against Israel. All soldiers were stationed along the Nile. Morocco, during the same war, sent three brigades. And a small force was also sent in 1967 to help Nasser in his war efforts. In 1970, Tunisia sent forces to Jordan to act as buffer between the Palestinians and Jordanians after "Black September," when tens of thousands of Palestinians were massacred there, not by Israelis but by the Jordanians and Syrians. Tunisia quickly understood that sending soldiers to battle does not make sense, and began to focus on UN peacekeeping missions, mainly in Uganda, Rwanda and Cambodia. In 2010, Tunisia's military consisted of 27,000 enlisted soldiers and 84 tanks.

Colonialism in North African countries was not the same as colonialism in Sub-Saharan Africa. But the anti-colonial theories were the same. The Arab intelligentsia adopted the anti-colonialist rhetoric of the colonizer and the colonized, Black and White, oppressed and oppressor. From Memmi to Fanon, independence and anti-colonialism became the agenda of the day. However, what was ignored in this struggle was the ultimate creation of an Islamic state without minorities, especially without Jews. Tunisia was part of this grand Islamist design disguised as nationalism, socialism, state building, non-alignment, or whatever. Within a span of 30 years Islamic States had succeeded in totally eliminating its Jewish population as well as its other minorities. They were pushed out and made to understand that Tunisia was not their home. The tragedy of post-colonial politics in North Africa is the ease with which these countries eliminated their minorities. It is highly ironic that these same countries now uphold Palestinian rights as central to their politics, embedding it in their constitutions. Millions of Jews are now scattered around the globe, leaving their Islamist brothers in peace so they can build their homogenous Islamist societies. The irony grows as millions of North Africans, this time Muslims, are now exiling themselves to Europe and the Americas. Disenchanted Moroccans, Tunisians, Algerians, Libyans and Egyptians have left their homelands which are run by corrupt politicians and religious Islamist interests.

It was irresponsible for intellectuals and journalists not to be alarmed by the idea that Jews may not have a place in the newly formed Tunisia. No one cared when they were persecuted and pushed out, and no one cared when the same was done to other minorities. The new politics of post-colonial governments basically left the exit door open to anyone who could not stomach dictatorial religious rule. This provided the government with an excuse for inaction, for continued poverty and underdevelopment and brain drain of those who were educated. In post-revolution Egypt the hate tradition has continued, and it seems like the Muslim Brotherhood cannot wait for the destruction of the State of Israel. The Brotherhood is helpless in resolving the economic crisis and preventing deteriorating living conditions, so it has turned to blaming Israel and the Jews again—a tactic which has worked for past dictators of the Arab world. In conclusion, it does not matter who owns the Spring Revolution: the Muslim Brotherhood, the military or another dictator. Every government will have to embrace Islamic practices, a military fist and a continued policy of ethnic cleansing.

Tunisians in European Camps

I have been following with amazement and sympathy the trend of Tunisians running far away from their Islamic homeland of Tunisia in search of a better life. This trend existed for a number of years, but it intensified after the revolution. My sympathy towards them exists because they resemble in some ways the exile of the Jewish people from Tunisia. Tens of thousands of young people have flocked to worn-out boats for a one-way sea trip to unknown European lands. Why would any Tunisian be ready to live in poverty, underemployment in Italy, France, Greece or Belgium? Why would Tunisians flee by the thousands to the small island of Lampedusa just off the coast of Tunisia? The island with its 6,000 inhabitants is now flooded with Tunisians running away, first from Ben Ali and now from the Ennahda party, searching for work and a way to make life better. One month after the Jasmine Revolution, some 5,000 Tunisians flocked there, instantly doubling the population of the island. The Tunisian government in post-colonial era was helpless in preventing this emigration trend. No government policies were able to tackle the problem because the problem was rooted in the way the Tunisian State had developed. Incompetent bureaucrats, corrupt religious elite and a "lazy intellectual class" had taken over the language and resources, leaving nothing to its aspiring young population. Nothing was left from an ancient idea that "Tunisia was the promised land." From Lampedusa they hope to be flown to mainland Italy for paper processing and work visas. But they will probably be flown to Palermo processing centers for a long and miserable stay. The Italian government cried for help from the EU while trying to figure out how to make it attractive for them to stay at home. In all, 54,000 North Africans reached Italian shores in 2011, and thousands more have died at sea, adding to the countless lives that have ended beneath the ocean over the centuries. So far, more than 1,500 boat people have drowned in the Mediterranean trying to reach Italy, Spain or France. And while writing these pages, another Tunisian boat, full of disillusioned citizens, ran into trouble and dozens drowned.

In April 2012, France temporarily suspended the Schengen Agreement, reintroduced border controls and even closed its border to Tunisians and their supporters from Italy. This was a response to Italy's agreement with Tunisia, which involved issuing visas to the 23,000 Tunisians already in the country and rejecting all who arrived after this time. They assumed that Tunisians would probably try to move to France, which is not implausible. Meanwhile, 3,200 Tunisians were deported from France, and Germany, and Austria also threatened to reintroduce border controls. Denmark, too, reintroduced border controls, though with some different arguments, referring to them as "illegal migrants," part of an alleged influx of criminals from Eastern Europe. The EU is struggling with responses to these issues, which are potentially threatening the EU's core values of open internal borders and free travel.

Dissociative identity disorder (DID)

Alysha Bedig summed up the conflicting messages coming out the Ennahda Party by labeling it an organization suffering from split personality syndrome. They are trying to please the secularists and the ultra-religious groups at the same. They want to sound liberal while pushing Sharia or at least a partial Sharia on a population that is largely still moderate manipulating the poor.[101] The party's ideological base is hopelessly trying to please too many masters at the same time. In this way the party is trying to replicate the successes of Bourguiba's Destour party, which put Tunisia on a path towards a homogenous society. This split personality was revealed in a secretly taped conversation between Ghannushi and the hard-core Islamic religious elements within the Salafists. In these now-public videos, he is heard instructing and advising the Salafists on how they should proceed with their Sharia agenda. Up until the ousting of Ben Ali's government, the Ennahda Party was a movement in exile, and its leader Ghannushi is now 70 years old. Everyone called the movement a moderate Islamic movement. However, there have been few signs of moderation throughout its short life as victors of the Jasmine Revolution. The movement, which later became a political party, was formed along the lines of the Shah of Iran, where an old man comes from exile to lead his people back to the true religion of Islam. The party was heavily inspired by the Muslim Brotherhood in Egypt and even supported overtaking the American Embassy in Iran at the time. Ghannushi also studied abroad, in Egypt and later studied philosophy in Damascus.

A few months after Tunisia was taken over by radical Islam, Salafists were calling for the killing of the few Jews who remained in the country. The Salafists' call for the extermination of Jews during a march for Sharia law on Bourguiba Avenue sparked a little outrage in Tunisia, though Roger Bismuth decided to challenge these atrocious words in the Tunisian parliament. Bismuth, the president of the tiny Jewish community of Tunis, pleaded with Islamist politicians for restraint. He should have received a Noble Peace Prize for standing firm against the negative forces of religion. "What this sheikh said is not part of our customs in Tunisia, and he cannot be Tunisian," he said. "We now have to be one hand, more than ever, to save the country's economy and bring in foreign investment and tourists."[102] Bismuth should be commended for asking for sanity and recognition of the fact that Jews are not foreigners in Tunisia and have never have been "temporary residents in the country." Human rights activist Saida Garrache added "Judaism is a divine religion recognized in Islam, like Christianity." Tunisian Salafists, however, are fully aware of Jewish history in Tunisia, which is exactly why they are trying to erase it. Mr. Bismuth did not leave Tunisia when everyone around him did, nor does he have any plans of leaving his homeland for Israel or France. He knows that Judaism is not just a divine religion like Islam or Christianity, because in Tunisia it preceded Islam, the Arab conquest and Christianity. But very few Tunisians today will agree that the handful of remaining Jews need the blessing of Mohammed to live in peace in Tunisia.

In May 2011, Ghannushi gave an interview that elucidated, unabashedly, the essence of his disturbing worldview. Not surprisingly, his ideology relies heavily on the destruction of Israel by jihad. Here is a translation from the Global Muslim Brotherhood Daily Report: "Ghannushi maintains that altogether the Arab revolutions are positive for the Palestinians, and threaten to bring Israel to an end. He says that the Palestinian problem lies at the heart of the Nation [Umma], and that all the land between the mosque in Mecca and Jerusalem represents the heart of the Islamic Nation, and any [foreign] control over part of this heart is a stamp on the Umma's illness. There is no doubt, he continued, that the revolutions opened a new age. The foundations of Western interests in the Arab countries are shaky. Sheikh Ahmad Yassin, he concluded, said that Israel will come to an end prior to 2027; this date looks far, and maybe Israel will come to an end sooner."[103]

I have no intention here of outlining the rituals, fatwas and laws relating to women, Jews, infidels, writers and others, today or in the past, done in the name of Islamic Arab conquest and expansion, because to do so would be exhausting and frankly depressing. In various forms and degrees, these practices still exist in some Islamic countries. What is important is the reference point of where we are today and what the past looked like a hundred years ago, or even a thousand years ago. Tunisian Jews viewed the Arabs as invaders and conquerors, a view shared by the different tribes scattered across North Africa. Robert Fisk of *The Independent* understood early the irony of the revolution quoting the Lebanese poet Khalil Gibran's famous line: "Pity the nation that welcomes its new ruler with trumpeting's, and farewells him with hooting's, only to welcome another with trumpeting again."[104] Rarely have these words sounded so painfully accurate.

The Salafist movement sprung immediately after the Jasmine Revolution, with a membership of around 10,000 Tunisians violently calling for Sharia law, seeing themselves as the reincarnation of Mohamed's Arab forces in the region. Thousands of them marched in a show of force on May 2012, calling for Sharia law and the ousting of all Jews from Tunisia. They are part of the "thugs and roses"—or in this case "thugs and Jasmine"—politics which was merely an extension of the Ennahda Party. Many of the demonstrators were wearing Afghan military uniforms and recited the usual hate slogans: "We are all the children of Osama (bin Laden)" and "Jews, Jews, the army of Mohammed is back." Ridha Belhaj, the leader of the outlawed Hizb Ettahrir party, claimed that the "revolution was made so Sharia can be implemented." This group of 10,000 Islamist extremists went on a 10-day rampage in Tunis, attacking shops selling alcohol, police stations and even randomly attacking individuals, men and women. The authorities so far have been silent about this. The army was deployed to protect public buildings, but the safety of the general population was at risk.

Creative imagination was booming after the Tunisian revolution, as a Tunisian troupe performed a play in Tehran about 9/11, depicting a Pentagon employee who had information about the attack but was kidnapped by the Israelis before he could inform his superiors. Hopefully no one will invite them to New York. Wagdy Ghoneim, a notorious Egyptian famous for his social and political issues, was invited to Tunisia to speak to his supporters and critics, which is also part of this cultural post-revolutionary awareness. But the creative political imagination had reached new lows with the recent (June 2012) visit of the AKP Turkish political delegates. Advisors and journalists gathered just steps from Tunisia's government building to exchange information and political know-how with their Tunisian counterparts. After all, Ghannushi and others in his party have been using the Turkish political model of Islamic democracy to explain their position—the only one available. According to the Turkish delegate, this visit of aspiring politicians traveled to Tunisia in order to "understand the situation in Tunisia after the revolution, and see what progress still needs to be made."[105] The delegate from the Turkish Embassy in Tunisia was quick to remind Tunisians that the Ennahda party is in political relations not just with the ruling AKP party but also with opposition parties. They quickly added, to calm the crowd in the room that "we (the Turks) are not here to colonize you" (again). They know perfectly well that hundreds of years of underdevelopment in Islamic Turkish colonialism were enough for Tunisians.

Can anyone see the historical irony here? Is Turkey really a model for Tunisia? Is Rachid Ghannushi the new Bey of Tunisia? Bernard Louise, a well-known scholar on the Middle

East and especially Turkey, who is now 96 years old, said in a recent interview that he is absolutely convinced that Turkey is in the process of reestablishing its empire again within the Arab world by presenting itself as a model for development; he is not surprised at all by the Muslim Brotherhood taking power in the Jasmine Revolution.[106] But he is also not convinced that Western style democracy is the answer in these North African countries.

In June 2012, a manifesto was published that was signed by many Tunisian intellectuals. It was very carefully worded not to offend the Islamists, and complained that "We hoped that the transformations that this Islamist party claimed to have performed were real. Many Tunisians hoped that this movement could be carrying a democratic agenda inspired by Islam. But the words and deeds showed otherwise as it aim to seize all the power to advance Islamist ideology and to impose Tunisian society's dogmatic order." Afterwards, the Minister of Communications Ben Jaafar condemned the media and the intellectuals with harsh words at the Parliamentary Assembly of the Council of Europe. He also complained that the revolution is being misunderstood, and that Tunis is not Kandahar, as it is being portrait in the media. As for the recent rise of the Salafists in Tunisia, he says, the interim government has chosen to give preference to seeking "dialogue and consensus" when resolving the country's social challenges. Ennahda is not using the same tactics implimented by the ousted dictator Ben Ali or Bourguiba before him. The government is using dialogue with people whose stated objectives included killing of Jews. The few remaining Jews of Tunisia cannot safely walk the streets, and those who have not converted to Islam have to hide their origins and their culture. He added, of course, that "The Tunisian Revolution has shown that there is no contradiction between Islam and democracy."

Anti-Colonialism and the Jews of North Africa

Every student of political science in third world countries (and often in the West) is made to read Frantz Fanon. It is one of the required readings for anyone studying African and Third-World politics, much like reading Karl Marx in studying socialism and anti-capitalism. Fanon analyzed the struggle for anti-colonialism and independence, but very few questioned his theories. There are not one[107] but two elephants in Fanon's theories and they are the absence of identifying Islam and Arabism as the character behind anti-colonialism in North Africa, and the absence of Jews, Berbers and other minorities in his theory. The real history of North Africa is nowhere to be found in his writings. The pluralistic fabric of North African society is absent; Fanon ignored it completely. He ignored minority and indigenous contributions to economy and society, and the role they played over the centuries. He also ignored the Islamists and their control over the countries of North Africa. Fanon lived briefly in Tunisia while hiding from the French, yet he never mentioned the amazing cultural diversity which existed in Tunisia, Algeria or Morocco before Independence, the Turks and Islam. His books *Black Skin White Masks* and *The Wretched of the Earth* were for many years, manuals for third-world students everywhere.

In February 2012, the Secretary of State Hilary Clinton went to Tunisia for another day of appeasement and was questioned in a "town hall" meeting by a young Tunisian about how political candidates, both Democrats and Republicans, when running for election "run towards the Zionist lobbies to get their support" and once elected they pretend to show support for Tunis and

Egypt. "How would you reassure and gain his (the citizen's) trust again, given the fact that you are supporting his enemy as well at the same time?" The Secretary of State answered that they should not worry about this kind of rhetoric and that the US is full of mosques: "If you go to the United States, you see mosques everywhere, you see Muslim Americans everywhere. That's the fact. So I would not pay attention to the rhetoric." There was no clear-cut support for Israel in front of the newly elected Muslim Fundamentalist Party in a country that eliminated their minorities. Little did she know that the student was really crying for help in understanding these complex issues! If she had known her history she could have answered this student that Israel is not the enemy of Tunisia; and that Israel is also not the enemy of Islam. She could have reminded this Muslim student, who probably has a university degree in political science, that Tunisia once had a large Jewish population. She could have looked at him straight in the eyes and reminded him of the role Americans played in the liberation of Tunisia, where almost 120,000 Allied soldiers died in the name of freedom stopping Nazism and Fascism.

Palestinians in Tunisia

I n 1982, two weeks after I landed at Ben Gurion Airport after being away for 7 years, I was drafted as a reservist and former paratrooper into the Israeli forces as they were preparing to enter Lebanon. Without much warning and little preparation, I soon found myself roaming the streets of Sidon. I came to Israel to protest the invasion of Lebanon, and found myself deep in it. Israel's harsh reality has a way of changing the normal course of living—I had to choose between a jail sentence for disobeying orders and the occupation of Lebanon, and I chose the latter. I was in the midst of completing my Doctorate degree, and this certainly was not something I had anticipated. Yet, almost ten years previous, I was deep inside Egypt during the Yom Kippur War, wondering how on earth I (and Israel) got there. In the mountains of Attaka, deep inside Egypt less than 100 km from Cairo, we voted in the general election and Golda Meir won again. Does anyone know how to make peace in this region? Does anybody here take responsibility for anything? These were the wrong questions in 1973 in Egypt, and certainly the wrong questions in Lebanon *in 1982. We did not know why we were in Lebanon. There was no visible enemy, and no clear objectives. We all agreed very early that our situation was not good, and decided in secret that the only objective we would adopt is to stay alive. None of us knew what we were supposed to do, or how, or why. We were posted in the middle of a heavily populated area, waiting for "clear objectives" to appear. At one point, we were sent to walk the streets of Sidon, waiting to be attacked, the same strange tactic I practiced in Gaza as a paratrooper with the current Defense Minister Moshe (Bogie) Ya'alon in 1970. Years later, Bogie, according to widely used publications, commanded the raid in Tunisia against Abu Jihad.*

In 1982, we were all experienced in warfare and various combat situations, and many of us already participated in other wars dating back to the War of Attrition in 1970 and the Yom Kippur war in 1973. But now we were all highly cynical of the Lebanese war and of our chain of command. We were five, heavily armed soldiers patrolling streets and orchards from morning to night. Two of us were born in Tunisia (including myself), one in Iraq, one in Georgia and one was an Israeli of Polish origin. The other Tunisian soldier was a young man who was just released from a lengthy jail sentence for his part in planning to blow up the Al-Aqsa mosque in Jerusalem. He was a religious ultra-nationalist—until he met me, that is. Every soldier knew we had no business entering Lebanon and no business staying there. It had nothing to do with one's political beliefs of Left or Right, or religious beliefs. Our objective remained...to come out of this place alive. During this war a few kilometers to the north of us, the PLO was completely surrounded. Thousands of PLO fighters, their families with Kalashnikovs in hand boarded a cruise ship headed for Tunisia, the only country in the Arab world which was willing to host them. The Israelis were determined to oust the PLO headquarters out of Lebanon, and under siege the PLO had no alternative but to yield and leave for the temporary safe haven of Tunis.

A few hundred people gathered on January 5, 2012 at the Tunis-Carthage airport to welcome Ismail Haniyeh, the Hamas leader of Gaza. As they waited for him, they sang anti-Semitic chants and slogans to the glory of Palestine and the liberation of Gaza. They carried Palestinian flags, the flags of the Ennahda movement, and the black flags of the Salafists and chanted:

Speaker: "Kick the Jews"

Crowd: "Duty" [wajib] (It is a duty)
Speaker: "Expel the Jews"

Crowd: "Duty"
Speaker: "Kill the Jews"

Crowd: "Duty"

The irony was that even though Haniyeh runs an oppressive religious rule in Gaza and has launched thousands of bombs on Israeli cities around Gaza, most of the affected civilians on the Israeli side were Berbers, and North African Jews from Morocco and Tunisia. He was now receiving a hero's welcome in North Africa for trying to kill as many Jewish North African Berbers. It was ironic that he was received as a hero determined to kill the indigenous population of North Africa. Amazingly, in 2009 when Israel defended itself against such attacks from Gaza the Federation of Moroccan Jews wrote an official letter to King

Mohammad VI of Morocco indicating that Israel has the right to defend itself, and that the attacks by Gaza were aimed at Moroccan Jews living in areas surrounding Gaza, Be'er Sheva, Sderot, Netivot, Ashkelon, Ashdod and other security-belt cities. The King of Morocco received the letter and added it to his sealed box full of local political grievances.

These types of chants were the sounds of Tunisia in 2012, in the so-called Jasmine or Spring Revolution. No jazz and no blues, only hateful lyrics. Dizzy Gillespie's "A Night of Tunisia" played by the world's greatest classical guitarist, Roland Dyens, a Tunisian Jew exiled in France, is but a tribute to a different Tunisia. It is also probably not an accident that Alain Boublil, another Tunisian Jew in exile, captured the heart of the world by writing the musical version of *Les Misérables* by Victor Hugo, making it a voice for social change from China to the US, and even in the Arab world. Also the Jewish musician and singer Cheikh El Afrit is now played solely by those who feel nostalgic about the old days of diversity in Tunisia.

How was it possible that Tunisians were uttering such hateful slogans? Israel is more than a thousand miles away and has no issue with Tunisians. No Tunisian Jew anywhere is capable of such hateful rhetoric towards Tunisians of any religion. The outburst of hate was rooted in the type of Islam awaiting Tunisia after the revolution. This type of Islam had been years in the making and at its roots was the Palestinian-Israeli conflict. The ethnic cleansing of Jews was by then a completed process. Who was next in line? First there was the pretext of war in the Middle East as an excuse for harassing Jews and making them leave, and now they take comfort that it was the "right thing to do" by adopting the Palestinian cause. Even Tunisia's new constitution with its clause to oppose Zionism and ties with Israel had to do more with psychology then with politics. The two largest Tunisian parties supported the draft of a new Tunisian constitution, which included clauses condemning normalization of relations with Israel.

In Israel, more than 20 percent of the population is Muslim, living in conditions of equality before the law—not perfect existence by any means, and often far from it. But, if Israel was to employ the same methods and tactics used by Morocco, Egypt, Tunisia and Libya against the Jews, the outcome would have been the same: no Muslims would be living in Israel. There would have been no Palestinian people, no Palestinian identity and no Palestinian refugees. The contrast between outcomes in these two countries, Israel and Tunisia, is clear, leading us to conclude that Israel cannot be accused of ethnic cleansing, at least not successfully. At the same time we have no other words to use for what had happened in the whole of North Africa and other Middle Eastern countries. It is evident that the Palestinians themselves cannot turn to any country of North Africa for moral support or comfort on issues of refugees, citizenship and land rights. North African Muslim nationalists have done a fantastic job of eliminating all minorities, especially their Jewish Berber brothers. On a psychological level Tunisians do not miss an occasion supporting the Palestinian cause. And, they do so for two reasons, one of which is guilt and the other is the silencing of opposition.

The average Tunisian is not without a sense of guilt on the absence of Jews in the land of Tunisia. Some Tunisians still remember the presence of a Jewish population. They cannot explain their sense of guilt, a product of generations which can easily be manipulated by Arab Muslims determined to control the agenda and exploit the country's wealth, physical and moral. Supporting the Palestinians eases their conscious and soothes their unexplained hatred towards Jews and Israelis. The Muslim Brotherhood was and is an expert in this kind of mass manipulation, and Muslims in Tunisia naively fell into this. This was also the reason why the head of the Ennahda party called the Jews to come back. It was his way of showing some form of forgotten liberalism and much-needed renewed humanism. He believed that this will help him look more progressive to the eyes of the Western world, something he desperately needed. He has nothing against Tunisian Jews and they are free to come back.

But these were only words, considering the moral fabric of the party he controls. He knows for certain that Jews will not come back to Tunisia, at least not as long as Islamists are in control. As mentioned in a previous chapter, historically, even radical Muslims in Tunisia needed the Jews for moral salvation on philosophical, historical and political levels, and they will continue to do so, long after they have thrown them all out. Tunisians are trying to have it both ways, exploiting the historical fact that Jews contributed to Tunisia, while at the same time making sure they are out of Tunisia. Indeed, the Sharia-law promoting party is in need of the handful of Jews still left in the country in order to show that it has still some sense of compassion. For Ghannushi, (the leader of the "moderate" Islamist party in power) there is no contradiction in calling for the destruction of Israel and at the same time inviting Tunisian Jews to come back. He is pleasing two masters—the West and radical Islam—all in one breath, and all in the name of Allah. He does not see any contradiction whatsoever—no one there does.

The irony lies with the Tunisian Jews who fled to France only to find out 50 years later that Tunisian Muslims have also fled to the same city, quarters, streets and buildings, sharing the same kind of life and memories in exile. The only differences between them were the reasons for leaving Tunisia and the numbers behind this exile. The Muslim population in France now reaching close to 10 percent of the population, which is enough to help determine the outcomes of elections at all levels of French politics. The relationship between the Tunisian Jews and Tunisian Muslims in France was not confrontational at first. Slowly, this normal relationship had broken down and became intolerable for some Jews. Tunisians, like other North Africans, could not miss an opportunity to bring the Palestinian cause into French politics on both national and municipal levels. Everything had to do with the plight of the Palestinians and the relationship between Jews in France and the Israeli Zionist State. Through the Palestinian question, the whole psychological internal debate naturally ended with the superiority of Islam over everybody else, and especially over the Jews. The economic crisis also did not help ease the friction among immigrants, and between immigrants and the State.

Another determining factor was that Tunisian Muslims have not kept much of the Berber heritage and were left open to Islamic Arab influence, often radical in nature. Apart from the food and music, the two communities had very little in common. By 2011, the two communities in France have had to work hard to figure out how to live together, if this is at all possible. Unfortunately, now that the numbers are not equal and the Islamic population is larger, Tunisian Muslims have developed a total indifference to the Jewish Tunisian population, ignoring the long historical links of the Jewish people in Tunisia, and in France as well. Many Tunisian Muslims have unfortunately become radicalized politically and culturally, and much work has to be done in order for this to change—and it has to be done before all French Jews are pushed out again. Tunisian Jews in France are torn and amazed at how history has tricked them once again.

With the old generation who still remember Jewish Tunisia slowly disappearing, soon nothing will be left of this ancient community scattered all over the globe, not just in Israel and France. The younger generation was often proud to be Tunisian because of the rather Liberal politics the Tunisian State held in comparison with other Islamic countries. But all this nostalgia disappeared quickly with the outcome of the Jasmine Revolution in 2011. Anyone with Tunisian roots cannot but shrug his shoulders at the emergence of another Islamic, Sharia-based country in the world. No one was left to be proud of anything Tunisian. Those in France, I guess, will have to wait a while longer for that to happen. Centuries of coexistence in submission with the Muslims in Tunisia left their mark. The unholy alliance between the French, the Left and the Islamists have not helped the situation, and Tunisian Jews are now in a precarious and unexplainable predicament. The only thing left in common was the color of their skin.

The outcome of the Jasmine Revolution caught everyone by surprise. For Tunisian Jews in France and elsewhere, the surprise was mixed with sadness and questions, even if they did not live in Tunisia. The outcome of the so-called revolution made them reflect more seriously on how and why they ended up in France or Israel. There are some 50,000 people in Israel who registered to vote in the recent French election, and only 9,899 voted. Most of the voters live in Netanya, Ashdod and Haifa, and 92.8 percent of them voted for Nicolas Sarkozy; it is estimated that 93 percent of French Muslims voted for François Hollande.[108]

In 2012, Facebook CEO Mark Zuckerberg canceled his scheduled visit to the oldest synagogue in Africa on the Tunisian island of Djerba, where he was to be a guest of honor at the pilgrimage. He was invited to attend a religious ceremony by the small Jewish community there. His visit was an opportunity to rehabilitate the image of Tunisia and promote international tourism, but the elected Ennahda party discouraged him from traveling to Tunisia. Around the same time, an Islamist who sits in the Tunisian Constituent Assembly had drawn attention to the sale of land on Djerba to Jews, comparing the situation in the largest island off the coast of North Africa with a "second Palestine." In response, Ennahda proposed legal restrictions on the acquisition of property by Jews. With this proposal the members of Ennahda discriminated against Tunisian Jews, and revived anti-Semitic sentiments in the streets of Tunisia. The leadership of the Islamist party did not condemn the racist and anti-Semitic proposals. Following the shameful public calls to kill Jews by some Islamists, the image of Tunisia became tainted. These sentiments were also expressed on Facebook, which did not go unnoticed by Western bloggers. Tunisian Islamists have yet to understand that anti-Semitism against members of the small Jewish population hurts the whole of Tunisia. These hate statements have shocked members of Jewish community in Djerba, who were supposed to have the same rights and duties as all Tunisians.[109] In April 2002, the Jewish synagogue in Tunis was the target of an attack by Al-Qaeda, which killed 21 people including 14 German tourists, five Tunisians and two French. The risk of further attacks cannot be taken lightly. Armed gangs and Islamist terrorists, linked to global Jihad or al Qaeda and other autonomous groups, could attack Jewish tourists and pilgrims. By the end of 2012, two additional synagogues were looted and destroyed by Islamist activists.

The Palestinians are well aware of presence of Israelis of Berber and North African origin. They are even aware of the claim that these Jews are refugees just like them. The Palestinians Remember website writes about this, stating that they don't believe these Jews left their homelands of their own free will. They agree that it is not the doing of the Zionist ideology, although this did not help the situation. However, Palestinians claim that they are not responsible for the faith of those Jews, nor for the actions of the states that exiled them.[110]

Yet, no Palestinian ideology can explain how their tragedy is different than those of Jews of LCA, except by pointing to the refugee problem which exists and has not yet been resolved by the neighboring Arab countries. They also point out that just arrangements resolved the Jewish problem but not the Palestinian problem. Interestingly, the Palestinians have no problem with the demands for reparations from all of the countries which ousted the Jews. They are not accepting any responsibility for actions of Arab states but are pushing these countries to even further anti-Jewish radicalism in thoughts and action. The Palestinians are in a better historical situation than the one million people who were forced to leave their countries of origin. There are no refugee camps; no cultural centers; no United Nations support, no libraries or museums...they have completely disappeared. We cannot but call this pure ethnic cleansing, done with Palestinian support and encouragement, throughout the Middle East and North Africa, and this continues to happen even today. I have argued above that the exodus of the Jews from Arab lands was directly linked to the Palestinian problem and to wars in the Middle East. I also argue that the reasons behind the disappearance of these Jews are also the key to providing a powerful ideological solution to the Palestinian problem and to the Arab-Israeli conflict. I am not talking about reparations but of recognition of the injustices done to many people in the Middle East, which may or may not be more serious than what the Palestinians have gone through over the past 60 years. Recognition, understanding of history, tolerance and the acceptance of responsibilities by states of Arab Conquered Lands over the centuries may provide a whole different set of truths sorely needed in this area of the world.

The Palestinian demand to take back all Israel's land and institute the law of return for the remaining refugees may be viewed as another layer in the politics of ethnic cleansing practiced throughout the Muslim world. Most Israeli Jews were pushed out of Spain, and then out of North Africa, and would again be threatened to be thrown out of the only country where history was prepared to meet them. The Palestinian claim that the "two exoduses are not identical in motivation and cause, and should be considered separately" is also unacceptable historically. Frankly, the world really does not need another Islamic, Sharia-based country, a la Gaza, and both the Palestinians and Israelis deserve much better.

In June 2012, the Palestinian Authority threatened the issue of a bill in a the US Senate amending the numbers of real Palestinian refugees, which will affect the peace process with Israel, urging Congress to recognize their refugee count of 1948. Jonathan Schanzer, a researcher at the Foundation for Defense of Democracies, estimated that the real number of refugees living in the Palestinian territories in 1948 was about 300,000, as opposed to several millions claimed by the United Nations Relief and Works Agency. The game of inflating numbers has been played constantly by various Arab interests and other actors. The real numbers pales in comparison with the number of displaced indigenous Jews of Tunisia and Morocco, Algeria, Egypt and Libya. The number also pales in comparison with any of the 10 Islamic countries where Jews formed part of the indigenous population for thousands of years. This is the untold secret to be revealed by the post-Jasmine and Arab Spring revolutions. The Palestinians will have to deal with a new world a new Islamic reality, making them a marginal issue in the Middle East and in the Arab world. The numbers and the history are not favorable to the Palestinians, who repeatedly call for the destruction of Israel. They are also not favorable to the Israelis who refuse to acknowledge errors done in the past.

One Tunisian Rabbi, interviewed in 2012 by Michael Totten of *World Affairs*, offered strange responses to simple questions, as though he would later be judged by the whole Arab world. Here is his response to a question about the possibility of normalizing or breaking off relations with Israel: "If Tunisia normalized relations with Israel, then the Muslims here might bother Jews. So we would rather Tunisia not have normal relations with Israel." His response is a typical ultra-religious response, whereby Jews have no need of any state or government in order to survive. Nevertheless, Totten turned to the church for a bit more openness to sensitive questions, interviewing Father Macmillan. There are churches in Tunis filled on Sundays by foreigners, though virtually no Christians are left in Tunisia. His take on the Jews of Tunisia: "I don't know the Jewish community here," he said. "There are Tunisian Jewish families who have been here for centuries. Their synagogue is of course protected. It functions, but I think they keep a fairly low profile. There's an amalgam of what is Jewish and what is Israeli. Many Arabs assume that anyone who's Jewish is also Israeli and Zionist, and is oppressing the Palestinians and so on. That doesn't make it easy for somebody who's Jewish to openly be known as Jewish. They are probably a more oppressed minority." [111]

Palestinian hijacking of Tunisia

Many argue that Bourguiba had a hidden agenda in his handling of Tunisian Jews, that his policies were not really aimed at protecting Tunisian Jews but rather pretending to do so and at the same time help push them out to France and Israel. Bourguiba was proud of his Western stance, as well as his peace initiative towards the Israeli-Palestinian situation. He was educated in political science at a Paris University and married a non-Tunisian woman. He spent years in French and Italian prisons, furthering his political education that way. But many key members of the North African Muslim Brotherhood also got their education in prison. Bourguiba was not naïve, at least not in the early years of his leadership. He was pragmatic and he worried about independence and economic development which had to follow. Islamic fundamentalism was not part of his agenda at the time, but Islam certainly was.

He was part of a long list of leaders of colonies demanding independence, struggling through the Cold War era. He was consistent in international handling of Tunisian affairs and was strangely consistent as far as the Palestinian problem was concerned. He made it clear, so Tunisians would not get overly enthusiastic, that Palestine is not "a Tunisian home" and would never be one, thus distancing himself from the Palestinian struggle and people, knowing well where all this was leading Tunisia. He obviously understood the political emotions that would flourish if he were to align himself too closely with the chaos and violence in the Middle East, knowing that that such a rapprochement would automatically bring radical Islam to the Tunisian dining room tables. He was not afraid to be different on this question and was the first and only leader of the Arab world who actually called to recognize Israel. However, he slowly became disillusioned with Israel and the US; foreign aid and new projects were not coming fast enough to Tunisia from the US, and any type of relations with Israel was problematic to say the least. At the same there were increasingly fewer Jews left in Tunisia and his Jewish card was already played. He helped push all the Jews out as requested by Islamic interests. Also, his age was a factor which contributed to him losing control of Tunisia, mainly to more radical Islamic interests.

Letting the PLO (Palestinian Liberation Organization) into Tunisia was probably the biggest mistake Tunisians ever made. It was the only country that was prepared to welcome a terrorist organization who in theory was able to take over a country just by physically being there. Every country in the Middle East knew this risk. They already witnessed what happened in Jordan in 1970, and in Syria and Lebanon. No other country was ready to take a chance again except Tunisia. Tunisians were suddenly confronted with a ship full of many armed PLO soldiers with their guns loaded, shouting death to Israel and the Jews as they came out of the cruise ships which brought them to Tunisia from Lebanon. The PLO was now ready for the good life and stability, which Tunisia was eager to provide. But it did not take long for for the Palestinians to realize that the good foods of "Tunisian cuisine were calming them down."

The reasons behind Tunisian involvement in hosting the terrorist organization were often misunderstood. Why did Tunisia agreed to be a host country? What benefits did they get from welcoming the PLO on their land? These questions cannot easily be answered even today. It was an illogical and dangerous move for any state, and even more so for Tunisia, one of the most moderate "Arab" country at the time. For years, Bourguiba and Ben Ali fought the development of radical Islamic organizations in Tunisia. They were afraid of religious fanaticism throughout their struggle for independence, yet were somehow not afraid of radical Palestinians, which automatically brought with them religious Islamic radicalism. On a psychoanalytical level, the move represented a historical breaking point of Tunisia's relations with the Jewish people. The link between the Jewish people of LCA and the Arab-Israeli conflict was already established years ago, and inviting the PLO into Tunisia was a national symbolic statement in line with decades of Tunisian ethnic cleansing policies.

Bourguiba and Ben Ali underestimated what the Palestinian quest for national identity meant: opening the door to an unknown but very radical route. The most peaceful and moderate Islamic state in the Arab world accepted the temporary entry of an international terrorist organization and were hoping that the damage will be limited. It took Tunisia a few days to understand the magnitude of the error, but by then it was too late. Their only hope was that the damage would be limited. At that time the PLO was considered a terrorist organization by most Western countries. Their short-lived stay in Tunisia is marked as a low point in their power and prestige over Palestinians in the occupied territories and even lower for Tunisians. The thousands of PLO members continued to plot against Israel, attacking Israeli yachtsmen in Cypress in 1985. The PLO could not have imagined that Israelis would retaliate, even in Tunisia, but Israel sent war planes to Tunis to bomb the PLO headquarters in the outskirt of Tunis. Israeli planes flew in low altitude over the Mediterranean covering a distance of 2000km. Sixty PLO members and some local Tunisians were killed in the raid. The PLO continued to do what they do best and this time kidnaped an Italian cruise ship. Israel again wasted no time and sent a commando team to take down Abu Jihad, Arafat's deputy who was responsible for plotting the attacks on Israeli targets. Recently, Tunisian lawyers have been trying to sue the Israeli government for these invasions.

The PLO under Arafat stayed in Tunisia for 12 years, and only in 1994, after his acceptance of Israel's right to exist and his renunciation of terrorism was he allowed to come back to the West Bank. Tunisians, by this time were in a panic mode over the hijacking of their country and the loss of control of its borders, ideologies and universities. They quickly made sure no Palestinians were left behind, but it was too late—the damage was irreparable.

The relationship between the Palestinians and their hosts was tense, as seen in media coverages at that time: "'we do not have a ghetto here,' said a journalist from the PLO press service, Wafa. 'We don't even have a social club. We try to integrate with the population.'"[112] This was exactly what the Tunisians did not want; they generally did not quite understood the Palestinians, their culture and their struggle. In 2011, a Western diplomat said, Tunisian authorities discovered a link between some Palestinians in Tunisia and plans for a bomb attack in Morocco. Here is a quote from the same article in the *New York Times*: "'As a result of that, there was some misunderstanding,' Abu Iyad said in an interview. 'But even during the crisis, they didn't ask us to find an alternative place for our leadership.'"

A Western diplomat was aware that the crisis prompted Tunisian authorities to post a watch list of unwanted Palestinian supporters at the country's tightly controlled airports. In late 1986, the Tunisians—troubled by upheavals among their own people and eager to avert other problems—withdrew the passports that had been granted to some PLO officials and canceled residence permits to others, the diplomat said.[113] Military planning, he indicated, was then switched to Yemen. Many PLO guerrillas are also said to have moved to nearby Algeria, and some are said to have infiltrated back into Lebanon. There are no reliable figures for such a fluid situation, but Western estimates are that as many as 4,000 guerrillas returned to Lebanon, that a few thousand are in Syria, and that there are a thousand or so each in Algeria, Iraq, Yemen and the Sudan. The Israeli air strike, a Western diplomat said, convinced the Tunisians they had "done their duty" towards the Palestinian cause.[114]

In 1993, another Middle Eastern "expert," Yael Dayan (the daughter of Moshe Dayan), went to Tunisia to meet the PLO leadership to find out, according to her own words, if there was one or two PLO organizations: "I wanted to learn for myself whether there were two PLOs, one outside and one inside the territories." She found out after two talks with Arafat and his aids that there is only one organization[115]...how clever! But then this fits perfectly with her father's "amazement" during the Yom Kippur War that "the Arabs were planning this for three years without us knowing about it." (*From recently published documents from the Yom Kippur War*). Underestimating Arab states' power and political abilities had been the hallmark of Israelis to this day.

Already by 1986, Tunisians were showing their discontent with the PLO's presence, and began delaying passport renewals and refused to allow reentry for 45 families who visited other Arab countries and wanted to come back. The situation was fragile, and Arafat at one point threatened not to come back to Tunisia until the government reassessed its position. The PLO tried in vain to argue that its military arm was no longer in Tunis and that only the political headquarters were there.[116]

The precarious situation the PLO found itself in is described by George Joffe in an article in the *Journal of Palestinian Studies*: "There is considerable bitterness—at least in private—in Palestinian circles over the Tunisian attitude. The problem is, however, to decide precisely where the PLO should now go [...] many potential havens are marred by serious disadvantages." Algeria was too distant from the Middle East, and there was the added danger of political interference. Sudan was too far way and too unstable. Jordan was too hostile, as were Libya and Syria, at least to the pro-Arafat PLO faction. Lebanon was too chaotic, and a move there would strongly be resisted by the country's Shi'ite groups, and by Syria and Israel. Egypt suffered from the stigma of Camp David, and in any case, there was the danger of political pressure from the Mubarak government. The choices for the PLO have not really changed. They still have nowhere better to go in the Arab world. The situation in every country that has undergone (or is undergoing) the "Spring Revolutions" deteriorated even further, as neither Jews nor Palestinians have anywhere else to go. Nevertheless, even among Israelis, the assassinations in Tunis drew serious criticism. As Yoel Marcus wrote in *Ha'aretz*: "The Abu Jihad operation may make us feel good, may be good for our egos, but it does not in itself really addresses the weighty problems this country should be struggling with. The killing of Abu Jihad is a symbolic illustration of what is happening to us. It was an operation that made for a nostalgia movie about the good old days of brilliant punitive raids—because it does not advance us one inch towards a solution of the problems that have produced this or that 'Abu...'"[117] This view was not a popular view in Israel at that time.

Suha Arafat (Yasser Arafat's wife), now living in Malta, is under investigation in Tunisia for her financial dealings with the wife of the ousted Tunisian dictator Ben Ali. She is thus not welcome in Tunisia, and going back to Palestinian territories for her was simply out of the question, even during the analysis of her husband's remains by French investigators as to the cause of his death. The future does not look bright, as Tunisia is now becoming a safe haven for terrorists and jihadist activities threatening the little stability left of Tunisian society. Al-Qaida cells were discovered in Tunisia, and Salafists are contributing their share to the overall insecurity felt by every Tunisian. In Bizerte in 2012, students and tourists were attacked in two separate incidents. In both cases the attackers were Salafists. Every Western country has a travel warning posted on their Foreign Affairs websites warning their citizens of the precarious situation and the risks of visiting Tunisia.

Palestinian Suspicion

The Palestinians were not really supportive of the Tunisian revolution, and this was mainly because Tunisians were now in the front line of Arab winds of change. Palestinians were no longer setting the agenda in the Arab world, as was the case since 1948. For decades the Palestinians were the spearhead of the Islamic Arabic world, feeding corrupt rulers who had every interest to continue the violent, dead-end struggles. The Palestinians were not after any comprehensible settlement, and their "all or nothing" approach led to nowhere except to more violence and further loss of land. The Jasmine Revolution laid bare the corruption behind the economic and political systems in the Arab world. The majority of the population, who has been subjugated for years to living in poverty, voted en masse for more of the same, and even more repressive political parties. They voted for more religion in countries where people are already suffering from too much religion. The Jasmine Revolution had made the Palestinian struggle secondary, but it will not remain this way for long. The Islamists in power will make sure the indoctrination will continue and get stronger, as the need for the ideological glue of repression was now greater because much more is now at stake. And the Palestinians are waiting to again play their traditional role in the Arab world.

When events were unfolding in Tunisia during the Spring Revolution, PLO advisor Ahmed Abdel Rahman said that the Executive Committee had not met and therefore had not issued an official statement of support. Still, he extended condolences to the families of Tunisian victims, the official Palestinian Authority news agency WAFA reported.[118] The Palestinians, like everyone else, were not sure what is going on and what their position should be. After all, there were demonstrations in the streets in an Arab country and they were not involved in any way. They were not the centerpiece of the revolution, at least not directly.

Ismail Haniyeh's speech in Tunisia a year after the revolution was an attempt to make a statement so Tunisians do not forget Palestine. His visit to Tunisia was also a reassuring act to support the new Islamic party in power and consolidate its hold on the population, that the Palestinian struggle will not be forgotten, and that the Jews of Tunisia will be forgotten forever. His words were but an attempt to re-hijack Tunisia: "Israel no longer has allies in Egypt and Tunisia; we are saying to the Zionist enemies that times have changed and that the time of the Arab Spring, the time of the revolution, of dignity and of pride has arrived. [...] We promise you that we will not cede a single part of Palestine, we will not cede Jerusalem, we will continue to fight and we will not lay down our arms." He further urged "the people of the revolution to fight the army of Al-Quds," as Jerusalem is known in Arabic. "To Tunisia we say: 'It is us today who are going to build the new Middle East'." He also stressed that "we will not recognize Israel," as the crowd chanted "Death to Israel," "The Tunisian revolution supports Palestine," and "The army of Mohammed is back." Some wiped their feet on the Star of David while others tried to figure out where the Jews of Tunisia were— there were very few Jews left to attack. What was left was the cry of a handful of Jewish residents in Djerba, who still think that Zionism and Judaism are two distinct entities and should be separated.

The Emir of Qatar at a Doucha conference in 2012 stated that Israel is now isolated like never before as a result of the Spring Revolution. He is obviously expressing a personal opinion because the situation in Islamic countries had proven to be lot more complex. The Spring Revolutions forced people to question their politicians and dictators, who can no longer bring the Palestinian conflict to the forefront as the cause of all evil, thereby avoiding the real social issues of corruption and development. His statement was basically a nostalgic expression of how easy it used to be to control local population before the upheavals across the Arab world.

Haniyeh's visit to Tunisia took place immediately after Ennahda party took power. It was a symbolic visit to remind the Tunisian people where the real struggle lies. It was not Abu Mahzen, the official PLO leader, who made the visit, but a leader of Hamas in Gaza who is set on the destruction of Israel and the institution of a strict Islamic, Sharia-based Palestine. Haniyeh's visit was also a psychological comforting act preformed in good company; where else in the world would he get such a warm reception?

Since the Jasmine Revolution, Palestinians were no longer headline news in the Arab and Western worlds. In the grand picture of events the Palestinians became but an important footnote. The corrupt leaders of the Arab world, who for years held the Palestinians as a propaganda card, have been ousted out of Egypt, Tunisian, Libya, Iraq, and soon, likely Syria too. There is no one to wave the Palestinian flag. The Palestinians' job now is to regroup because they too were awed by the social and political upheavals all around them. So in way, Haniyeh's visit to Tunisia was designed to promote their cause once again to a sympathetic radical ruling party and radicalized crowed.

Behind the Silence

On November 4, 1995, Yitzhak Rabin, Israel's Prime Minister, was assassinated, marking another new era in the tumultuous and confusing world of Middle Eastern politics. I was in my car with my family driving from Herzliya to our (overly priced) rented apartment in Tel Aviv when the music on the radio was interrupted to bring us the shady details of the assassination.

A few weeks earlier, I had handed Rabin the latest copy of my yachting magazine. At that time, I organized a massive regatta of yachts of all size sailing from all marinas in Israel to the newly built Marina in Ashkelon to celebrate the opening of this wonderful project of peace, a model for leisurely peacetime activities for all people of the region, if only they would or could participate. The Mediterranean Sea, after all, is not just for fishermen, Tunisian pirates and American and Russian war ships. On reaching Ashkelon marina in full sails with a huge Al Italia banner, in Freda and David's yacht I was told that Rabin and his security entourage had entered the marina. I rushed to shake his hand and to give him a copy of the latest edition of my magazine only to be stopped almost immediately by a circle of security men. From a distance, I saw that he received the magazine, but I never got to shake his hand.

Under Rabin's watch, Israel was under terrible terrorist attacks. Buses, banks, restaurants and beaches were targeted, and a few bombs had exploded too close to me and my family. It was an unbearable life for everyone, everywhere in Israel, including the holy city of Tel Aviv. Palestinian Jihadists had implemented a level of terror never before seen. So, when Rabin and Arafat were finally talking peace, you could feel it in the Mediterranean breeze; in the Middle East tension travels through the air. You could actually measure the level of tension in the region just by breathing. You don't even need to turn on the radio or television; there was no need for internet, Facebook and Twitter and other useless social media. This time, the tension that everyone felt was being transformed into the euphoria of real peace, or at least the end of violence. For a few days, the air in the morning was thick and sweet. It was also a bit scary because it was irrational, almost like a war was about to start. One could not explain what a peace treaty with the Palestinians would look like, yet enthusiasm and optimism infused everyone, whether religious or unreligious, Left and Right. Everybody wanted peace, and the only remaining question was how? Yitzhak Rabin managed to make this happen as this was the only way to radically change things in the region.

It was like stepping into another dimension, literally. Menachem Begin the Prime Minister of Israel and Anwar Sadat the President of Egypt had done this before him in 1979, with the peace treaty between Israel and Egypt after the Yom Kippur war. And, it was happening again. Lawyers in such situations come after and are in the margins of the process, their proper role. It was a powerful situation which made opposition to peace impossible. There was nothing anyone could do to stop the peace train—except assassination, a scenario which happened to Sadat in Egypt and now Rabin in Israel. No politician can replicate this optimism artificially. Hate marches can be planned, as during the Spring and Jasmine revolutions, but the feelings of change and optimism for the future has a way of spontaneously absorbing everyone. With the assassination of Rabin, Israelis and the Palestinians gave the file back to our beloved lawyers to figure out a just solution measured with cash, stone gravel and graveyards.

On the weekend following Rabin's assassination, we organized another sailing regatta in Marina Tel Aviv, only this time each boat put on its main sail a black stripe in remembrance of Rabin, and in remembrance of yet another failed revolution for peace. It was a sad sailing day, and the project I worked on for years, organizing a Peace Regatta from Israel to Malta to Tunisia came to a halt, reminded me once again that planning and forecasting are notoriously difficult concepts in this region.

The story of Israel's social and immigration policies leading to a mass absorption of exiled Jews, refugees, immigrants and Holocaust survivors was a social and political experiment not seen anywhere in human history. Such a massive absorption of people was done at least twice in the short history of Israel. But did it succeed? Absolutely. It succeeded, considering that all Jews of LCA communities completely disappeared as identifiable groups. What the Arabs, the Turks and European interventions, invasions and colonialism in Tunisia could not achieve in 1,400 years, Israel achieved in 65 years.

Zena Herman clearly expressed the Zionist objectives in the early days: "The ultimate aim is the emergence of a well-knit homogeneous national unit."[119] This was exactly the same grand objective in Tunisia under Bourguiba. Israeli nationalism and Arab nationalism were in good company, feeding off of one another's energies and "primitive" religious and nationalist-based ideologies. Bourguiba for years was impressed with Israel's state-building abilities and was determined very early to follow the logic that "if Israel can become a social democratic Jewish state, then there is no reason why Tunisia could not become a social democratic Islamic state." In Israel, it was the Palestinians who prevented this idealistic picture, and in Tunisia it was the Jews of Tunisia. Israel's political and cultural state apparatus was designed as such that no communities of LCA were to retain their ethnic identity and history, including their religious traditions. This was easy to do, considering Israel was surrounded by hostile countries, and the Mediterranean Sea in the west. It was easy to do because Israel is an extremely small country, almost ghetto-like. The influx of Jews from Eastern Europe, North Africa and the Middle East, and later Russian Jews, Ethiopian Jews and recently Sudanese refugees was an adventurous plan concocted by overly imaginative minds, and it succeeded for completely unforeseen reasons. At times, the influx of exiled people surpassed the local Israeli population. Why did anyone in the decision-making hierarchy in Israel think it would work? Did they have any choice? What were the real motives behind all of this? Some party politicians were accused of bringing North Africans because Israel needed cheap labor and soldiers, maybe. When the Russians immigrated to Israel en masse in the 1990s they were accused of trying to "Europeanize" Israel (in terms of skin color) again.

Most Tunisian Jews left for France and other countries. Some 40,000 native indigenous Jewish Tunisians left for Israel in different emigration waves since Israel's independence in 1948. The periods of fleeing Tunisia, as I pointed out, were closely related to the tensions and wars in the region. The years 1948, 1956, 1967 corresponded to wars in the Middle East, and each one also corresponded to further migrations of Jews from Tunisia to Israel, France and other countries. The first wave was in some respects a direct result of the Nazi occupation of Tunisia and the Second World War. The German occupation, together with Arab Tunisian Muslim nationalism, led to this first phase of exile. Very few Tunisian Jews even thought of moving to Palestine pre-WWII. During the 1920s a few young Tunisians went on fact-finding missions to Palestine and returned with terrible stories of hardships, reinforcing their beliefs that Tunisia was their home and that they have nowhere else to go. In fact, very few Tunisian Jews before the war wanted or accepted French passports, even if many of them could obtain one.

Archives show that no more than 10,000 Tunisian Jews held French citizenship since 1887, and of those, most refused to move away from Tunisia. So, Zionism was not the determining factor in their exile, despite the endless and meaningless energy invested in trying to make them move to Israel. Belonging to Tunisian Zionist youth organizations in Tunisia was one thing, but moving to Israel was a different story. Every Middle Eastern war brought with it further radicalization of Islam and of Muslims and of Arabs. This radicalization culminated in a strange show of madness when in 2011, during the "Spring Revolutions," people were marching towards the main synagogue in the city of Tunis, stopping by the main entrance and chanting death to the Jews—but only 1,500 "token" Jews were left in the whole country. How were Tunisian Muslims able to make the connection between their present so-called revolution, getting rid of corrupt dictator, and the anti-Jewish sentiment against their own disappearing indigenous population? The demonstrators went wild when they saw the large Star of David staring at them at the gate of the ancient Synagogue. To them, it seemed, the symbol and the building were recently planted there just to get them upset. You can find pictures and videos from these demonstrations on the internet, and seeing them broadcasted on the news brought sadness and even tears to Tunisian Jews everywhere. For some unexplainable reasons, they were expecting a higher level of human conduct from Tunisians. They expected from Tunisia what they once hoped to expect from Israel, respect and acknowledgment of their distinct history in North Africa and Europe. Instead, Tunisia was proving to be no different from any of the other Muslim countries of North Africa and the Middle East. The perceived fundamental differences in politics and history, between them and the rest of the Arab world, have largely evaporated during the two years since the revolution. Many Tunisian Jews living in exile today continue to be naïve and refuse to acknowledge that Tunisia is now a totally different country and that they have stopped having a part in its history or in its politics. Tunisian Jews in exile cannot believe that for Tunisians they do not exist, and for Islamists they were never there to begin with. Soon, no one will remember who they were as a people—the new generation has moved on.

The head of the Islamic party that took power after the Tunisian revolution came out with a statement that Jews are welcomed to come back to Tunisia. Was it a sub-conscious reaction or political maneuvering? There was also a response from another "enlightened" politician in Israel. Israel's vice-Prime Minister Silvan Shalom, who happens to be a Tunisian-born Israeli, was calling the remaining Jews in Tunisia to come to Israel, to make *Aliyah*. The headmaster of a synagogue in Tunisia replied in public that they as a small community have no interest in moving to Israel, that Tunisia is their home. He added that he is not afraid to remain there in Tunisia. Muslim leaders backed by mobs and the Deputy Prime Minister of Israel, all wanted a Tunisia without Jews. This politician was not content with the present situation and wanted to complete the process of achieving zero Jews in Tunisia, as in Egypt, Iraq and other countries. This obviously does not make any sense as we can explain and somehow understand the Islamic Arabic reaction, but it is difficult to digest the view of this Israeli Tunisian politician, only a few decades after the Grand Exile. In 2013 the tiny Jewish community in Tunisia was invited to take part in the current Tunisian parliament. Incredibly, they turned this offer down, on the grounds that Tunisian Jews can be represented by qualified people of any faith and that state representatives should not be elected based on their religion. Yamina Thabet, the leader of Tunisian Association for the Support of Minorities agreed, but went a step further on her Facebook page, calling to "criminalize all forms of discrimination, stop protesters who call for the murder of Jews, stop imams who call for the torture of non-Muslims, and non-Muslims should be allowed to serve as president." Roland Sa'ada, a member of the community stated: "I am a Tunisian like any other Tunisian, and I want a parliament where people are elected based on their qualifications to serve the people and not on their religious confessions. I might be Jewish, but I know many Muslims who could represent my ideas in parliament who I would vote for."[120]

A similar story is unfolding in Ethiopia, as Jews there were brought to Israel en masse under the pretext of saving this Eastern African Jewish people. It did not matter that historically the Falasha Jews have never considered Israel to be the Promised Land. But Israelis and the Jewish Agency made it their business, influencing their decision to stay or be lifted out in order to prove to the world how open the Zionist movement is—hardly a reason to eliminate the Jewish population from Ethiopia, one of the last Jewish populations in Africa.

Tunisian Jews were living as a community for thousands of years, and it was not the business of an Islamic ruling party to move them or even think about pushing them out. Tunisian Jews preceded Islam and they have as much right to remain and live in peace in their native country as its native people and Berber population. Islamists have no more right to live in Tunisia than the handful of Jews who still remain there, or any other Tunisian Jew living elsewhere. In fact Tunisia does not belong to Islam or to Muslims or to Arabs. It belongs to Tunisians, all of whom were not Muslims to begin with. The building of a homogenous society was never part of its history, even during its peak Islamic periods; its diversity was its strength. In fact, any glory Islam professes to have had in its history is necessarily due to the roles minorities and locals played, especially the Jews and the Berbers. Acknowledging this in itself might even help us have a better grasp of Middle Eastern and Northen African conflicts. Almost every country in the Middle East and North Africa was going through similar processes of Islamic nationalism and ethnic cleansing. Opening the books and re-educating Israelis and Tunisians on the history of Jews of LCA will also help us understand the Palestinian situation, the Palestinians' miserable status as citizens, individuals and as a people in and outside of Israel. It's all one subject, one history, and both Israelis and Palestinians have to learn all of this—it has nothing to do with ethnicity; rather, it's all political.

The first wave of Tunisians Jews exiling from their country took place in 1948-1953. Still under the traumatic experience of a massive Nazi brutal occupation which completely destroyed their traditional links and relations, Jews started packing.

News of the creation of the State of Israel was all over the front pages of national and local newspapers and on the airwaves in Tunisia. The media at that time did not miss a chance to remind everyone where the real crisis is, pointing to the faith of the Palestinians in the Middle East and setting the political tone in the subsequent years. By 1956, the year of independence for Tunisia and the war between the Arab world and Israel, Jews packed even less belongings and hurried out before it was too late, to their life in exile. In 1961 France decided to continue its naval presence in Bizerte, leading to a full-blown crisis and a state of war, which eventually affected the Jews of Tunisia. France attacked the port by sending paratroopers and war ships. Tunisian Arabs again targeted the Jews, burning their factories and shops, including the famous Boukah Bokobsa (Jewish Fig Vodka) production plant. By 1967, after the Six-Day War, everyone had left Tunisia. No one stayed behind. These were impossible times for the people who endured every possible colonial/invasion combination imaginable. Hassan, the King of Morocco, said just before independence that Morocco had it really hard because they did not have just one (French) colonial power to worry about but two, the Spanish and French. The Jews of North Africa can also add an even greater colonial tragedy, that of Arab nationalism and the rise of radical Islam. The Jews of Tunisia also had the German occupation in their collective memory, knowing perfectly well that they had barely escaped the fate of their brothers in Europe.

For Tunisian Jews the story of survival continued once in exile in Israel, France and elsewhere. They were scattered all over Israel in small communities from the far north, to the Sinai desert in the south. They were to form an instant forced and artificial working class to be settled along Israeli borders, north and south, replacing the local Palestinian population. For years public buses were always full of these North African travelers searching for contacts, news from relatives and friends, thirsty for continued cultural exchange. Until late 1970s most did not have phones to communicate, so they travelled, the young and the very old, stayed in other people's modest homes for a day or two and returned back to their own homes recharged and ready for another challenging day of discrimination and hardship. This practice was common among Tunisian Jews and probably with other communities as well. (The search for friends and identity continues today using the internet, increasingly less, as fewer and fewer people are around to visit.) They needed reinforcement from each other. They needed to figure out how to survive in this new environment where they were just another strange, primitive and misunderstood ethnic group stripped of their traditional sources of livelihood, relying on the State and party affiliations for support and survival.

During the early days of exile, the younger generation had a totally different story to tell, as they were trying to bridge between the new cultural and political order, and their parents—a near impossible task. Indeed, many failed and ended up in Israeli jails. At one point, more than 90 percent of all Israeli inmates were Jews from North Africa and the Middle East, along with local Palestinian youth. The situation is not much different today. This state of affairs was unheard of in their country of origin and rare among Jews who did not move to Israel. It is interesting to note that France is now undergoing a similar trend with Muslims from the Maghreb crowding its jails.[121]

In the early days, Israel was in an impossible social, cultural and political situation. The State was controlled by Eastern European Jews who saw the world through a colonial lens disguised as Zionist ideology. They were the founders of the State and its ideology, and thus developed a whole culture in order to maintain their superiority. There were no major differences between how European colonists viewed Africans, for example, and the Israeli ruling class in desperate need of a ready-made working class. Better still, they needed Jewish people who physically and naturally fit the region in order to justify their land holdings and their Zionist dream. The young were entrusted with an impossible role not knowing the cultures of their ancestors and not taking part in the newly imposed, corrupt and unfamiliar culture. Most were not permitted from a very early age to speak their native Arabic in its various dialects, nor could they continue to hold their native traditional customs, which were very Jewish and very ancient. At the same time they could not enter new society as equal players anywhere, nor in any capacity. Their entrusted role was doomed. Preying on this fragile situation and profiting from it all were the Jewish equivalents of the Muslim Brotherhood, the various extreme religious organizations and religious political parties, and, of course, the various Zionist political parties, both Left and Right.

The interchange among all ethnic groups in the early days turned Israel into the most pluralistic and colorful country on the planet. But not everyone was able to appreciate this amazing diversity, and finding individuals who did was a constant but rewarding challenge to anyone living in Israel at the time. This is the Israel some of us wish to remember. There are many examples of these colorful ethnic situations, from the people who manned the heavily fortified bunkers along the Suez Canal during the war of attrition in 1970, to the curiosity surrounding the country of origin of sailors on board the Israeli Dakar submarine, which disappeared in 1968. There were 68 soldiers

Silencing The Past:

on board, who were born in 20 different countries. There was one Tunisian-born sailor, as well as Moroccan, Turkish, Egyptian and Yemenite Jews, and others from Eastern Europe and Israel itself. The Tunisian Boujnach family, like many others, was devastated by the loss of their son, and their leadership role within the Tunisian community in Israel collapsed overnight affecting the community as whole. This colorful, multi-cultural situation lasted only for a short period of time. With the older generation heartbroken and gradually dying, nothing from the past remained, and nothing was there to replace it, except distorted religion, nationalism, violence and more wars. The creation of a homogenous society was now a fait accompli in both Israel and Tunisia.

By the time Jews of LCA understood that the political and economic game in Israel was rigged against them, it was too late—the wealth and employment were already distributed and the Jews of LCA were increasingly marginalized, rarely considered or mentioned. This population was unarmed against the injustice, crime, inequality and total disrespect of Israeli mainstream ideology, both Left and Right. They quickly understood that behind the façade of Zionist ideology, there was very little culture, tolerance, understanding, or even Jewish history. It all started and ended with "never again" and the (East European) "Jewish homeland" mentality presuming to be the only answer to the "Jewish Question." People who managed to survive and at times flourish for thousands of years in Middle East and African countries now found themselves having no role in shaping the political character of their new home of Israel. In essence they were all "ethnic footnotes" in Israel's internal and external politics. It did not matter that they made up more than 50 percent of Israel's population. They were divided, cleaned and stripped of any remnant of meaningful political existence. Their history did not matter and never even existed prior to their arrival, neither in State history books, nor in the Jewish experience everywhere.

This is why the introduction of these issues in 2012 caught everyone (both Jews and Muslims) by surprise, and most had no idea how to deal with this new information. In the early days of Zionism, many, including prominent politicians such as Golda Meir, could not comprehend the fluid ethnic situation and were continuously asking, "why are they (North Africans) so ungrateful"? The political elite pretended, like the colonialists, that they were emancipating and re-educating this secondary Jewish population. Imagine the horror this had on the order of things when the Jewish Eastern European population in Israel was strongly made to believe (as many do even today) in their cultural and political superiority; this just a few years after the Holocaust, when the real Wretched of the Earth were not Africans but Europeans refugees, Holocaust survivors and displaced people. Imagine the humiliating situation and the irony whereby the ideologically driven peasants in the Kibbutzim were employed to "educate" North Africans and Yemenite Jews in transit camps. What could they possibly teach them? I'm convinced that the "educating" should have been the other way around. There was so much they could have learned from these ancient Jewish people of Yemen, Iraq and North Africa.

Ancient Jewish civilizations were reduced to being called Sephardim, meaning Spaniards, or Spanish Jews (in exile), Orientals or even "Arab" Jews, and other useless terms. Not all North African Jews were of Spanish descent, and Middle East Jews had no direct connection to Spain. They were North Africans, Berbers. There were of Portuguese, Spanish,

Italian, Greek and Turkish origin. None of them was Arab in identity. Yet, anyone whose skin color was not white was called Sephardic or Mizrahi (Easterner, Oriental) and was instantly in need of emancipation (Jewish submission) and a socialist party membership card. This over-simplification still holds today as well. Every political party or political movement continues to search for the token dark-skinned individual to ease their guilt and their conscious—and get more votes in the process. The need for simplification of complex realities was nothing more than a powerful control mechanism implemented by the elites in power. The colonialists used it for hundreds of years to control the indigenous populations in Africa and the Americas, and the Israeli establishment has done it for the same reasons. Indeed, even the Palestinians in this story were not at the bottom of the social hierarchy—the Jews of LCA were. The Palestinians had built their identity and demanded rights and recognition within a specific territory, something that North African and Middle Eastern Jews could not have possibly done or gotten away with unless they were prepared to use same tactics which was violence and more violence.

But it all began years ago in North Africa, in Tunisia and other countries. Ideologically driven Eastern European Zionist missionaries from different political parties (Shlichim) really believed that their mission was to save and educate the Jews of North Africa. They were often close-knit socialist party members and held full-time positions. It is strange to consider now, as though societies that had lasted for 3,000 years and survived more than a handful of violent foreign invasions of Europeans and Arabs really needed their help. Tunisian Jews at that point had to deal not only with the Turkish Bey, the French colonialists, Arab Nationalists, Muslim radicals, and later the Italian Fascists and Germans Nazis, but also with the Shlichim and other shady Jewish religious organizations whose job was to indoctrinate the local population through foreign education, foreign cultural activities and pseudo-religious teachings. Indeed, their Judaism and political philosophy was completely foreign to Tunisians Jews. This one-way indoctrination of course continued in Israel, assuring that no traces of these ancient communities survive.

Overall, North African Jews were put under immense pressure from the three great and opposing forces of Islamism, Zionism and European colonialism. Each for its own purpose and grand design wanted the same outcome. The Islamist nationalists and religious organizations in Tunisia wanted the Jews out, while the Zionists jumped on the occasion to push their plan further, justifying it with all kinds of outdated nineteenth-century colonial ideological arguments. They needed soldiers and workers, and they needed them young (Selection). Most importantly, however, they needed solid historical and political justification for the control of Palestinian lands, and without the Jews of LCA, Israel may not have had a chance for survival. Obviously, the political elite could not possibly admit this, and the result was a complete reliance on modern technology and weapon systems to insure that another Holocaust will not happen again. They also relied on the rigid ideology of Eastern European Zionism. The colonial forces were also interested in having the Jews out of Tunisia so they could better control and exploit the colonies and its peoples.

And so, North African Jews ended up in Israel not as equal partners in the building of the country but as an oppressed and discriminated against group, literally building the country, but receiving no political credit at all. It is important to understand that the most difficult part of their journey and life in Israel was not due to the economic hardship or the security situation. They could have dealt with these realities, as most were used to harsh and complex living and business conditions in their countries of origin. The hardest part was the deafening silence by the State and by all political parties, Left and Right, in recognizing their ancient unique history, culture, and politics. They did not exist as people nor did they exist as individuals or as family units, and especially not as political entities. The combination of nationalism and socialism was for North African Jews not an appealing situation, neither in Israel, nor in Tunisia. Homogenous Eastern-European communist Zionism was also unattractive on many levels, and was in fact part of the shock treatment they received. The Kibbutzim did not want them in, nor did they really want in. They felt the same with Bourguiba's new cooperatives, which later incidentally destroyed Tunisia's economy. The complete reliance on the State for their livelihood was a foreign concept to them. It was these vulnerabilities, exploited by all political parties, the political elite, and especially by strange North African religious movements which sprung up like mushrooms in Israel after independence—these became their only acceptable political expressions.

Their political situation has not changed. It cannot change without the full recognition of their unique history as it unfolded. Integration and the melting pot processes will also not resolve any of the existing conflicts, especially not the Israeli-Palestinian one.

It is no wonder that the Left and Liberal forces in Israel and abroad could easily relate to the Palestinian cause, but have a difficult time relating to the Jews of LCA. Militant Jews everywhere would join hands in exposing Israel's apartheid, discrimination and occupation towards the Palestinians, almost completely ignoring the complex fabric of injustices in play which affected Israel, North Africa and the Middle East, determining the region's future and future levels of violence. These same groups will point to the right-wing tendencies of Jews of Arab lands in Israel, a claim which is totally unfounded; I would even argue that the opposite is true. The total disappearance of worlds of these indigenous cultures somehow escaped their attention. The wiping out of Jewish populations from Arab lands had no place in their interpretation of the current conflict in the Middle East. But from my perspective, it is impossible to understand the Palestinian issue without understanding what happened to the Jews of LCA. Their stories are interconnected in history and politics and in language and in religion, and this story must be told in order for productive dialog to emerge.

Here is an excerpt of a 1949 article published without shame in *Ha'aretz*, by Aryeh Gelblum, which gives a glimpse into the existing worldview Jews of LCA had to confront in the early days of Israeli independence: "This is the immigration of a race we have not yet known in the country. We are dealing with people whose primitivism is at a peak, whose level of knowledge is one of virtually absolute ignorance and, worse, who have little talent for understanding anything intellectual. Generally, they are only slightly better than the general level of the Arabs, Negroes, and Berbers in the same regions. In any case, they are at an even lower level than what we know with regard to the former Arabs of Israel. These Jews also lack roots in Judaism, as they are totally subordinated to savage and primitive instincts. As with Africans you will find among them gambling, drunkenness, and prostitution [...] chronic laziness and hatred for work; there is nothing safe about this asocial element. [Even] the kibbutzim will not hear of their absorption." Similar articles, also without shame, were published in the same newspaper in 1983 by Dankner, and in other newspapers as well. These kinds of racist articles are somehow absent today because the subject has been totally suppressed, silenced for the sake of political correctness, which explains in part the massive vote for Yair Lapid's party, as well as the specific character of the current coalition government, which only has four members of Middle East or North African origin.

The Tunisian Jewish community in Israel is not an identifiable ethnic group, not anymore. Israel's melting pot proved to be exactly that. Today this concept has transformed itself into a pressure cooker. Years of silence on the most important political issue have resulted in unimaginable violence and hardship in the Middle East for Jews and Muslims alike, for Israelis as well as Palestinians. What was left of the Tunisian community and all other communities of Jews of LCA was the color of their skin, an unknown and never told history and much silence from all directions. For both known and unknown reasons no one seems to be interested in our story, including young Jewish Israelis.

The Jewish population of Tunisia had no choice but to embrace in part the French and its political and economic culture in order to survive the Bey, the Sultan of Tunisia and later even Zionism. The French Protectorate did not serve them well but it served them better than the dark Islamic laws and rules under the corrupt Turkish Sultan and later corrupt Islamic nationalism. France was exporting colonialism to the rest of their subjects in the empire in the late nineteenth century, packaging it as "Liberté, égalité, fraternité," an added presumed security belt for the Jews of Tunisia. The French, along with Italy and to a lesser degree the English, promised another layer of political and social protection for minorities, among them the fragile Tunisian Jewish population. Tunisia to this day has kept this French protectorate heritage in trade, industry, science and culture. France is still the country's most important trading partner. So, anti-colonialism in Tunisia paved the way to eliminating the Jews and all other minorities in order for Tunisia to become an all Muslim-Arab society. Colonialism was about exploitation, and anti-colonialism was about turning Tunisia into a pure Islamic state. Colonialism was not about modernization nor was it about education. Every policy and agreement (written or oral) was designed in order to maintain the present and future exploitative system of resources, material and human. Nothing else mattered and Tunisia in this world economic reality was no different—olives, dates and phosphates are still the main exported products. The Sultan knew what the Europeans wanted, and he had no choice but to go along with their scheme of specific type of colonization in the form of a protectorate, as long as his personal riches were kept to an acceptable level. The colonialists calculated the price they had to pay to colonize Tunisia without war and excessive violence, with the blessing of the Sultan who was well taken care of in this process. His role continued unhindered, to operate his bureaucracy, government and mosques in order to prevent upheavals and unrest by the local population, enabling a peaceful takeover, towards a protectorate. The Bey was working for the French and was allowed to remain in power until independence in 1956. Thus, history has tricked them all in Tunisia. The Jew's reliance on the French for moral, legal and cultural salvation was also what brought them to their knees, out of Tunisia and off the world maps forever. Anti-colonialism "en bloc" was based on opposition against anything which was not Arab and Muslim. It did not matter that most of Tunisian Jews did not speak French nor adopted its culture. This, for the Islamic nationalists, was a golden opportunity to purify and cleansed Tunisia of its Jews. History has tricked them all again in Israel and in France where they simply disappeared, not to be counted or even remembered.

The majority of Tunisian Jews who came to Israel were not religious. They had their own customs and traditions developed over many centuries. Religion played an even smaller role in their social organization in Israel, summed up by a weekly visit to a synagogue and partial celebrations of the various Jewish holidays. Religious fanaticism came much later when religious leaders exploited their precarious social and political situation. Religious fanaticism was mostly borrowed from the Eastern European traditions, but some of it also from Islamic traditions. Most, if not all Tunisian Jews were neither part of the Zionist dream in Israel or elsewhere, nor part of Tunisian Islamist nationalism and anti-colonialism. They were politically doomed to be in this disadvantaged position, manipulated by three powerful historical movements. Jews of other LCA countries were confronting similar forces with different colonial powers.

Israel's main daily newspaper *Yedioth Ahronoth* published an article in 2012 on the sorry state of the Arabic language among Israeli students, exposing another great irony of the silence surrounding this issue. Tomer Velner writes that this is a real crisis, and even identifies it as Israel's "Achilles's Heel" from a national security perspective. Half of the population in Israel originated from Arabic-speaking countries, yet all of them were forced to abandon their language in favor of Hebrew at a very early age. For decades, people were ashamed to speak Arabic, and Jewish schools certainly did not teach it. Sixty-five years later, Arabic has to be learned as a foreign language. Matriculation exams are held for 170,000 students, and only a few thousand apply for Arabic as a language of choice. The government had been pushing Arabic as an elective language with the stated official objectives of learning the customs and culture of the Arab population in Israel. The customs and language of half of Israel's population were completely ignored. Dr. Basilious Bouardi, the head of one of Israeli college's, stated that it is absurd that Arabic is taught as the language of the "enemy." He continued, saying that "Reality in the region will change the minute a new generation of Israelis will start speaking Arabic." Apparently, very few of Arabic teachers speak Arabic as a mother tongue. The teaching of Arabic in most schools was done in Hebrew using outdate textbooks and teaching methods. I will conclude this sad section by mentioning again that this situation is completely incomprehensible considering that half of Israeli population used to be not just fluent in Arabic, but spoke it as a mother tongue. Conversely, the Hebrew language was for centuries also part of the Muslim world, was used by millions and influenced local dialects everywhere in North Africa and the Middle East.

Tunisian Jews in Israel gradually lost every link they ever had to their homeland and anything Tunisian. The popularity of North African religious and political organizations in Israel had more to do with the unfavorable conditions in Israel than with how they were organized in their country of origin. But then, these organizations tried at least to cater to this disadvantaged segments of the population, something the Eastern European Left and Right, and especially the Labor Party in Israel were incapable of doing. Most Tunisian Jews in Israel lived on the margins of Israel's political life. They kept to themselves in silence and expressed their political discontent passively on voting day, waiting for their children to recount their story—not knowing that it was really too late.

The total misunderstanding of the history of Jews of LCA continues to this day; nothing has changed in this respect. Jonathan Kaplan, the director of Rothberg International School at the Hebrew University of Jerusalem, wrote an article in 2012[122] which sums up this distortion in line with the accepted but erroneous interpretation of history. "The 'culture shock' for immigrants from developing countries was of particular significance, [...] the shock and disorientation that the new immigrants from developing countries faced upon arriving in Israel. These people came from pre-industrial societies [from] large and extended families. [...] Israel, on the other hand, was a modern, industrial society." As in Tunisia, Israeli intellectuals are as scared and as lazy. It does not matter that this was absolutely not true in the 1950s. Israel was not a modern state at that time, nor was it an industrial state. The two states (Israel and Tunisia) were not at all comparable. The living conditions, as well as the standard of living in Tunisia, could not be compared with those in Israel, not in the 1950s, and not in the previous centuries. Kaplan was probably comparing the living conditions of people in the Tunisian Hara (Jewish Ghetto) with the living conditions of Israel's aristocracy. How was Israel a modern state in 1950? Kaplan obviously does not elaborate on this statement. In Israel, the extended family of Jews from LCA was replaced with a variety of Eastern European youth organizations, boarding schools and Yeshivas (religious seminaries) making the country a haven for child abusers, national and international criminals and pseudo-intellectuals in almost every field. Israel's social fabric at the time had nothing meaningful to replace the traditional family and the economic set-up which Tunisian Jews had brought with them.

When Yaruzalomsky Yerushalmi was sent to Tunisia in 1938 as a missionary by the Jewish National Fund, he pleaded to remain in Tunisia as long as he possibly could. He was well guarded and fed by the Jewish community. Yerushalmi, an unemployed Russian pretending to be a journalist after writing a few articles for *HaTzofe* newspaper in Israel, was sent to Tunisia in order, among other things, to teach Hebrew to the most ancient Hebrew community on the planet. It was a comical situation, and Mr. Kaplan should read a Tunisian perspective of his stay in Tunisia. Mr. Yerushalmi quickly found out that he was the one in need of emancipation and re-education. He could not understand their biblical Hebrew, nor could he understand their many languages—Berber, Jewish Berber, Arabic, French and Italian—needed in order to operate efficiently within the Tunisian Jewish community at the time. During the 1920s, Zionist propaganda material was sent to Tunisia only in Yiddish and in German. His inability to comprehend and integrate led him to do the only thing he could, which was spreading crude Zionism to justify his monthly salary transferred to his family in Jerusalem. He stayed there for seven years, and kept refusing to come back to Israel, even when he was relieved of his post. Unsurprisingly, he was unable to convince anyone to leave for Israel. He was living in a dream world in comparison with the living conditions in Israel or Eastern Europe which were suffering from a deep economic depression. Others quickly deciphered this man's character and his "primitive" ideological intentions. He even kept begging Jewish organizations in Israel to send him back to Tunisia, even after his return to Israel in 1945.[123] Ethnic and party affiliation has since continued to be a determining factor in selecting foreign representatives in the decades following the Independence of Israel. Some of the Israeli foreign representatives sent to France and Belgium in the late 1980s could not even speak a word of French.

The sources I consulted and the people I interviewed all point to the simple truth that Zionist activities in Tunisia, from the beginning of the twentieth century until WWII, were seen as a charity enterprise, much like today and similar to how Tunisians viewed the Jewish community in Jerusalem over the centuries. In the 1930s, Tunisia had some 22 different Zionist organizations operating in the country, and seven newspapers in Hebrew and Jewish Berber. The community did not change its centuries-old perception of who they were as a people and on what territory.

It may help to remind Mr. Kaplan that many of the Tunisian Jews coming to Israel were not just part of the ancient peoples of North Africa, the Berbers, but also part of the Livorno Jews who centralized trade and commerce in the Mediterranean and also linked Europe to Asia; these were the same Spanish and Portuguese Jews who in in the fifteenth century were welcomed to settle in Livorno to enhance the port activities under the Medicis and were known as the *nazione ebrea*. Trade between Livorno and Tunisia continued well into the nineteenth century. Does he even know how important this community was in facilitating trade in Western Europe and within the Ottoman Empire? Unfortunately Kaplan's distorted views are also mainstream views held by most Israelis, as well as by most Jews in the Western world.

The shock Tunisian Jews received once they reached Israel was exactly the opposite of the accepted narrative held by Israelis today and in the past. They were shocked to find a backward society—culturally, economically and morally. Every Tunisian still alive will be able to describe this shock they experienced by the level of discrimination unjustly imposed on them, and the corrupt distribution of wealth. They were shocked to find out that they had no friends in the system, and to find a bureaucracy which was in a sense far worse than the bureaucracy of the Bey and the French protectorate combined. And they were shocked when they could not practice their professions and had to rely on a centralized government bureaucracy for work, food, education and medical assistance. Above all, they were shocked to find out that they were building a new Jewish super ghetto in the Middle East. This was not what they had in mind. Furthermore, Jews of LCA were not immigrants; as Kaplan writes, they were not even refugees as some want us to believe today. They were forced out of their country and moved on, refusing to become refugees. There is plenty of evidence that Tunisian Jews did not see Israel as an alternative home country prior to WWII. Kaplan's article is scandalously wrong on so many levels, and the fact that it was written in 2012 demonstrates that nothing has really changed. Our children continue to absorb such one-sided stories of a complex reality. Once again, silence has been replaced by unapologetic distortions.

The Open Files

"Naiveté is often an excuse for those who exercise power. For those upon whom that power is exercised, naiveté is always a mistake." – Michel-Rolph Troullot

My objective when I started to write this book was modest, dealing mainly with Tunisia and the Jews of Tunisia. But like many projects, the direction I ended taking changed considerably in the process. I called my North African Israeli friends and presented them with some of my findings, only to find out that they were all aware of what was going on in Israel at that time. One Moroccan friend who knew I was writing a book asked me, "why do you think we want to know what happened?" His reaction has made a powerful impression on me, and it kept surfacing in my mind throughout the rest of my work. Some really preferred silence over investigations. I called my Eastern European Israeli friends, and they were so shocked that, like me, they spent weeks deeply disturbed, not knowing how to make sense of it all. I spent months researching every publication, videos, books and articles I could find, because frankly I could not believe what I was learning. My immediate reaction, like every "patriotic" Israeli, was to think that these were hoaxes invented by anti-Israel elements which exist in every corner of the internet. I ended up using only my conclusions and lessons instead of presenting facts to convince the reader of the open files. The following two pages are but a summary of my findings. I can only add that something went terribly wrong in the early days of the Israeli State.

Unfortunately, it is impossible to talk about Israel and North African Jews in Israel without opening deep wounds dating back to the early days of Israel's existence, days almost no one from North Africa and the Middle East wants to remember. In contrast, we have Avraham Burg (son of German-born Jewish Knesset Member Yosef Burg) who recently announced[124] that he longs for the 1950s, claiming, "it was an age of dreamers and builders who sought to create a new world, one without prejudice, racism or discrimination." Was he referring to Israel? Does he know who the Health Minister was when tens of thousands of North African children were kidnapped from schools and from the streets, and illegally irradiated under Dr. Scheiber (Sheba), as "treatment" against nonexistent Ringworm?

I'm absolutely certain that Dr. Sheba (many North African Israelis call him the Jewish Joseph Mengele, and not because they are both the same age and went to the same schools system, in Vienna and Frankfurt, respectfully)[125] and his collaborators did not read anything in French written by the Tunisian-French Doctor Charles Nicolle, who received a Nobel Peace Prize in Medicine (1928) for his contributions in fighting infectious diseases. I'm also certain that they did not read any medical journals in English coming out of the US in late 1940s and which dealt with treatments of Ringworm without x-rays (for example, Stephan Rothman in *Science Newsletter*, September 1946). Furthermore, no one ever talked of x-ray treatments as preventive medicine for all babies and children. Above all, they did not consult our grandmothers. No one from this era was held responsible for these crimes (not negligence) committed against North African Jews. No one to this day knows what on earth happened, to whom exactly, nor why.

Like the Palestinians, most if not all North African and Middle Eastern Jews view this era as a terrible nightmare. They were betrayed again, this time not by their Muslim brothers, but by their Jewish brothers. Even the Conception theory leading to the catastrophic Yom Kippur War is embedded in this betrayal. The wounds from the 1950s are still open, reminding us of the Missing Children[126] (Yemenite, Tunisian, Libyan, Moroccan and others) and the Ringworm Children[127], which involved many North African Jews, including Tunisians.[128] These affairs were dealt with not as national political or ideological problems, but as ethnic problems, medical and social mistakes which happened a long time ago in a country under serious economic crisis, the result of mass absorption of "uneducated and poor Jews" from LCA. The people responsible were never charged or accused, and some even had streets and hospitals named after them. Others—like Karl Frankenstein (yes, this is his real name) who was, a German-Jewish "educator"[129] with an extremely racist ideology—were upheld as contributors to Israel's social development, winning academic and literary prizes. In 1968, "Dr." Sheba was awarded the Israel Prize in Medicine, even though more people were injured from his criminal conduct than in all of Israel's wars combined throughout its history.

In 1998 Ehud Barak, Chairman of the Labor Party and later Prime Minister, published a letter asking for "forgiveness" for what the "Labor Party had done to them" during the 1950s. It was a good start. Nevertheless, too many files are still open and no one dares to look inside. Everyone is waiting for the issues to die or to go away by themselves; the Palestinian problem is also viewed in a similar way.

Jews of LCA were extremely naïve and totally divided, but in the absence of friends, they adopted silence as a tactic. Their quest for answers as to what happened to them during the early days of Israel was never transformed into any meaningful political expression.

The Search For Arab Jews

Edward Said was a leading intellectual of the Arab world pushing for Palestinian rights and using the theory of Orientalism to diminish Western influence and untangle the

Islamic ideological deadlock. He viewed himself as a Christian Palestinian who grew up in Egypt and lived in the US during the height of a Palestinian violent phase. He hoped to replace pan-Arabism and non-alignment ideologies with his own scientific "unified theory of everything," Orientalism. He couldn't live under or agree with pan-Arabism which was the ideology adopted by Nasser in Egypt, Bourguiba in Tunisia and other leaders in the Arab world. This direction was "too Arab," so he needed something else to enhance Palestinian demands, making them universal at least as far the region is concerned. In fact, he had the same existential problem that every non-European Jew in the region had at the time. He could not be Arab or an Islamist, which was a mainstream ideology, so Orientalism was a perfect concept, used also by Israelis labeling the Sephardim Jews as Mizrachi or Arab Jews, Orientals. This concept, while full of contradictions, had no foot hold anywhere, neither among the Palestinians nor among Israeli Jews. Said's quest for a non-Islamist "unified theory of everything" in the Arab-Israeli conflict has led to an absurd and reinvented theory of Jewish and Arab history and ultimately, a unifying theory of nothing.

According to Said, the Jews immigrated to Israel from LCA of their own free will[130] forgetting that he, too, was part of the process of Arab-Islamic ethnic cleansing. Jews of LCA did not decide one day to forget their language and culture and leave behind friends and family, their properties and houses and just move to another small alien world to start all over again. According to Said, people immigrated to the Americas, Israel and France from Tunisia, Algeria, Morocco and Egypt. Said, and those who adopted his theory in Israeli universities, point to the failed melting pot and to the Black Panthers in Israel as signs of the failure of Zionism, ignoring completely the failure of

Islamism. He spoke of Orientalism and loved to mention Israel as a case in point for his adopted ideology where millions of *Mizrachis* ("Orientals" in Hebrew) live. Said sees a real common front between the Palestinians and the margins of Israeli society, the Orientals. This was a naive attempt because it is historically false and also useless in terms of the harsh realities on the ground. The Jews of North Africa did not immigrate to Israel; they were forced to leave their homelands. The rights of Christians and Jews and other minorities were not part of the Islamic revolution. According to Said's philosophy, "the Jewish immigrants from Arab countries were de-Arabized upon arrival in order to fit the Zionist dream," but he glosses over the historical fact that they were never Arabized in the first place, not even after 1,400 years of Arab colonialism and submission.

We also have Noam Chomsky, who became a leading Leftist expert on the Jewish people, and like many he completely avoids the issue of North African and Middle Eastern Jews, without which it is impossible to understand the Middle East and Israeli politics of conflicts and history. Exposing this story will necessarily reveal the half-truths or rather distortions in Chomsky's political thesis on Israel, the Palestinians and the region as a whole. Chomsky is a popular speaker in Arab circles exactly because he brings to the table only half of the story, the same half that Arabs like to hear again and again. No one, it seems, can handle the full story of Israel and its people.

English universities love to glorify the Orient and its tolerance towards Jews over the centuries. Here is an example of an essay requirement for a university course that states, "In political and scholarly debates, in literature and the arts, the 'Orient' was depicted, for centuries, as a place where Jews were said to be at home." That the Islamic world was a good place for

Jews to live had become an acceptable narrative, an indication of the glory of the Orient and Islam. The Arab world was delighted with Said's theory that we do have Arab Jews, that indeed they too suffered under Zionism, that Jews and Arabs lived happily for centuries and that peace with the Palestinians is possible after all. This is why Said concentrated on the history of the twentieth century; the other 13 centuries were not counted because they would have undermined the foundations of his Orientalist theory. However, the full story can only be revealed when we realize that the Arabs invaded North Africa and subjugated the local population, the Berber and the Jews into submission, as they have done everywhere else in the world. For Said, North African countries and their populations were Arabs in the same sense as all Jews from North Africa and Middle East are *Mizrachim*.

Even Albert Memmi, a Tunisian Jewish philosopher living in France, fell into this minefield, erroneously calling North Africans Arabs (at times including himself on his father's side, as his mother was Berber) and by adopting the Orientalist agenda. Even his daughter thought she was an Arab while trying to make sense of the identity confusion plaguing North Africa. However, to his credit he was fully aware that independence, nationalism and decolonization did not lead to a separation of state and religion. My argument is that there was never a question of such separation since the Arab conquest 1,400 years ago. It was the Arabs who were foreigners in North Africa, not the Jews, and certainly not the Berbers, who at one point in history were one and the same. In essence there was no difference between European colonialism, the Arab conquest and the forced submission of indigenous populations under the various Islamic Turkish rules.

This Islamization process continued unhindered until the era of nationalism, all the way to the Jasmine Revolution.

North African Jews were neither Orientalists nor Arabs, and no argument by Edward Said can change anything in this regard. At most, he convinced a few Leftist Eastern European Israelis that Jews of LCA were "Arab" Jews, enhancing further discrimination and distortion. What he did not know was that North African Jews were and probably still are the most moderate elements in Israeli society, in spite of the hardships and discrimination they suffered. North African Jews are not Arab Jews, they never were. They are also not "en mass" Sephardic Jews as many labeled them. These historical issues were ignored for decades and continue to remained taboo subjects; no one is permitted to take the "ethnic genie out of the bottle".

Arab Jews became a term used quite openly by many in the Western world and by racist elements within the Jewish, Israeli and Arab communities. The Berbers in North Africa are not Arabs, neither are the Iranians or the Turks or Afghans or Pakistanis. The people of Egypt know that they too are not strictly speaking Arabs, as their historical monuments overshadow Islam. Its territorial continuity since ancient times, its unique history as exemplified in its Pharonic past and later its Coptic language and culture had already made Egypt into a nation many centuries ago. Like Tunisians, Egyptians saw themselves, their history, culture and language as specifically Egyptian and not "Arab."[131] The Arabs were borrowing and adopting cultures and civilizations from North Africa—not the other way around.

In exactly the same context, North African Jews were not and are not Arabs. The Berbers and Jews both preceded the Arab invasion in the seventh century. Both viewed the Arabs as colonizers, invaders, no different than the Europeans who took their turn in colonizing and occupying their lands. Tunisians know that theirs was a pluralistic society made up of Arabs, Muslims, Berber, Jews and Christians of different origins and from all corners of the Mediterranean and the Middle East, and as far as Yemen. None of the existing indigenous populations felt they were Arabs even if they spoke Arabic, except maybe Edward Said, who was a Christian arguing for a Muslim Arabic struggle. Said made his living writing about the Palestinian struggle and had a deep-rooted dislike for Israelis and Jews. 1,300 years of Arab domination, irrespective of who controlled Tunisia, never resulted in the Berber or the Jews becoming Arabs. The Arabs in North Africa were conquerors from Egypt to Morocco, and the Berbers in Algeria never forgot their history, wanting to take back control of their customs, culture and history.

This is the reason why Pan-Arabism did not work, and why the current Arab Spring is leading to nowhere. Egypt's dream of leading the Arab world was also doomed to fail because it clashed with the real history of the region. In the final analysis, Israel had become a major factor in the push for Arab unity and the further radicalization of Islam. It also adopted the current cultural division between Israeli as Eastern European and everyone else as Oriental. Minority rights and separation of religion and State were never part of any discussions within pan-Arabism. Islamic nationalism, vague socialist principles, and anti-West, and above all anti-Israel, sentiments were the foundations on which unity was supposed to work. So, anti-Israel and anti-Jewish became synonymous with Pan-Arabism, and later with Islamism.

Jacob Taieb, Paul Sebag and others agree as well that the term "Arab" Jews for Tunisians and other North African countries are false notions. As Taieb writes, "these terms were never used in Tunisia, and they do not correspond/coincide to the religious and socio-historical context/reality of the Jews in Tunisia or the rest of the Arab world." Jewish identity was firmly established before the Arab invasion in the seventh century and it remained intact over the centuries. Only a small percentage converted to Islam (as far as we know, and we don't know exactly), those who survived the hardships of living under Islam endeavored to keep their own culture and religion. We have seen this also with the indigenous Berber population throughout North Africa, who are determined to this day to try and figure out how not to be Arabs. In fact, it is possible to argue that all the recent spring revolutions have to do with this struggle of identity; between what is Arab and Muslim and what is indigenous. And how can this be resolved without its indigenous Jewish population? The forces suppressed throughout the centuries of invasions and Islamic and Arab control were now out in the open, putting into question the existing value system of the whole region—politically, culturally, morally and economically. The difficulties these revolutions are now confronting stem from post-colonial Islamic nationalism, which ousted everyone who was not a Muslim or refused to become one.

Now We Are Called Refugees...

Jews of LCA were labeled as Arabs, Sephardim, *Mizrahim*, and Orientals. A new label is about to take over the conversation; trying to convince us that now we are all refugees, like the Palestinians. Someone is trying to make us victims, again. Serge

Moati, the great Tunisian movie maker has said that Tunisian Jews feel like they are orphans without a country and without history, without land and without memory.[132]

It was only recently that the Israeli government, along with a few ad hoc organizations, decided to bring the suffering of Jews from LCA into the Palestinian-Israeli discussions. They are now calling these Jews refugees, same as the Palestinian refugees. Their logic is simple, and it goes like this: over a million Jews from Arab lands were forced to leave, turning them into refugees. During the same period, some 600,000 (probably fewer) Palestinians also became refugees. An exchange of population and a dollar value of abandoned property would make things even and right. According to this brilliant logic, a solution to the Palestinian refugee problem had now been found. Israel's elites have recently discovered the Jews of LCA and are determined to use a European (German) formula for future negotiations with the Palestinians, in which it is either a question of reparations with a value sticker, or a question of population (refugee) exchange between the displaced Palestinians with Jews of Arab Lands.

This logic, now in the open, was also used to lure Jews of LCA to leave everything behind and come to the new, "amazing" world of Israel in the 1950s. Some Iraqi Jews actually believed that once in Israel they would be compensated for their abandoned properties and businesses by Israeli authorities, and that they would be paid out from what was left behind by Palestinians in Palestine. They did not realize that the Israeli government was really using the value of their abandoned property as bargaining tool in future talks with the Palestinians. In other words, their property was nationalized, thus stolen twice. Once by the Iraqi government in 1951, and again by the Israeli government,[133] who has no intention whatsoever to compensate anyone from LCA for anything, not now and not in the future. The complexities of history have led to a bizarre situation in line with previous historical distortions. The recent request in July 2012 by Israeli Deputy Foreign Minister Danny Ayalon (of Algerian origin) and the Minister of Foreign Affairs Lieberman to set a day in the Jewish calendar remembering the exile is designed to be a bargaining chip for all future negotiations with the Palestinians in the Arab-Israeli conflict. The State of Israel had not taken the issue seriously to this day. The story is merely a propaganda tool for the continuation of the present political and social situation. The Jews of LCA have already disappeared, and it now seems safe to speak about them: there is no one around to remember anything, and no one to demand anything. Nevertheless, Ayalon organized the first UN Symposium on the subject on September 2012, despite opposition by Arab states. He vowed to continue to bring the issue to the UN every year, slightly breaking the long silence.

There is another Tunisian group demanding reparations, this time from the Germans. In 2001, I received a call in Montreal from a Tunisian Jewish lady who invited me to a meeting of Tunisian Jews in the city. The subject was reparation for Jews who suffered from Nazi occupation during WWII. From 1940 to 1943, Tunisia, as we already know, was under brutal control for some 7 months, and then under no less brutal Vichy control, until it was liberated by the Allies. Attending the meeting was also a member of the Canadian Government of Tunisian Jewish origin. The issue of reparations was a hot issue after WWII, and a divisive one within the Jewish community in general and Israeli society in particular.

In 1940, there were three times as many Jews living in North Africa than in Palestine. The official records show that the

Jewish population of Palestine increased naturally and through immigration from 174,606 in November 1931 to 488,600 in September 1940.[134]

North African Jews were silent partners for many years since the creation of the State of Israel. The incidents of Black Panther unrest, and other small demonstrations for justice and equality in Haifa and Jerusalem were insignificant and limited in scope and demands. Their story of survival continued under totally different conditions. The economic conditions were painful, but the moral and historical aspects of their story even more so. Most North African Jewish communities kept to themselves. Their history, culture and customs were kept for a short time and gradually let go in silence. Israel's short history was packaged as a European country by a population who was mostly Eastern European; the Jews of LCA could not possibly understand nor relate to the dominant Eastern European segment of Israeli society, nor did they want to integrate. The early story of Israel's existence was in this sense so complex that one can cannot but marvel that the grand experiment actually worked. All these communities that survived for thousands of years in the Middle East and North Africa were now reduced to ethnic groups in Israeli society. Obviously, wars and the process of state building did not permit the luxury of questioning all this. Those in power had their own agenda, while universities for decades blocked entry to North African students and faculty.

No one today denies the inequalities, discrimination and other hardships these communities were subject to by their Eastern European brothers. The melting pot worked better than anyone could ever imagine. The integration was so one-sided that whole communities simply disappeared as unique entities before they even got the chance to have their say politically.

The passing of older generations, the education system, the army service, intermarriage and the economic hardships made sure no community survived as an independent cultural entity. It is therefore no wonder that no one really knows what this integration meant. What were they integrating into? Still, the merit of integration remains, and measuring it is nothing but an academic exercise as these communities no longer exist, leaving the doors wide open for other class-based struggles. Over one million people from rich, ancient cultures disappeared under the watch of a quasi-socialist and Zionist ideology.

It is also obvious that the Left had no sympathy for the Jews of LCA, and not because they did not understand their ethnicity, but because they do not understand the history and politics of the countries where they lived for thousands of years. And by consequence, they did not understand the Palestinian problem. The Palestinians also have a problem with Jews of LCA. They had adopted readymade anti-colonialist theories developed for third-world countries, and Jews of LCA did not fit their nationalist Islamic aspirations. The Palestinians know that unraveling the history of Jews of LCA would also lay naked some of the unreasonable political demands and beliefs they themselves hold.

These arguments may be naive, but they may also provide a solid logical and unshakable political basis for the continued existence of Israel in the Middle East. The history of Jews of LCA provides the clue to successful peace initiatives in the region. However, merely having more Jews of LCA in powerful positions would not guarantee change. It is not an ethnic issue, so a North African prime minister of Israel would not necessarily resolve the Palestinian-Israeli conflict. The new generation of Israelis from Muslim countries now must figure out a way to find their political voice, and the key to doing this lies in their historical and political experiences in Muslim-conquered lands of North Africa and the Middle East, as well as their short experience in Israel.

Two-State Solution

Nearly everyone agrees—Left and Right, Europeans, Americans and Arabs—that a two-state solution with agreed upon borders is the only viable direction to resolving the Palestinian-Israeli conflict. Israelis are suspicious, but they believe that in the final negotiation they have outsmarted everyone else. There is a perceived notion that a two-state solution would finally put to rest the whole question of Israel's existence. Benjamin Netanyahu, the current head of the Israeli State, insists on a Palestinian declaration recognizing Israel as a Jewish state, even if a large percentage of his population is not Jewish. Such a declaration will satisfy Israel and assure that Palestinians across or behind the erected walls have finally came to their senses. I have argued in this book, through the Tunisian experience, that Israel's academics, politicians and thinkers alike have outsmarted no one. Instead of developing strong relationships across the Middle East and North Africa with open borders, cultural exchange and free trade, they have closed themselves, building a huge ghetto in the area, relating to no one, and making no friends in the past 65 years.

Day of Remembrance

The Jewish people, especially in Israel, have all kinds of Remembrance days: commemorating the exile from Egypt, the death of soldiers, the Holocaust, the Maccabees and the Second Temple, and so on… It's depressing having so many sad days to remember, and they are often grouped together. It is therefore very appropriate to either cancel a few or add another day to a people who are used to crying: A day of remembrance for the total ethnic cleansing of Jews from North Africa and the Middle East. This day should be up there just below the Holocaust. It should equal the Palestinian Nakba (Palestinian exodus) in terms of importance, though the Jewish exile was more disastrous in number and intensity. The Palestinians went through a process of partial ethnic cleansing, while Jews of LCA experienced a total process of ethnic cleansing. The Palestinians were never purged completely from their homeland. Some were ousted or ran away, and most are alive and well, thriving within Israeli territories and in the West Bank and Gaza. No one in Israel speaks of total ethnic cleansing, not even the most radical elements of the various nationalist Eastern European and North African parties. Instead, we have the "enlightened" Left that speaks of fences all around, thus creating a ghetto of physical and moral ignorance, furthering the deafening silence. Very few Jews are left in in Morocco, Tunisia, Libya, Algeria and Egypt. What was done to Jews in Arab lands in the Middle East and North Africa by Arab nationalists was a conscious act of ethnic cleansing amongst the worst found in the history of mankind.

I read in one example of Israel-bashing by a professor of North Eastern University that "historians describe the expulsion of Palestinians in 1948 as the largest ethnic cleansing project in the century," and my immediate reaction was, "not so fast." Real ethnic cleansing happened elsewhere, in countries of North Africa and the Middle East, in the total elimination of ancient Jewish indigenous communities. The Jasmine Revolution has helped unravel this history, still unknown to many, which contains the keys to resolving many current political issues in a very troubled region of the world, from anti-dictatorial revolutions to the Israeli-Palestinian problem.

Raising these issues during the 1980s and 1990s in Western and Israeli universities was an impossible task. I know this because I went through it. The subject of Jews of LCA was not mentioned even briefly in any courses of political science, history, Israeli politics, international affairs, third-world politics, or even human rights. Jewish professors did not want to hear about the subject and Muslim professors brushed it aside violently. There will probably never be a remembrance day for Jews of Lands Conquered by Arabs. They will also not ask for reparations, nor will they ask for their houses and properties. They retained whatever culture they could hold and left for Israel and elsewhere, avoiding becoming permanent political refugees. People who lived for thousands of years in conquered lands accepted the ultimate defeat in order to survive and tried somehow to put the pieces back together. And they survived patiently, trying to keep their memories, waiting for history to do them justice.

Jews of LCA living in Israel, Europe and America have marched on with life, demanding nothing from anyone. They knew that their lands of origin were all Arab and Muslim conquered lands. They knew long ago what historians and intellectuals everywhere avoided talking about, that ethnic cleansing was taking place in the whole of the Muslim world in the Middle East and the whole of Africa under the noses of the UN and Human Rights Organizations. They are the living proof of this ethnic cleansing…over one million of them. For some, it was the second time in history they were unjustly and violently exiled. Tunisian Jews all knew about the extermination of Jews in Europe, and they had no plans to be next in line. These same people were determined to resolve their situation in order to survive building better lives for themselves in the process. In fact, their story was about human survival. They chose to live and prosper away from Islamic submission, refusing to become permanent refugees.

Why Tunisian Jews Will Not Return

The Spanish government recently extended a citizenship offer to Jews whose ancestors were exiled and pushed out of Spain at the end of the fifteenth century. At the time they were told to convert or leave Spain. It is estimated that between 140,000 and 200,000 people were exiled, about the same number of Tunisian Jews forced out only a few decades ago. In both instances, the economies of both countries suffered greatly. In fact, it is said that the Ottoman Sultan found the Spanish move illogical and counterproductive, and offered to host every Jewish family in his Empire.[135] So far, some 900 people have received this recent special historical citizenship by the Spanish government, and about 6,000 inquiries have been made. The Portuguese Parliament is also voting on whether to allow Jews to come back to Portugal in an historic gesture acknowledging its history.[136]

Can anyone imagine such a situation in the Arab world? Would anyone want to live under Sharia law in any Arab country, including Tunisia? A Muslim woman in Tunisia was quoted in *World Affairs* as wishing Tunisian Jews were back in Tunisia. Ben Ali invited the Jews to come back before being ousted, and so did Ghannushi after the Jasmine Revolution. All suffer from the same Tunisian Jewish syndrome. Even though Jews were a meaningful and a powerful minority at the heart of Tunisian society, in the early days of independence they were made to leave Tunisia, in exactly the same way that Palestinians were made to leave their land in 1948. But now that the Jewish community is virtually non-existent they want Tunisian Jews to come back. It is "wonderful" to see how liberal-minded Tunisians still are, even if they espouse a radical version of Islam. They know that a significant part of Tunisia's liberal tradition is due to the historical existence of a large and influential Jewish community. Still, in the early days nationalists were unable to choose a different political path, considering world order following WWII and the Cold War that followed. The real breakdown of the political system happened when most of the Jews had left Tunisia. The door was open for anti-Israel and anti-Jewish sentiments, aided by the nationalists' newly acquired (imaginary) Palestinian friends.

All those who hope that Tunisian Jews will come back forget that there are just no Tunisian Jews anywhere anymore. They seemed to have disappeared into the thin air, assimilated into the new societies where they found themselves. New generations of Tunisian Jews have nothing to do with Tunisia, and even more so now, as Islamism take further hold in the country. It is even increasingly difficult to find Tunisian Jewish intellectuals in Israel who would take the time to investigate anything Tunisian. One researcher told me that studying Tunisian Jewish history is "too depressing and useless," especially considering that no one really wants to know. So there are no Tunisians Jews left to go back to Tunisia, and there is really no Tunisia to go to—it works both ways.

Speaking to Tunisian students of political science in Canadian universities has helped shed some light on the precarious Tunisian political base, as well as on their fragile psychological state of mind in relation to this topic. These students were once much more liberal than their Muslim brothers in other Muslim countries because of the country's history and traditions. But this is no longer the case. Anti-Zionist and anti-Israel sentiments has captured Tunisian logic at almost every level of political discourse. The same people who pushed their own Jews out are now calling for justice to the same number of people pushed out in Palestine, 2,000 miles away. It doesn't make sense. Tunisian students are lost in terms of their own history and their own political future. And when the subject is pushed even further, the confusion becomes total. The statement that "There is basically no difference between what happened to the Palestinians and to Tunisian Jews because both were pushed out" will make a nationalist Tunisian speechless and sometimes aggressive. Some Palestinians also left Israel to be exiled in other countries in the region. They were promised that once the war would be over they would be able to return. They believed their Muslim brothers. Similarly, the Jews of Tunisia were made to believe that Tunisia was an Islamic state and their presence was no longer desirable.

There is one important difference between what happened to Tunisian Jews and what happened to the Palestinians: the latter disappeared completely from the map, never to appear again, while the Palestinians are still there in the same territory, living their lives—some as Israeli citizens, some under Israeli control, some in semi-occupied territories, and others in refugee camps in countries surrounding Israel. Tunisian Islamic nationalism was responsible for completely ousting one of the most ancient peoples in the world.

There are many reasons why so many prominent Tunisian politicians and public figures want Tunisian Jews back, all of which have to do more with the internal psychological and political contradictions of their own existence, because, as I've argued above, Tunisia without its Jewish population is not Tunisia. I would even argue that the Salafist position is an extreme psychological reaction to this situation. Tunisian Muslims are unwilling to take responsibility for what happened to Tunisian Jews; they are in denial. Without the Jewish community, the Tunisian liberal character has no base, leaving the doors wide open to an extreme form of Islam, Sharia Law, the Muslim Brotherhood, the Salafists, and other shady pseudo-religious and political organizations. Thus we return to the theme of silence, whereby everyone knows what happened, but no one speaks openly and freely about it—neither in Israel, nor in Tunisia. The Salafists are the shield preventing discussion of this scary topic. The more they expand and become visible, the less anyone questions the true historical motives. Algerian Jews in France are starting to break the silence by attempting to figure out who they were and why they left Algeria, as Arab dominance is threatened there by the rise of Berber nationalism. Interest in Judeo-Berber

Algeria has been recently renewed, as many students (Algerian Jews and Muslims) in France are embarking on field studies, before all remnants of their past disappear completely. Israel has remained silent on this for decades and is now incapable of dealing with the complex issues resulting from such discussions.

Sylvain Hayoun,[137] a Tunisian who was himself expelled in 1967 and ended up in Israel, has questioned the Tunisian President's call for Jews to return, following the Jasmine Revolution. Here are a few of his questions: "Can we go back with our spouses and descendants? Can we go back and ask for restitution for everything we lost when we fled in 1967 and even before (including real estate and other assets we left behind)?" Knowing his people, he is convinced that the call is not sincere, nor was it made in good faith. But, like all Tunisian Jews he says, "But let me dream and let me believe that it is an opening to a new era, with an apology to the population of Jews for the pogroms we have been victims of, restitution of everything we have left behind, and offering the friendship of the Tunisian government and population to Jews." I'm afraid that Mr. Hayoun will not see this dream realized for many generations to come. I'm also convinced that there is not one Tunisian left to even remember what had happened and how to dream about it. Decades of silence everywhere have eroded the memories and dreams that often comprise the life of a people, and their journey in the development of the human race.

Now What?

The Tunisian revolution has brought radical Islam to Tunisia in full force. Before this, Bourguiba replaced the Bey to become another Bey for life, and in the process managed to rid Tunisia of its indigenous populations, the Jews, the Berbers and other minorities. He was replaced by another modern Bey, Ben Ali, who continued to rule aimlessly, amassing obscene wealth for him and his extended family. As in Israel, religion was naively seen as a liberating force in the face of this corruption. So, they voted for the Muslim Brotherhood, the ultimate religious savior who has naturally become the new beloved Sultan. But the revolution continues, with new demonstrations calling for less Islam and more democracy and economic prosperity. Tunisia can easily have both by recognizing and engaging with their own history, with the tragedy done to Tunisian Jews, who for thousands of years were an important and inseparable part of the country.

Notes

1 http://www.rawa.org/statues.htm

2 http://rt.com/art-and-culture/news/egypt-library-fire-heritage-destroyed-163/

3 http://www.fairobserver.com/article/post-revolution-tunisia-still-waiting-its-economic-recovery?page=1

4 http://www.telegraph.co.uk/travel/destinations/africaandindianocean/tunisia/737926/Tunisias-ancient-history.html

5 Sheikh Omar Bakri Muhammad, audio debate, http://www.mrctv.org/videos/dr-wafa-sultan-exposes-islamic-values-sheikh-omar-bakri-muhammad

6 http://meria.idc.ac.il/journal/2000/issue2/jv4n2a7.html

7 http://meria.idc.ac.il/journal/2000/issue2/jv4n2a7.html

8 Israel and Ishmael: Studies in Muslim-Jewish Relations
 By Tudor Parfitt, p.118

9 http://archive.jta.org/article/1965/04/26/3080535/israel-cabinet-discusses-bourguibas-call-for-arabisrael-peace-talks

10 http://blog.sami-aldeeb.com/2012/04/09/tunisie-lillusion-de-lislam-devoile-lillusion-de-la-liberte/

11 (Sir Richard Wood was the British Consul-General in Tunis from 1855-1879).

12 http://topics.nytimes.com/top/news/international/countriesandterritories/tunisia/index.html

13 Agreement between the French authorities and Sultan Malai Hafiz making Morocco a French protectorate.

14 Moshe Dayan, address to the Technion, Haifa, reported in Haaretz, April 4, 1969

15 http://www.nationalmuseum.af.mil/factsheets/factsheet.asp?id=1735

16 Colonialism in Question, Frederick Cooper 2005, University of California Press
16a http://historum.com/european-history/50072-madagascar-real-reason-british-conquest-3.html

16b www.history.army.mil/html/books/072/72-12/CMH_Pub_72-12.pdf
17 From the Ottoman Conquests to the Present Time, By Haim Zeev Hirschberg, Eliezer Bashan, Robert Attal

18 http://www.jstor.org.ezproxy.bibl.ulaval.ca/stable/pdfplus/3777449.pdf

19 http://www.historynet.com/raid-on-rommels-railroad-in-tunisia-during-world-war-ii.htm

20 http://kefteji.wordpress.com/tag/war-cemeteries/

21 Montreal Gazette May 1943)

22 http://nosharia.wordpress.com/nazi-islam-collaboration/

23 http://www.ushmm.org/wlc/en/article.php?ModuleId=10007667

24 Nazi Propaganda for the Arab World, By Jeffrey Herf

25 Ashraf Amin, 339

26 Carl Brown, 2004
http://kms1.isn.ethz.ch/serviceengine/Files/ISN/46329/ipublicationdocument_
singledocument/5f9b96c0-ab26-4e65-aee9-ed5937e5db85/en/doc508.pdf

27 Jeoffery Brainard, Patton Tank Marks suggest a long recovery, 1998, Science News

28 http://www.lonesentry.com/germansoldier/index.html

29 The Abolition of Slavery in Tunisia (1846)1 A study into its historical backgrounds
and its juridico-theological legitimization

30 Islam without Extremes: A Muslim Case for Liberty, By Mustafa Akyol

31 http://en.wikipedia.org/wiki/List_of_Beys_of_Tunis

32 http://www.vqronline.org/articles/1944/autumn/macleod-mellimelli/

32a http://www.vqronline.org/articles/1944/autumn/macleod-mellimelli/

33 http://archive.org/stream/mordecaimanuelno00wolf/mordecaimanuelno00wolf_
djvu.txt

34 Travels p.308

35 The Traveler

36 The Berber Identity Movement and the Challenge to North African States By
Bruce Maddy-Weitzma

37 History of the Berber p.180, el Khaldun

38 Thirteen Tribe, Arthur Koestler

39 http://en.wikipedia.org/wiki/Curse_of_Ham#Incest_interpretations

40 http://eelhaik.aravindachakravartilab.org/ArticlesPDFs/MissingLink2012.pdf

41 http://www.economist.com/node/303168

42 http://www.mondeberbere.com/societe/manifest-index-en.htm

44 http://www.mondeberbere.com/societe/manifest-index-en.htm

45 The Land of the Moors, 1900, Budget Meakin, 1899

46 Tunisia Live 2012

47 Moroccan World News 2012

48 http://www.moroccotomorrow.org/new-york-study-defines-the-origins-of-north-african-jews-for-the-first-time/

49 Jews and Sciences in German Contexts: Case Studies from the 19th and 20th ... edited by Ulrich Charpa, Ute Deichmann

50 Population Genetics in Israel in the 1950s, The Unconscious Internalization of Ideology By Nurit Kirsh, 2003

51 Carthage and Tunis, 1906

52 Tunis. The Land and the People, **Ernst von Hesse-Wartegg**

53 Tunis: The Land and the People, Ernst von Hesse-Wartegg

54 Esther Schely-Newman. Our Lives Are But Stories: Narratives of Tunisian-Israeli Women. Detroit: Wayne State University Press, 2002

55 Cultures of the Jews: A New History, By David Biale, 2002

56 http://www.projetaladin.org/holocaust/en/muslims-and-jews/muslims-and-jews-in-history/history-of-the-jews-in-tunisia.html

57 A Mediterranean Society: The Jewish Communities of the Arab World as Portrayed in the Documents of the Cairo Geniza, S. D. Goitein (Mar 1, 1972)

58 Studia Islamica, The Unity of the Mediterranean World in the "Middle" Middle Ages S. D. Goitein, #12. 1960

59 http://www.tabletmag.com/jewish-news-and-politics/88249/out-of-tune-3

60 http://www.tabletmag.com/jewish-news-and-politics/88249/out-of-tune-3

61 The Absence of Islamism in Fanon's Work, Islam: The Elephant in Fanon's The Wretched of the Earth Author: Fouzi Slisli, St. Cloud State University

62 http://en.wikipedia.org/wiki/Historical_Jewish_population_comparisons

63http://www.ushmm.org/wlc/en/article.php?ModuleId=10007311

64 Land Tenure in Tunisia, Raymond E. Crist, Scientific Monthly, May 1941

65 Elliott Abrams - Elliott Abrams is a senior fellow for Middle Eastern Studies at the Council on Foreign Relations. http://www.theatlantic.com/international/archive/2012/03/destroy-all-the-churches-saudi-arabias-poor-treatment-of-christians/254650/

66 http://www.northafricaunited.com/Rally-for-sharia-law-in-Tunisia_a1017.html

67 http://www.scoops.co/dgQXF3bE

68 Africa since 1935, By Unesco. International Scientific Committee for the Drafting of a General History of Africa

69 http://www.tunisia-live.net/2012/09/17/director-of-american-school-in-tunis-recounts-day-of-looting-and-vandalism/

70 http://mondoweiss.net/2012/03/hundreds-of-soccer-fans-crowd-jerusalem-mall-death-to-arabs.html

71 A Voice Called: Stories of Jewish Heroism, By Yossi Katz

72 http://www.jstor.org.ezproxy.bibl.ulaval.ca/stable/pdfplus/2935279.pdf

73 http://www.nytimes.com/2012/05/15/world/middleeast/deal-to-end-hunger-strike-awaits-palestinian-prisoners-approval.html

74 http://www.americanthinker.com/blog/2012/05/ny_times_spotlights_palestinian_naqba_ignores_jewish_naqba_in_arab_lands.html

75 Dr Andre Nahum, Sarcelles

76 Les refugies echanges by the author, journalist and academic Jean-Pierre Allali http://jewishrefugees.blogspot.co.uk/2008/10/how-bourguibas-tunisia-pushed-out-its.html

77 http://www.hsje.org/displacement_of_jews_from_arab_c.htm

78 http://www.hsje.org/displacement_of_jews_from_arab_c.htm

79 http://www.hsje.org/displacement_of_jews_from_arab_c.htm

80 http://jewishrefugees.blogspot.ca/2011/10/shabi-puts-positive-spin-on-tunisian.html

81 http://www.wikiislam.net/wiki/Persecution_of_Non-Muslims

82 Bittersweet Nostalgia: Memoirs of Jewish Emigrants from the Arab Countries: Review Article, 1981 Jacob M. Landau

83 http://www.timesofisrael.com/tunisia-to-support-annual-jewish-pilgrimage/

84 Army in the Service of the State, By Tom Bowden

85 http://dar.aucegypt.edu/bitstream/handle/10526/2965/2012mestseanhaley.pdf?sequence=1

86 Harold D. Nelson, Country Study, American University, Department of the Army, 1986

87 http://en.wikipedia.org/wiki/Italian_Tunisians

88 http://ephraiyim.wordpress.com/2011/01/02/al-qaeda-targeting-christians-in-canada-austria/

89 Newspaper report, Ma'arive, July17 2012

90 http://bcc.rcav.org/canadian/672-deborah-gyapong

91 http://www.nytimes.com/2012/11/01/opinion/tunisia-a-sad-year-later.html

92 http://www.tunisia-live.net/2012/04/05/tunisian-judiciary-investigates-case-of-jewish-community-president-roger-bismuth-against-salafist-preacher/

93 http://berkleycenter.georgetown.edu/resources/quotes/habib-bourguiba-speaks-on-muslim-unity-in-jericho

94 http://www.americanthinker.com/2012/04/obamas_america_why_black_grievance_will_never_end.html

95 http://www.atimes.com/atimes/Middle_East/ND11Ak01.html

96 http://www.americanthinker.com/2012/04/arab_riots_then_and_now.html

97 http://www.jewishvirtuallibrary.org/jsource/talking/jew_refugees.html

98 http://joshuapundit.blogspot.ca/2012/03/tunisia-secularists-accuse-obama.html

99 http://joshuapundit.blogspot.ca/2012/03/tunisia-secularists-accuse-obama.html

100 http://www.michaeltotten.com/2010/01/why-they-hate-us-middle-eastern-politics-and-the-principle-of-the-strong-horse.php

101 http://www.fletcherforum.org/2012/04/08/ennahdas-split-personality/

102 http://www.magharebia.com/cocoon/awi/xhtml1/en_GB/features/awi/features/2012/04/04/feature-01

103 http://www.americanthinker.com/blog/2011/10/the_jihadist_vision_of_tunisias_new_democratic_leader.html

104 http://www.independent.co.uk/opinion/commentators/fisk/the-brutal-truth-about-tunisia-2186287.html

105 http://www.tunisia-live.net/2012/06/29/is-turkeys-akp-party-a-model-for-tunisia/

106 Ma'arive 06.2012

107 http://ouraim.blogspot.ca/2008/03/absence-of-islamism-in-fanons-work.html

108 http://www.gatestoneinstitute.org/3064/muslim-voters-europe

109 Ftouh Souhail http://www.terredisrael.com/infos/?p=50780#more-50780

110 http://www.palestineremembered.com/Articles/General/Story2127.html
#Why did the Jews Leave?

111 http://www.worldaffairsjournal.org/blog/michael-j-totten/last-jews-tunisia

112 http://www.nytimes.com/1987/06/24/world/plo-in-tunis-is-shadow-of-former-
power.html

113 http://www.nytimes.com/1987/06/24/world/plo-in-tunis-is-shadow-of-former-
power.html

114 http://www.nytimes.com/1987/06/24/world/plo-in-tunis-is-shadow-of-former-
power.html?pagewanted=2&src=pm

115 http://www.wrmea.com/component/content/article/146/7141-yael-dayans-visit-
to-the-plo-in-tunis.html

116 Tunisia and the PLO, George Joffe, Journal of Palestinians Studies, Winter 1987

117 http://middleeast.about.com/od/arabisraeliconflict/a/me090420_2.htm

118 http://israelmatzav.blogspot.ca/2011/01/surprise-plo-walks-back-support-of.html

119 Zena Herman, The Assimilation of Immigrants into Israel. Vol. 5, 3 (Summer
1951)

120 http://www.nrg.co.il/online/48/ART2/456/870.html

121 http://francestanford.stanford.edu/sites/francestanford.stanford.edu/files/
Khosrokhavar.pdf

122 http://www.myjewishlearning.com/israel/History/1948-1967/Building_the_State/
Absorbing_Immigrants.shtml

123 Haim Saadon, Missionary in education in Tunisia, Nachum Yerushalmi 1938-
1945

124 NYT August 2012

125 Jews and Sciences in German Contexts: Case Studies from the 19th and 20th ..
edited by Ulrich Charpa, Ute Deichmann, 2007

126 http://www.leftcurve.org/LC35WebPages/QXWhitewashingHistory.Shoshi.pdf

127http://pod.icast.co.il/Media/Index/Files/cbec0eeb-153b-4821-af7c-33f7889bbdd9.icast.mp3

128 http://www.shoa.org.il/files/344.28609723.pdf

129 http://archive.org/stream/ChildCareInIsrael#page/n0/mode/1up

130 Edward Said: A Legacy of Emancipation and Representation By Adel Iskander, Hakem Rustom

131 Haeri, Niloofar. Sacred language, Ordinary People: Dilemmas of Culture and Politics in Egypt. New York: Palgrave Macmillan. 2003, pp. 47, 136.

132 http://www.amit4u.net/newsarticle/10683,1305,25881.aspx

133 http://www.ha-keshet.org.il/articles/lands/perfect_yehuda-shenhav.htm

134 http://www.nature.com/nature/journal/v147/n3727/abs/147413b0.html

135 http://www.bbc.co.uk/news/magazine-21631427

136 http://www.jpost.com/JewishWorld/JewishNews/Article.aspx?id=309447

137 http://boulderjewishnews.org/2012/a-view-of-the-new-tunisia-from-boulder/

Index

SILENCING THE PAST:

Made in the USA
Middletown, DE
30 January 2017